The Catholic Enlightenment

The Catholic Enlightenment

The Forgotten History of a Global Movement

ULRICH L. LEHNER

OXFORD
UNIVERSITY PRESS

Library of Congress Cataloging-in-Publication Data
Lehner, Ulrich L., 1976–
The Catholic enlightenment : the forgotten history of a global movement / Ulrich L.
Lehner.
pages cm
Includes bibliographical references and index.
ISBN 978-0-19-023291-7 (cloth : alk. paper)   1. Catholic Church—History—Modern
period, 1500–   2. Enlightenment.   I. Title.
BX1330.L44 2016
282.09′03—dc23
2015023905

1 3 5 7 9 8 6 4 2
Printed in the United States of America
on acid-free paper

Contents

The Catholic Enlightenment

Introduction

WHEN JORGE MARIO Bergoglio was elected pope in March 2013, many considered this the beginning of a new era for the papacy. The choice of his papal name Francis was seen as a primary example for this paradigm shift. Like the medieval St. Francis of Assisi the pope would now stand at the side of the poor and try to reform a self-content, often lethargic church. He is largely seen as a radical reformer who does not shy away from discussing hot-button issues in a direct and pragmatic way. Yet what is usually overlooked is that Pope Francis is merely continuing a long tradition of reforming popes of modernity, picking up ideas in particular of the so-called Tridentine Reform of the sixteenth and seventeenth centuries. The most famous exponent of such reform was also a namesake, St. Francis de Sales. Reform was in the air then as it is now; attempts were being made to retrieve the spiritual power sources of faith and to eliminate sources of scandal from within the church. For each Francis, however, "reform" has not been primarily a political thing: it is the constant struggle to let the church be the salt of the earth and a light to the world. In the footsteps of De Sales and St. Alphonsus of Liguori, an eighteenth-century saint, the pope tries to be a sensitive pastor who takes human frailty seriously while admonishing bishops and priests against shepherding with harshness and rigor. Like his forerunners De Sales and Liguori, Francis is also a journalistic missionary of sorts, using social media to reach out to millions of people—Catholics and non-Catholics alike. His brisk, simple spiritual advice is perfectly suited for the Twitter generation. The reforms and the style of Pope Francis did not fall from the sky but are deeply rooted in the reform movement that found expression in the Councils of Trent and Vatican II, but also in the Catholic Enlightenment. These events all took place in a time of turmoil and have in common the realization that a self-content church that is not dynamically reaching out beyond the pews is doomed to wither away.[1]

"Christianity claimed to bring light, hope, and truth, but its central myth was incredible, its dogma a conflation of rustic superstitions, its sacred book an incoherent collection of primitive tales, its church a cohort of servile fanatics as long as they were out of power and of despotic fanatics once they had seized control."[2] This was, in a nutshell, the belief of most of the key figures in the Enlightenment, according to historian Peter Gay's 1968 assessment. Almost fifty years later, there has been a dramatic change in perspective. Today, historians recognize that only a small fraction of Enlighteners was anti-religious; the overwhelming majority was interested in finding a balanced relationship between reason and faith. Such religious Enlighteners (Catholics, Protestants, Jews, Orthodox) were not necessarily obedient churchgoers; in fact, some were radical critics of the hierarchy and inclined toward belief in an impersonal god—a position that is usually called deism. The religious Enlightenment was like a "great series of congregations, with some common doctrines but numerous paths to salvation."[3] Common to all was the conviction that new discoveries in science and philosophy should renew the faith. The religious Enlightenment cut across national and confessional lines. It drew in Lutherans, Calvinists, Unitarians, Catholics, Jews, and the Orthodox. It could be found in the heartlands of Europe but also on its periphery, in Lithuania and Poland, in Malta and Portugal, in the Americas, and even in India. Its leading lights believed they could create a more tolerant society, more efficient government, more effective education, improved morals, and greater happiness.

While many Protestant Enlighteners have received attention from historians, less has been said about the struggle of Catholicism to come to terms with the Enlightenment. Is such a thing as a "Catholic Enlightenment" even possible? Did Spain, Portugal, France, and their overseas colonies contribute to the Enlightenment or should they be seen as merely "conservative Catholic regimes"? Is Catholicism compatible with the values modernity cherishes?

When I began asking these questions, I was often greeted by frowning faces or sometimes patronizing smiles. I had the impression that my colleagues thought I was chasing sprites. I was told that Catholics did not believe in science, that they were superstitious, and that they were never great supporters of democracy. The Catholic Church had subjugated women, they said, and its missionaries had helped destroy the Native American population. The fact that my learned colleagues harbor such simplistic views has convinced me that it is necessary to tell the forgotten story of the Catholic Enlightenment. Long before there was a Pope Francis, there existed an open-minded Catholicism that was in dialogue with cutting-edge intellectual trends.

Why has this history been lost? A great deal of the blame falls on the church, which until the 1960s felt embarrassed that there was a positive engagement with the Enlightenment and decried it as heretical and un-Catholic. The other reason may be the lenses through which historians like Peter Gay looked at the Enlightenment: if only anti-religious thinkers were enlightened, then there could not be a Catholic Enlightenment. It would be a contradiction in terms. Therefore, historians did not bother to investigate with more thoroughness Catholic life of the eighteenth century until, due to the work of brave pioneers like R. R. Palmer, a more differentiated view began to take root. He, Bernard Plongeron, and many others have worked tirelessly to demonstrate that Catholicism and Enlightenment, faith and reason, progress and religion were not incompatible. It was these historians who also refuted the widespread misunderstanding that Catholicism equated with the papacy. In the eighteenth century, Catholicism was not centered around the pope but was much more locally organized. The pope certainly had a say, but often only a very limited one. In many countries, the pope could not even publish a public announcement without prior approval of state authorities. Thus, even if many popes proved to be enemies of the Enlightenment, it does not follow that Catholicism was hostile to it, too.

Yet a closer look at history reveals that many progressive reforms within the Catholic Church predate even the Enlightenment. Some of the most cherished values of modernity can be traced to the *pre-Enlightenment* Catholic Reform that began in the sixteenth century.[4] The rejection of arranged marriages originated in the Catholic Reform movement, as did prohibitions against domestic abuse, criticism of the denigration of women, and also the protection of the indigenous tribes of South and Middle America, and much else.

Much of the blame for the neglect of this history lies with the Catholic Church itself. After the French Revolution, the church retreated to an intellectual ghetto from which it did not emerge until the twentieth century. During this dark period, any discussion of progressive Catholics was unwelcome; most were labeled "heretics" or persons of "questionable character." Everything modern came under suspicion; modern thought was something to be denounced, not engaged. Not until the 1960s did sound historical studies of Enlightenment Catholicism begin to appear. It seems that, slowly, the Catholic Church is again beginning to reconcile with modernity, having realized that to shut out modernity—which was common practice between 1850 and 1950—only prevented the updating of theology and church practice. Many proposals that are hotly debated by Catholics today—a new role for the papacy, a preferential option for the poor, married priests, divorce and remarriage—first emerged in the 1700s. Yet most Catholics are completely unaware that the question, "How can I remain Catholic and yet be part of the modern world?" is far from new. Looking at the answers of the past helps us to identify roads not taken, roads that led followers astray or into the abyss—and perhaps even roads to which the church might return.

So what was the Catholic Enlightenment? To understand what was happening in the eighteenth century, one has to begin two hundred years earlier. When the Protestant Reformation shook Europe, Catholicism lost its hegemony. Suddenly new churches sprang up. They were divided on many things but agreed on one: that the Catholic Church had lost the true faith through corruption and decay. Getting over the shock, Catholics responded with a meeting of bishops, a council, in the city of Trent, which lasted from 1545 to 1563. The council addressed what had to be reformed in the church—for example, it determined that future priests should be properly educated and guided to become authentic pastors—but it also codified what Catholics believed in contrast to Protestants. Thus, for example, the council stressed that human freedom is a crucial feature of theology. This particular teaching was part of a new, more optimistic view of the human person: one could do good deeds without faith or divine help and could freely reject God's grace. This prepared the ground for ongoing controversies over the question of predestination, but most of all it became the foundation of the Enlightenment belief in individual freedom and the natural capacities of the human person. It was the beginning of Catholic Reform, also called Tridentine Reform.

One of the most important products of the council was the Roman Catechism, a handbook that taught parish priests to teach doctrine intelligibly and appealingly. A new edition of the Bible followed later. Reform bishops such as Charles Borromeo in Milan spread the word about the renewal of Catholicism, and new religious orders such as the Society of

Jesus (the Jesuits) preached about it across Europe, from royal courts to poorhouses; and through missionaries it was eventually preached to the ends of the earth. The church was emerging stronger from the shock of the Reformation and was back on track to eradicate the deviant behavior of its clergy, homogenize teaching, and centralize administration.

But the pronouncements of the council were not embraced everywhere. In countries where sovereigns enjoyed strong influence over the church, the council, which called old privileges into question, was perceived as a threat. The council insisted that people had the freedom to choose their own spouse and declared that nobody could force a Catholic to legally marry another. This undermined the rights of the French kings, who therefore opposed the publication of the decrees of the council for a long time. Trent also had another, often overlooked, result: it encouraged new forms of religious life and religious fervor. It not only embraced the reform movements of religious orders, but it also encouraged new orders centered on particular missions. These orders increased exponentially the works of mercy administered by the church. Some began caring for abandoned children and orphans, others for the sick and mentally ill; yet others provided education. This trend toward more practicality is also obvious in the new definition of sainthood that became prevalent after Trent. It was the heroic virtues of the candidate for sainthood that now mattered and not whether he or she had performed miracles, or had visions, or suffered stigmata. This idea of Christian heroism stressed, furthermore, that *everyone* was called to holiness. The saints again became role models for the laity, as they originally had been, and the universal call to holiness, especially emphasized by Francis de Sales, was increasingly preached, even though this was not defined as explicit church teaching until the twentieth century.[5]

This brings us to the Enlightenment. Most historians today understand the Enlightenment as a cultural process that stressed the sovereignty of reason and questioned authority and tradition. It contained so many diverse ideas that some scholars no longer speak of a singular, homogenous Enlightenment but of multiple Enlightenments. The movement had roots in the Renaissance of the fourteenth and fifteenth centuries when a new and fresh look was cast at ancient thought; but its most important impetus was the philosophy of Baruch Spinoza. Writing in the latter half of the seventeenth century, Spinoza sought to demonstrate that there was only one substance—namely, the material world—and consequentially, no spiritual realm. God and world were identical, and the Bible was merely a piece of literature in which eternal and natural truths were explained to an uneducated readership through fantastic stories. Moreover, Spinozism stressed freedom of expression, democracy, and religiously untainted reason as the only sources of a happy life. Spinoza's disciples disseminated these ideas—clandestinely at first, then, by the middle of the eighteenth century, more openly. In France, Spinozism merged with an already existing anti-clericalism. Denis Diderot and Paul-Henri Thiry d'Holbach became its most influential voices. Spinozist arguments—along with Jansenism, a radical branch of Catholic thought—were the main drivers of eighteenth-century theology. Most Enlighteners, however, did not share the radical views of Spinoza but rather developed moderate ideas for reforming society, often supported by governments. Among these, one can group thinkers like Charles-Luis de Secondat Montesquieu, who is best known for his thoughts on a separation of powers; John Locke, who propagated empiricism and toleration; and also Voltaire, who, despite being fiercely anti-Catholic and anti-clerical, never questioned the belief in a supreme deity.

How do Catholic Enlighteners fit into this scheme? Most are best classified as moderates, favoring a modernization that compromised with tradition and reigning authorities. The problem with this categorization is not that it differentiates between a more progressive and radical wing, on the one hand, and a more moderate, even conservative, wing on the other. Rather, the problem is that the inventors of the term "Enlightenment" assigned value only to the first group: only the radical Enlightenment, with its hostility to religion, was—we are told—responsible for the development of the modern values we cherish today, such as equality, freedom, democracy, cultural diversity, and tolerance. Certainly, Spinozists argued at one time or another for all those values, but their support for these tenets is, frankly, as inconsistent as that of their moderate counterparts. To take just one example: Spinoza himself supported allowing the government to mandate religious adherence in order to preserve peace within the commonwealth. The result is not, as Spinoza scholars have claimed, a separation of church and state but rather a new political theology, and one that is not nearly as tolerant as some would like to believe. Specifically, Spinoza's tolerance leaves out smaller, independent religious groups, such as the Mennonites, who believed that the state should not be obeyed in questions of violence and warfare and who would therefore easily be classified by the radical Enlighteners of the French Revolution as enemies of the state's "natural rights." This was the label applied to critics of the

Revolution, and because they opposed the rule of reason and "natural rights," they could be disposed of as "enemies of the human race"—and they frequently were, as the Great Terror shows.[6]

What was on the agenda of Catholic Enlighteners? Their aim was (a) to use the newest achievements of philosophy and science to defend the essential dogmas of Catholic Christianity by explaining them in a new language, and (b) to reconcile Catholicism with modern culture. If anything held these diverse thinkers together, it was their belief that Catholicism had to modernize if it wanted to be a viable intellectual alternative to the persuasive arguments of the anti-clerical Enlighteners. Catholic Enlighteners differed among themselves as to how such a modernization should be brought about, but all agreed that Aristotelian scholasticism could no longer serve as the universal foundation for theology.

Some thought that the empiricism of John Locke looked promising: if one could show that all human ideas originated in sensory impressions, then this might explain why there were so many different views of God. The more one could control the senses and purge them of selfish influences, the clearer the idea of God would become. In the end, however, God would have to reveal himself because not everybody had time for such a long, ascetic search for truth. Others believed that the philosophy of Immanuel Kant enabled a new way of conceptualizing Christianity. If Kant was right that no knowledge about God existed and that every proof for the existence as well as the non-existence of God was impossible, one still had to postulate His existence for the sake of morality. Atheism was thus refuted, and the necessity of God for the realm of morality was established—which seemed enough for some. Many such proposals for reconciling philosophy and Catholicism were circulating at this time.

It also became clear that Catholics were falling behind in the natural sciences as the whole world began conducting experiments and teaching Newtonian physics. Against the resistance of conservatives, Catholic Enlighteners urged the church not to bind itself to outdated science and instead introduce the sciences into the curriculum of its universities. The Benedictine university of Salzburg in Austria was the first European institution of higher learning to introduce the discipline of experimental physics in the 1740s. Lectures in this field focused on demonstration experiments in hydrostatics, electricity, mechanics, pneumatics, and optics, and often attracted a wide public. Roger Boscovich, one of the greatest astronomers of the century and a Jesuit priest, said that "the greatest harm that can be done to religion is to connect religion with the things in physics which are considered wrong. .... The youth then ... say that such and such a thing in physics is wrong and consequently religion is wrong."[7] Instead, the church had to be, according to the Jesuit, in a dialogue with scientists, and it had to abandon disproven theories from the past, such as the Pre-Copernican worldview. When Boscovich's friend Pope Benedict XIV removed Copernicus from the list of forbidden books in 1757, this was an important signal of the return of intellectual openness to the church.

Catholic Enlighteners, however, also faced an internal battle: the attacks of both radical and moderate Enlighteners on church teachings and institutions increased. While a substantial number of Catholics simply dismissed criticism without engaging it, Catholic Enlighteners saw some merit in the criticisms and tried, to the best of their ability, to refute them thoroughly while also ceding some ground. For example, although some counter-Enlighteners would not engage with Spinoza's radical statement that the biblical books were the product of a long process of editing and development, the French theologian Richard Simon took such an argument seriously. He nevertheless attempted to defeat it, but not without reinforcing his own theology with what we today call "historical criticism." The same goes for Nicholas Bergier, whom Jean-Jacques Rousseau and others called their smartest critic. The Catholic Enlighteners were open to discussion, to science, to new philosophies, to everything, just as long as the main dogmas of the faith—the incarnation, the Trinity, the sacraments—were not undermined. It was an eclectic enterprise. This is sometimes seen as a negative: shouldn't church teachings be based on one solid philosophical system? This argument is usually put forward by systematic theologians, but it overlooks the simple historical fact that the church has been most creative, and has won more new members, when it was open to an eclectic dialogue with the cultures around it. In the first centuries, the synthesis of Greek philosophy and Christianity came about because of such interactions, and in the Middle Ages a new worldview was created through the reception of Aristotelianism. Only through continuous dialogue with culture is the church able to identify what is good, true, and beautiful and to incorporate these gems and riches into its treasury—a view that was officially embraced until the Second Vatican Council in the 1960s.

One can identify a few concrete ideas that almost all proponents of the Catholic Enlightenment shared, despite the intellectual diversity of the movement. Most important, perhaps, was the desire to communicate their message more widely and in a more conceptually clear manner. While literacy was spreading in Europe, the majority of the church's authors were still writing in Latin and thus for a small circle of specialists. Moreover, they followed a style called scholasticism. A thesis was introduced, then arguments were listed for and against the thesis, all leading to a conclusion. One read such accounts to study arguments but not for enjoyment or personal edification. Also, the terms were often confusing and burdened with subtle distinctions. It was an arcane world that an outsider could not penetrate. The vernacular was increasingly seen as the most suitable way of disseminating the church's message, and alternative literary styles were being established by authors who wanted to display critical judgment, engagement with contemporary thinkers, and erudition—but also orthodoxy.

Catholic Enlighteners sought to show the public that they could successfully grapple with their intellectual counterparts and that they possessed the same intellectual abilities. They became much more conscious of the history of doctrine. Careful historical research made it clear that traditions—whose changelessness had been previously assumed—had in fact developed, and sometimes decayed. Now, using eighteenth-century "criticism," it became possible to distinguish the wheat from the chaff, to discern the essential core of Catholic teaching and separate it from overgrowth. Monastic historians especially contributed to this change of mentality, which ultimately led to the conviction that if things were different in the past, they could also change in the future.[8] Underlying this zeal for reform was of course the belief in the perfectibility of structures and organizations, or simply put, that things could change for the better—an idea common to secular Enlighteners and Catholics. Catholic Enlighteners developed plans for improvement of the individual, the human race, the church, and the state. Certainly, these plans were not always equal to the problems they hoped to address, but still, the proposals for "taming" capitalism or promoting a just wage were quite remarkable given their context and the unimpressive results of such ideas introduced by the Enlighteners' secular peers.

Yet another concrete motif that one finds among Catholic Enlighteners, as well their secular peers, is their shared disgust for enthusiasm, superstition, and prejudice. Enthusiasm was a synonym for fanatic religious zeal, which was irreconcilable with the ecumenical agenda of the Catholic Enlighteners, that is, their peaceful and benevolent attitude toward other denominations. Superstition was regarded as the unenlightened use and abuse of religion. Prejudice, finally, impeded the proper use of reason and thus progress. All three presupposed a limited use of discernment and reason, both of which were essential to true faith. The faith of the Enlighteners was opposed to blind obedience; echoing St. Paul, they affirmed only "rational" obedience (Rm 12: 1).

The papacy was yet another target of Catholic Enlightenment critique. While certain popes displayed some sympathies for the Enlightenment, the majority of Catholic Enlighteners were unhappy about how the papacy sought to control the local and national churches. Many suggested that the church should revitalize the institution of regular councils, and make clear that the pope was a servant and that the local bishops were not his vicars but successors of the Apostles. In some regions, such as Tuscany and Germany, such criticism blossomed into open opposition to Rome. Last but not least, Catholic Enlighteners discovered the human person as an important topic of theology, albeit with no references to the groundbreaking anthropology of Thomas Aquinas (1225–1274), which would heavily influence theological developments in the twentieth century. They developed new anthropologies and considered how doctrines could be useful for the fulfillment of human persons and how the church contributed to the happiness of mankind. Certainly, such theologies often became quite utilitarian, but as with any new discipline, most mistakes are made at the beginning; never before had Catholic doctrine been in such close dialogue with Protestants of all denominations, with the Eastern Orthodox, and with Jews, but also with self-avowed agnostics and even atheists.

Catholic Enlighteners often worked very closely with state reformers. Both the church reformers and the state had common goals. The more the reformers felt disappointed about the lack of renewal coming out of Rome, the more they placed their hopes in state sovereigns. Meaningful church reform could only be brought about, they thought, if the state forced the church's arm. Catholic Enlighteners and the state had common enemies and common goals. Both identified papal influence as harmful and instead sought to strengthen the national character of the church; both believed that the church's freedom from taxation was no longer defensible, and thus they demanded that the church contribute more to national coffers; and both felt that the church should yield to modern states in disputes over jurisprudence.

The last point needs some clarification. In many Catholic states the Holy Inquisition still prosecuted religious dissent and blasphemy. Enlightened reformers suggested that such prosecution be stopped, or at least heavily curtailed. Every instance in which the church claimed privileged rights over the sphere of secular law was being revisited. A major example was internment. For centuries it had been common practice for priests, monks, and nuns who had committed crimes or acted defiantly to be incarcerated in secret ecclesiastical prisons. In the eighteenth century, however, the state claimed that a criminal monk was first and foremost a citizen and should be punished under the code of secular law. Often the inmates in these prisons had been deprived of any legal defense during their trials, or had been incarcerated at the despotic whim of their superiors.[9] The church could no longer be granted the right to have a parallel structure of legislation that rivaled the state's. Enlightened jurisprudence put an end to the ancient understanding of the church as a "state within the state" and began seeing it as a religious corporation, though the extent to which such a secularization of law was implemented differed greatly from region to region; it was stronger in Central Europe than in Spain or Portugal.

Until 1789 nothing seemed to impede the rise of Catholic Enlighteners, but then a series of events changed the course of history. The French Revolution disillusioned many Catholics who might have embraced the idea that modernity and Christianity were really reconcilable. After all, the Revolution had mercilessly persecuted Catholics who did not succumb to the state's new church, murdered a hundred thousand Catholic peasants in the Vendée, and attempted to replace Christianity with a cult of reason. Every crime the revolutionary government committed was attributed to "the" Enlightenment. Throughout the world, intellectuals distanced themselves from the once-adored intellectual revolution. A conservative reaction set in. This alone would not have stopped the reform of the church, but the Revolution, because it spawned Napoleon, also meant the beginning of the end of the close alliance of church and state throughout Europe. When Napoleon occupied the Rhineland he enabled the German princes to dissolve all monasteries in 1802–1803, by then strongholds of Enlightenment, and seized all Catholic institutions of higher learning. The church lost its intellectual bastions, its charity organizations, its religious orders, and its bishoprics. Catholicism was stripped naked. Pope Pius VI had died a prisoner of Napoleon in 1799, and in 1802 it looked as if his successor would share this same fate. But, being deprived of leadership, Catholics looked upon Napoleon's prisoner as the new moral authority who could lead the church after the failure of local bishops and prelates. The rest is history. The popes happily accepted the public endorsement and gained a power over the church they had never before possessed.

In this new environment, Enlightenment Catholicism had no niche left; it was considered a remnant cancerous growth that had to be eradicated. The few independent thinkers Catholicism had produced in the nineteenth century prove this development: Bernhard Bolzano and Franz Brentano, both brilliant logicians and "grandfathers" of modern analytic philosophy, were Catholic priests who were ousted because the church was too intellectually narrow to contend with their thought. Matthias Scheeben's merging of systematic and romantic theology had almost no influence until the 1950s, and biblical exegetes who applied the historical-critical method had to fear the loss of their positions. Catholicism withdrew more and more into an intellectual ghetto that was not in dialogue with modern thought but rather in a defensive crouch against everything modern. Certainly, Catholic Romanticism produced great contributions to art, philosophy, and church life, but unlike the Catholic Enlightenment it believed that the glorified past, for example, scholasticism, held all answers and was thus not willing to engage with the intellectual currents of the time. At the turn of the twentieth century, questions that the Catholic Enlightenment had posed long ago reemerged in the so-called Modernism Crisis; the suppression of the modernists almost tore the church apart. In the 1960s, however, the Second Vatican Council (1962–1965) reiterated the same questions about the compatibility of modernity and Catholicism.

When the Second Vatican Council articulated a new vision for the encounter of Catholicism with other Christian denominations and used the phrase "separated brethren" to describe their status as not in union with the Holy See, it used a phrase Catholic Enlighteners had already adopted in the late 1780s. Likewise, ideas about tolerance and religious liberty were already being circulated by Catholic Enlighteners two centuries before the council. Most striking, however, a core idea of the council's dogmatic Constitution on the Church, *Lumen Gentium*, was at the heart of Catholic Enlightenment, namely, that "whatever good is in the minds and hearts of men, whatever good lies latent in the religious practices and cultures of diverse peoples, is not only saved from destruction" by the actions of the church but "also cleansed, raised up and perfected."[10] Such "exchange between the Church and the diverse cultures of people,"[11] as the document *Gaudium et Spes* calls it, had already been tried by Enlightenment Catholics, yet none of the council fathers referenced them. Even the liturgical reforms of the council were anticipated: while Muratori emphasized the centrality of the Mass as devotional act, the active participation of the laity in the Mass, and stressed that it was all the faithful who offered the holy sacrifice, the German Benedict Werkmeister even went so far as to demand the vernacular for Catholic liturgies. Finally, Febronian theologians emphasized the collegiality of bishops and saw the role of the papacy primarily as a "center of unity," thereby anticipating the ecclesiological changes of the twentieth century.[12]

This book tells the story of this forgotten reform-minded Catholicism, which anticipated so many crucial ideas of the twentieth century. Yet this book does not glorify the past but undertakes to describe Enlightenment Catholicism with its bright and dark sides, and to leave any judgment about the value of its projects to the reader.

I

Catholic Enlighteners around the Globe

THE CATHOLIC ENLIGHTENMENT, which had its roots in the Council of
Trent and in Renaissance humanism, aspired to integrate modern science
and philosophy into a religious worldview. This movement was provoked
by modern philosophy, which in the late seventeenth century began challenging Catholic thought more and more assertively. One philosopher
whose challenges were especially pointed was Baruch Spinoza. Born into
a Dutch Jewish family, he studied under Francis van den Enden, a former
Jesuit priest and freethinker who introduced him in the 1650s to the philosophy of Rene Descartes, which the gifted young man eagerly absorbed.
Yet Spinoza radicalized Descartes' insights, and in 1670 he presented his
famous *Theological-Political Treatise* to the world. At the time it was one of
the most erudite attacks on established religion ever written; it not only
advised that the Bible should be read as a piece of historical literature
but also argued against the concept of miracles as divine interventions.
Spinoza advocated a free and tolerant society as well as the separation of
state and religion. Then, in 1677, he went even further. In his *Ethics*, he
contended that there was no supernatural, spiritual realm but only matter, and that everything happened by necessity. For Spinoza, the religions
of men were their own inventions, rooted in their superstitious nature.
Catholics felt compelled to respond to such an attack on the foundations
of the faith. They did so by producing philosophical arguments for the
existence of mind and matter, historical arguments for the reliability of
Scripture, and myriad other writings arguing for the intelligibility of
their faith. Catholic intellectuals also had to battle deists, especially from
England, who were not atheists like Spinoza but who taught a radically

de-Christianized religion; whether they believed in an impersonal deity or a personal God, none affirmed Jesus Christ as divine savior. Deist authors such as John Toland, Matthew Tindal, and Anthony Collins were of course ideologically buttressed by skeptics such as Pierre Bayle. The sharpest deist criticism of Christianity and of Catholicism, however, was offered by Voltaire. Although he merely reformulated what others had said before him, such as pointing out alleged contradictions in the dogmas of the faith or biblical texts, the cantankerous and entertaining Voltaire said it more memorably.[1]

When Spinoza claimed that miracles were impossible because the universe was governed by eternal and necessary laws, the French Oratorian priest Nicholas Malebranche tried to refute him with the concept of God's "general will." He agreed with the Dutch thinker about the eternal laws of the universe, but he claimed that these were set up by God such that the universe operated independently, without any divine guidance or special interventions. This theory "saved" providence against radical deists, yet at the same time it minimized divine action in the world. Consequently, this theory of providence was invoked both by Catholic Enlighteners who intended to defend the faith as well as by thinkers whose goal was the elimination of a personal God for the sake of an impersonal principle of creation. Nevertheless, Malebranche had always insisted that the ultimate goal of history and the purpose of nature was the incarnation of Jesus Christ.

While for Spinoza and rationalist Enlighteners, reason was the only viable key to unlocking the mysteries of nature, Catholic Enlighteners appealed to reason illuminated by faith. "Reason," as invoked by Catholics in the eighteenth century, no longer necessarily reflected only scholastic philosophy but also integrated new philosophies, such as the empiricism of John Locke. Drawing on reform ideas that grew out of the Council of Trent (1545–1563), Catholic Enlighteners constructed a worldview that defended the traditional faith while giving the utmost consideration to science, "the improvement of civilization, the increasing attractiveness and livability of this nether world," and individual moral progress.[2] This Catholic Enlightenment spread from Portugal to Austria, from Italy to England. It was a Catholicism that, at least during the first few decades of the eighteenth century, was able to interact productively with Enlightenment thought. Only the anti-clerical and anti-Christian attacks of Enlighteners—and especially the terror of the French Revolution—put a stop to this conversation.

Devotion and Reason

One of the most common arguments against Catholicism, employed by Enlighteners but also by Protestants, was that it was a superstitious religion that grossly overemphasized the supernatural. Miracles could easily be explained by natural causes, they said, and thus prove Catholicism false. It was argued that devotional practices—such as reciting the rosary, practicing Eucharistic adoration, or offering prayers for the souls in purgatory—were irrational. Such prejudice was widespread in Protestant countries, especially in England, where since the Reformation—with a short interlude—Catholics had been a persecuted and proscribed minority. However, the Council of Trent had already attempted to purge Christian theology of superstitious elements, and the English priest Thomas White, president of the English college in Lisbon, had answered critics with his book *Devotion and Reason* of 1661. He not only insisted that the rosary and adoration had profound biblical precursors but also that prayer for the deceased had nothing to do with ghost stories. He believed that when reason was used honestly, when it was unprejudiced, faith could not be disturbed or challenged by it.[3] Exiled English Catholic priests even founded, in 1745, a network of scholars, the Society of St. Edmund in Paris, which imitated the Royal Society in London. The society aimed to give missionaries to England rigorous training in Enlightenment thought, including the natural sciences. Founding president Augustine Walker believed reason should guide the participating scholars, whether they discussed Jewish thought, Newtonian physics, or theology, leading society and Catholicism from the darkness of scientific backwardness "into a new world of light."[4] Other English Catholic Enlighteners, such as Cuthbert Wilks, Joseph Berington, and John Lingard, attempted to appeal to their educated, rationalist peers by purging Catholicism of supernaturalism.[5]

Catholics in the Netherlands faced a similar challenge: they also were a religious minority, albeit a tolerated one. Thus, it is no surprise that one of the most cogent works attempting to prove the intelligibility of Catholic doctrine was written in Dutch in 1765, then translated into German, by a priest named Gerard J. van Sterck.[6] In France, Father Claude Houtteville had taken up his pen to defend the existence of miracles twenty-five years earlier. While Spinoza had declared that miracles were impossible because the laws of nature were immutable, Houtteville insisted that God could establish laws according to his will and could include miracles in his eternal plan for humanity. God did not have to change his mind in order to bring this or that miracle about. Instead, such miracles were predetermined from before all time.[7]

Intelligible and rational Catholicism was propagated even in Hungary, where the rural population still believed in superstitions such as vampires.[8] The Hungarian Pauline monk Johann Bartholotti wrote in 1779 what may be the most sophisticated contemporaneous Catholic treatise on superstition. It boldly joined church reform with the Enlightenment project to defeat ignorance and prejudice. The monk made it clear that no Catholic dogma was in danger if fantastic stories about miracles were purged from the lives of the saints, and that religious fanaticism counted as superstition since it confused human ideas with divine instructions. Bartholotti thus articulated an insight that one frequently finds among Catholic Enlighteners, namely, the abhorrence of fanaticism as an irrational religious force. Even theologians could be guilty of it, he wrote, especially those who downplayed the importance of reason or who sacrificed the intellectual coherence of the faith by insisting on doctrinally irrelevant marginalia (such as some unbelievable miracle in the life of a saint). Such fanatical theology distorted the faith and rendered it unintelligible to the Enlightenment world. What the Catholic Church needed instead, if it desired to remain an intellectually serious alternative to secular worldviews, was an open-minded evaluation of modern philosophies, a critical and honest examination of its own history and theology, and ultimately a serious updating.[9]

Shared Governance in the Church

To the contemporary observer, the Catholic Church can appear to be fiercely opposed to democratic government. Nevertheless, in the eighteenth century the "democratic"—or, perhaps better, constitutionalist—element in the church, which favored decision making based on the votes of clergy representatives rather than papal fiat, seemed to emerge victorious. The history of this movement dates back to the Council of Constance (1414–1418), which was supposed not only to end the Western Schism but also to reform the church. The decree *Haec Sancta* declared that the council had supreme authority over the church; only a congregation of all bishops could speak for the church, not the pope alone. Consequently, frequent councils should be called to express the will of the faithful, to enact reforms, and to address other pressing matters. These ideas, associated with the term "Conciliarism," survived despite papal efforts to eradicate them. The idea of provincial synods and local councils was even adopted by the Council of Trent. In France, Conciliarism inspired the *Declaration of Gallican Liberties* of 1682—a declaration of the independence of the French (or Gallican) church from Rome, which granted the king almost universal control over day-to-day ecclesiastical matters, such as the appointment of bishops and abbots (though not spiritual matters, such as the administration of the sacraments and catechesis).[10]

In the following century, especially in Germany, papal ambassadors kept intervening in local church affairs, and as a result, resentment against the papacy grew. Nikolaus von Hontheim, auxiliary bishop of Trier, expressed his anger in a pseudonymously published book titled *On the State of the Church* (1763). Febronius—the pseudonym Hontheim used—revived classic Conciliarist principles and adapted Gallican ideas. Most important was his claim that the authority of the bishops came not from the pope but from their status as successors of the Apostles. The papacy should lead the church but not understand itself as an absolutist monarchy, because Christ never left the keys to the kingdom of God to a single pope but rather to the entire church. The bishops were not the vicars of the pope, Febronius explained, but divinely appointed ministers. All church government therefore had to be collegial and not monarchical. Hontheim's bold book was immediately censored by the pope, but it inspired reformers across Europe. In Austria, a whole generation of canonists considered Febronius's work their Bible for ecclesial reform, as did the Italian bishop Scipione Ricci, who had called a synod of bishops and clergy in Pistoia on the command of the archduke of Tuscany. The pastoral ideas that surfaced during the discussions of the Synod of Pistoia (1786) were very similar to those discussed two hundred years later at the Second Vatican Council (1962–1965), yet the papacy of the time condemned Pistoia. Many of the theologians who were involved in the synod, such as Pietro Tamburini, were Jansenist, and some drew their inspiration from the sixteenth-century theologian Edmond Richer, who had stated that the authority of the church rests with local priests; Richerism was the most radically democratic ecclesiology in the Catholic Church. Though the popes rejected democracy in ecclesiastical affairs, they did not reject it as a governing form for states. The most famous example is a homily of Cardinal Chiaramonti, the future Pope Pius VII, preached at Christmas 1797, in which he argued that democratic government was not contrary to Catholic tradition. "Be good Christians and you will be excellent democrats," he preached.[11]

In England, support for a collegially governed church merged with enthusiasm for constitutional rights. Every English citizen enjoyed God-given, inalienable rights, which papal supremacy seemed to threaten. Moreover, English Catholics had to defend their faith against the accusation that they were subjects of a foreign tyrant, the pope. Sir Richard Throckmorton, Lord Petre, and Charles Butler organized the Cisalpine Club, where they articulated their Anglo-Gallican vision of a Conciliarist church. The Cisalpine Catholics oriented themselves on the northern side of the Alps (cis-alpine), and thus in a strong local church, placing themselves in opposition to Ultramontane Catholics, who looked beyond the mountains, toward the papacy, for such guidance. The Cisalpines believed that the church should be governed like the English state, with a strong constitution and institutions that provided checks and balances. Cisalpine theology denied papal infallibility and held that, in extreme cases, the faithful should appeal papal decisions with which they disagreed to a general council, and even that bishops should be elected by the faithful. It was Conciliarism seasoned with English individualism, and it was a view that was eventually exported to the British colonies (see Chapter 4, "Catholic Enlightenment in the Americas, China, and India").[12]

Contending with Philosophy: France

There were two main camps of Enlighteners within the French Catholic Church. One strongly supported the Jansenists, a group named after seventeenth-century bishop Cornelius Jansen, which stressed religious austerity, the importance of the ancient church for contemporary church reforms, and the moral progress of Catholics through individual piety and Bible reading. Jansenists also insisted that with the fall of Adam and Eve human nature had been irreparably wounded, while their opponents, the Jesuits, claimed that the fall had stripped humans merely of the right to live in Paradise and the special friendship with God but nothing more.[13] The Jesuits and their supporters believed Jansen was a heretic, and supported the papacy's fight against Jansenists. What is most fascinating, however, is that both groups were inspired by the philosophies of the time, in particular the empiricism of John Locke and the physics of Isaac Newton. These English thinkers were embraced as catalysts to reform

Catholic thought, to bring it up to date so as to again demonstrate its intellectual viability to the world.

Because the papal bull that declared them heretics was also state law in France after 1730, the Jansenists were in a defensive position, and the second group of Catholic Enlighteners, which had papal support, grew influential. While the Jansenists had stressed that it is impossible for humans to do any good deed without God's help, the Jesuits emphasized that human nature was amenable to and capable of good works by itself. Jesuit spirituality was more focused on the individual. It was therefore much closer to many secular forms of Enlightenment thought, which focused on human progress and responsibility, than the rather pessimistic Jansenists. Such openness to new academic currents, however, did not affect most Jesuit college curriculums; the education students received there was considered outdated because it was still based on the 1599 Jesuit *Plan of Studies.*

The Jesuits Claude Buffier and Rene Joseph Tournemine even tried to develop a philosophy that respected the insights of the Enlightenment but avoided the extremes of Spinoza's materialism and Descartes' skepticism. Like the Scottish common-sense philosophers, both priests argued that through self-awareness one could verify one's own existence as a thinking being and also the existence of a material world that functions according to certain laws. The initial perception of one's self was akin to scientific inquiry based on observation and experience. For these Jesuits, all ideas were based on sensory experience, including the idea of God.

This had a number of advantages. First, the Jesuits could show that Catholicism was open to empiricism and thus to scientific progress. This view was motivated in part by a common desire among French Catholics to engage in the sciences—botany, biology, astronomy, and medicine.[14] A good example of the latter is the early Catholic endorsement of vaccinations. Catholic missionaries, mostly Jesuits, began inoculating Amazon Indians against smallpox in the 1720s. The practice spread from there, saving countless individuals. In Europe, Catholic orders set up modern hospital care, and church officials, such as the archbishop of Bamberg in Germany, introduced public vaccinations in the 1780s. In Rome, Pius VII voiced support for the treatment, and already in 1805 more than eight hundred newborn babies were vaccinated. The claim that popes rejected vaccination as an interference with divine providence is nonsense, which even renowned historians unknowingly repeated.[15] Second, there was hope that Jesuit common-sense philosophy could promote an overhaul of scholasticism, which marginalized experiential knowledge. Third, this new synthesis of traditional scholasticism and modern philosophy was compatible with established doctrine. If all ideas derived from sensory experience, including the idea of God, then humanity needed divine revelation because otherwise views about the divine would be too diverse and false ideas would spread. Fourth, the teachings of the Bible were depicted as an exact fulfillment of philosophical expectations, and thus their accuracy could be proven by historical research.

The Jesuit emphasis on intuitive self-awareness also influenced ethics. Catholic theologians increasingly attempted to show that moral rules were self-evident, revealed by reason alone, and that a natural law existed for all humans. Thus, in 1769, the Jesuit Camier wrote that "independently of the existence of God, man is bound to do good and to avoid evil, or what is the same thing, moral principles impose obligation independently of the existence of God."[16] Similarly, Luke Hooke, an Irish priest teaching in Paris, wrote: "There is a certain sense of right and wrong placed in nature in the minds of men. ... We know by conscience that this moral sense is in us and would be vain to try to demonstrate it by argument. ... This sense is so natural, so constant and uniform, that it can be stifled by no prejudices and extinguished by no passions."[17] By defending the concept of natural law, Camier and Hooke agreed with the Enlightenment principle that revealed religion and morality as belonging to separate spheres. Yet while secular Enlighteners such as the materialist Denis Diderot thought such a separation meant that the church was unnecessary, the theologians believed they had proved the opposite. For them, the natural cognitive faculty that informed all humans about God's laws needed to be supplemented by revelation. Only then could one gain more detailed information about the ultimate lawgiver and one's obligations. The intellectual openness of the Jesuits impressed many, including the enlightened future royal minister Robert Turgot, who graduated in 1750 from the Parisian Jesuit college with a thesis on the usefulness of Catholic doctrine for individual and societal progress.

Two years later, however, the tides shifted when a young priest, Jean-Martin du Prades, defended a dissertation in Paris that was highly offensive to the silent Jansenist minority, especially because it seemed to discount any difference between the healing miracles of Jesus and those of other ancient healers. A publicity campaign against him and the Jesuit Enlighteners began. Suddenly on the defensive, branded as heretics, the Jesuits began to withdraw from their open engagement with Enlightenment thought and took a conservative turn. Then, to make matters worse, during the next decades even more radical works of Enlightenment philosophy appeared, especially from the pens of Jean-Jacques Rousseau and Paul d'Holbach. Instead of engaging with these works, a strong anti-Enlightenment force began to form.[18]

For French apologists, the most pressing task was to prove that the mysteries of Christianity did not clash with reason. For theologians such as Hooke or Houtteville, the world was not so much the creation of God's reason but of God's will, and therefore it made little sense to ask whether a special revelation of God was reasonable. Such thought did not occur to most theologians; if everything depended on God's will, it was pointless to ask about its rationality. The mysteries of faith were, after all, inaccessible to reason. All a good theologian could do was to prove their inner intelligibility or coherence, but not their truth. Furthermore, while one could not prove the content of the mysteries, one could prove the historical reliability of the witnesses of revelatory events such as the resurrection and thus argue for the probability of miracles. Catholic Enlighteners and critics of the church both accepted the idea that the first Christians must either have been trustworthy witnesses or frauds. While Diderot and d'Holbach believed the latter, the Catholic apologists tried to prove the former. For their argument to work, however, the apologists first had to address the criticism of the Scottish philosopher David Hume, who famously claimed that no testimony whatsoever could validate the report of a miracle. In response, the theologians stated that without trust in the testimony of men, all human knowledge would vanish. As Gabriel Gauchat wrote in the midst of the century: "The testimony of men has a preponderant weight even in the objects of reasoning. . . . On matters of fact it is testimony that decides, and not only does testimony assist our reason, but without it it is wholly impossible for reason to know the facts. . . . In this respect all witnesses have the same authority."[19]

The man who most courageously refuted the attacks on his church was Nicholas Bergier. As a parish priest, he wrote a bestselling book, *Deism Refuted by Itself* (1765), which convinced the French bishops to free him from all pastoral responsibilities and make him a full-time writer and apologist. Bergier did not disappoint them; in dozens of tomes he refuted critics of Christianity, generally in an irenic and generous tone. In *Deism Refuted*, he set out to unveil inconsistencies in the works of deist Enlighteners, who did not believe in the biblical God but rather in an impersonal divine principle. Bergier also responded to Jean-Jacques

Rousseau. While Rousseau was in many ways an easy target, since he did not defend a strictly rationalist philosophy, he was probably the most influential critic of Christianity at the time. A staunch individualist, Rousseau complained that Christianity created too many intermediaries between the divine and the human person. As an alternative, he proposed that God should be experienced through the fecundity and beauty of nature. Without priests, bishops, popes, or any teaching tradition, Christianity could be an acceptable religion, he reasoned. Bergier immediately understood that this argument was much more powerful than any flat denial of God's existence, and it shook the walls of the church more than any biblical criticism. He took up Rousseau's challenge and argued that religion was not merely a private affair but always a covenant between God and man. In particular, Christianity was not a private revelation but instead a revelation to all humankind through a body of witnesses, the writers of the Gospels. One cannot be a Christian without accepting their testimony, Bergier argued. Rousseau also rejected rituals, which was a position that made sense for someone who believed that religion was only a set of moral rules. But Bergier again challenged him; he denied the reduction of religion to morality and insisted that rituals like the sacraments were a necessary part of the covenantal alliance between God and man. Moreover, without rituals no religion could survive.[20]

Bergier also targeted Paul d'Holbach, whose anonymously published works were the most ardent expressions of atheism at the time. In *Christianity Unveiled*, d'Holbach attempted to show that Christianity led to barbarism because it perverted natural human behavior. Bergier, of course, argued for the opposite and showed, with enormous erudition, how Christian morality did not destroy human instincts and virtues but perfected them, and thus led to happiness. Unlike his colleagues, however, Bergier really tried to understand what motivated the unbelief of the radical Enlighteners, and he frequented their salons. He was a personal friend of Diderot, which shows that Catholics did not necessarily shy away from hot topics or from civil and friendly relations with their intellectual opponents. Beginning in the 1770s, Bergier also became convinced that the thing that damaged the reputation of Catholics the most was adherence to St. Augustine's teachings about grace. According to Augustine, only the baptized could be saved. According to Bergier, however, the grace of God was available to all mankind, even the unbaptized "savages" of the Americas and Oceania. Since many of them could not clearly conceive the idea of God, their reluctance to accept the Christian

faith must not be sinful. This was a remarkable step toward acknowl-
edging the possibility of salvation for those outside the Catholic Church,
including adherents of other religions—themes that only came to promi-
nence two hundred years later at the Second Vatican Council. Bergier's
boldest book, however, was *A Treatise on Redemption*, and it was never
published. Most of the manuscript was lost during the turmoil of the
French Revolution, but based on what scholars have been able to recon-
struct, Bergier truly was a tolerant theologian who insisted on the infinite mercy of God for all people of good will, and on the possibility of
salvation for all, albeit always through the grace of Christ. For Bergier,
Catholicism was not entirely comprehensible, as it contained mysteries of
faith, but it was never contrary to reason. This was of course nothing new,
as already Thomas Aquinas had stated that some truths of faith were
beyond the grasp of human reason and therefore supra-rational. Bergier
also criticized Catholicism for focusing too strongly on the unmerited
election of sinners without their assent or good works; such Augustinian
Catholicism, as he called it, had missed the chance to successfully communicate its message of faith seeking understanding.[21]

As mentioned, Jesuit Enlighteners rejected radical skepticism and
instead believed that one could establish historical certitude about church
teachings and revelation. Nobody took up the challenge to provide such
certitude more seriously than the Jesuit Jean Hardouin. Hardouin
had learned to appreciate the tools of biblical criticism from the great
Oratorian and early Catholic Enlightener Richard Simon, but Hardouin
carried Simon's insights to the extreme. He believed that atheism was the
greatest enemy of the church and that secret atheists had been plotting
against Catholicism for several generations. Hardouin was a conspiracy
nut. Immensely erudite, he mined whole libraries and, in the end, came
up with one of the strangest theories ever conceived: according to him
all written records dated before the fourteenth century were forgeries,
except the Latin text of the Bible, Homer, and a few others. Everything
else—whether the Hebrew or Greek Bible, the works of the Church
Fathers, the councils, and even the corpus of St. Thomas Aquinas—were
forgeries by atheist monks meant to bring about the Reformation. Despite
this, Hardouin still believed that tradition, as a living, orally transmitted
faith, was infallible, and that the pope was the supreme judge of tradition.
For Hardouin the church was in no need of written historical witnesses
because it was the source of its own authority. Although his works were
placed on the *Index of Forbidden Books*, Hardouin found at least one gifted

disciple, Isaac Berruyer, who in the spirit of his teacher rewrote the entire Old Testament under the title *History of the People of God* (1728–1758). It was a modernized paraphrase that added a lot of material concerning the unknown personal thoughts of the patriarchs, along with other insightful details. While the Roman Curia censored his work as well, it was remarkable that Berruyer—who is unacknowledged by modern historians and philosophers—had developed a sophisticated theory of historical interpretation. He sensed that it was difficult, if not impossible, for a modern reader to understand an ancient text because we live in a different intellectual climate. Because ancient writers wrote for human beings of their own time and according to their interests and limitations, their texts were unintelligible unless they were translated so as to correspond with the modern intellectual milieu. It was therefore futile to assume that texts like the Bible could serve as objective authorities because everyone reads in light of his or her own prejudices: "Whether Catholics or Protestants, we all read Scriptures with the prejudices of our own dogmas. These dogmas being already in our minds, we look for them in the Scriptures."[22] Berruyer was therefore among the first in the history of scholarship to acknowledge the impossibility of purely objective interpretation, long before Protestant scholars such as G. E. Lessing or Johann David Michaelis became famous for this historicist insight.

Because the best intellectuals of the time proved the rationality of the faith in abstract terms, talk about the biblical God as the triune unity of Father, Son, and Holy Spirit was replaced by the notion of a "supreme being" or "God." The religion of the "heart," whose importance Blaise Pascal had emphasized in the seventeenth century, was forgotten, and religion became for many an intellectual exercise. Theologian Michael Buckley has even argued that such early modern Catholic theology had essentially transformed into philosophy and given up its theological distinctiveness, such as the centrality of the mysteries of faith, thus paving the way for religious indifference and atheism.[23]

The Church, Marriage, Celibacy, and Divorce

Throughout the eighteenth century, Jansenism spread widely in the European heartlands of what are today Austria, Germany, and the Czech Republic. It was Jansen's teaching about the importance of a well-educated clergy, his aversion to the extroverted piety of the Baroque, and his support for the reading of the Bible in the vernacular that attracted most followers. The German Emperor Joseph II was deeply influenced by these ideas, and after he gained power he merged them with an agenda to further centralize his lands. The church became an important pawn in his political chess game and, like any other institution, was forced to accept government control; even seminaries were no longer free from government intrusion. This policy, called Josephinism, was heavily influenced by Enlightenment thought, and it was already partially in place during the reign of Joseph's mother, Maria Theresa. This period produced a number of radically liberal theologians, including most prominently Joseph Valentin Eybel, who attempted to completely rethink what "church" and "religion" meant. For Eybel religion was the fulfillment of all duties toward God, and since reason could demonstrate the necessity of worship, one could deduce from this the necessity and the existence of a *natural* church. Such a natural church was, for Eybel, a community of women and men whose goal was to venerate God and to maintain a pure concept of the divine.[24] Since this was achieved through interior, private faith, and not through public action, ecclesiastical power would have to be restricted.[25] On the basis of this insight, Eybel developed six theses that, he argued, should define the relationship of church and state. Accordingly, the state not only has the right to defend the church, to reform it in the case of harmful activities, and to inspect the church, but it also has the right to convene councils or synods to end theological controversies, to censor theological books, and to tolerate other religions.[26]

Josephinist theologians were particularly concerned about the possibility of divorce and remarriage, especially because the state also aimed at gaining sole control over matrimony. Traditionally, the church set up impediments to marriages—such as rules against marriage for close relatives—and these laws could be dispensed on a case-by-case basis, but the state increasingly questioned the validity of these rules. In 1783, Joseph II promulgated a decree that defined marriage as a civil contract. Consequently, government officals alone had the authority to decide about impediments to marriage, marital duties, and the dissolution of the marital bond—only the spiritual or sacramental side of marriage was left to the church. The deeper theological problem was that, traditionally, the contractual and sacramental aspects of marriage were indistinguishable, and now their separation made the spiritual side of marriage look extraneous instead of essential. An even sharper attack on church doctrine was the introduction of civil marriages after the French Revolution, at which point church marriages were increasingly marginalized.

Another theological problem caused by the increasing influence of the state on marriage law was the question of divorce. If divorce was suddenly possible in state law, how should the church react? Should it acknowledge that two previously married persons were suddenly no longer conjoined in a sacrament, or should it maintain its teaching that a valid marriage between two baptized Christians was indissoluable until one of the partners died? Beginning in 1741 the city of Breslau, which housed one of the most liberal theology departments in Germany, came under Prussian rule. One of its intellectual contributions to the Catholic Enlightenment was an academic essay contest hosted in 1817. Reflecting on the previous three decades of theological controversy, in which the ex-Jesuit Karl Joseph Michaeler and Benedict Werkmeister argued for the possibility of a divorce for a valid sacramental marriage, the department posed this question for the contest: "Is it a Catholic dogma that the marriage bond between two living spouses cannot be dissolved?"[27] Anton Frenzel, a student of the Catholic Enlightener and Carmelite Anton Dereser, won the prize. Frenzel amassed a remarkable number of sources and argued that the indissolubility of marriage was not contained in Scripture, nor in the utterances of the Fathers, nor the councils, and could therefore not be regarded a dogma. Instead, he found ample evidence that the Church Fathers had a more nuanced view, and that several particular councils (e.g., Toledo in 681 or Compiègne in 756) even allowed divorce and remarriage in cases of adultery. Frenzel argued that the Council of Florence's decree for the Armenians (1439), which had confirmed indissolubility, was not legally binding because the decree was written after the council had officially ended. Even in the canons of the Council of Trent (1545–1563), nothing was said against the possibility of divorce and remarriage. After all, Frenzel explained, Trent had only taught that adultery was *no* reason for the dissolution of the marriage bond, but had not stated that marriage was per se indissoluble. Frenzel's was a very idiosyncratic way of reading the tradition of the church, but we must not forget that the understanding of "dogma" was still in flux when he was writing; it was not defined until sixty years later at the First Vatican Council (1870–1871). It is fascinating to see how Frenzel tries to use the Council of Trent to support his view that a sacramental marriage was dissolvable. Because, he insists, the council states that one cannot interpret Scripture differently from the Church Fathers, and since they leave open the possibility of dissolving the marital bond through divorce in the case of adultery, one must come to the conclusion that divorce is theologically possible. Since the Greek Eastern Rite Catholic Churches, which kept this tradition, were never condemned for it, it seemed to Frenzel possible that the Latin Church could follow suit.

Even celibacy for priests was openly debated, especially in the 1780s. Canon law professors at the University of Vienna stated that celibacy was not of divine origin but was merely an ecclesiastical law that could be changed by the state sovereign. Critics argued that celibacy hurt the church. They claimed it was a violation of human rights and of natural law: since every person was endowed with the natural instinct to procreate and to find companionship with a partner, it would run against nature to ask someone to give this up. Secret marriages of clergymen, their affairs, and rumors of widespread immorality were used to buttress this claim. It is hard to say whether these were as common as then-contemporary critics described. The scarce paper trail for such cases makes the argument seem vastly exaggerated. In fact, archival records suggest that the reforms of the Council of Trent to improve the moral life of the clergy had been widely successful. The number of explicit public admonitions—such as the case in the Archdiocese of Paderborn in 1783, in which priests were reprimanded and ordered to abandon illicit relationships, and to live chastely—were quite rare.[28] Every accusation of immoral behavior was investigated, and if the priest was found guilty he was sentenced. In the case of a priest serving the nuns of Hersee, who had fathered a child with a farmer's daughter, it was not the bishop but the Mother Abbess of the monastery who served as the judge. She sentenced him to a substantial time of penance in a Capuchin monastery and offered the mother generous child support until the boy was of age.[29]

Some opponents of priestly celibacy even argued that it was detrimental to the economy because it slowed down population growth. In Speyer, the Catholic physician Johann Peter Frank, father of modern public hygiene, argued vehemently that sexual abstinence harmed the human body and should be avoided. Another Catholic layman, the Freiburg professor of jurisprudence Kaspar Ruef, claimed celibacy was a medieval invention to prevent priests from bequeathing church property to their offspring. The former Jesuit Karl Michaeler went even further. For him it was clear that the church could neither invent a new dogma nor introduce a new basic law for all its clergy if it was not previously prescribed by the Apostles themselves. Therefore, he said, celibacy had no legal ground within the Latin church. One of the most radical voices of the Catholic Enlightenment, he proclaimed that priests could get secretly married to "compensate their natural urges." Moreover, he believed that the state should acknowledge the secret marriages of priests as legally valid, thereby reinforcing the difference between marriage as a contract and as a sacrament: while the priest cannot enter a sacramental marriage because he is bound by church law, he can enter a civil marriage, thus giving his secret spouse legal recognition and his offspring the corresponding rights. Michaeler's hopes rested on Emperor Joseph II, but the Habsburg ruler ultimately decided not to act. Yet in the 1783 decree, he made it clear that the right to abolish or to keep celibacy was within his rights as a Catholic sovereign.[30]

Nevertheless, it would be wrong to assume that all Catholic Enlighteners were opponents of celibacy. In fact, most moderate reformers supported it. One of the most common arguments in favor of celibacy was that in order to be a good pastor, and to be readily available to meet the needs of the flock, one had to forgo family responsibilities. Thus, the Enlightenment idea of usefulness and practicality was used to defend church law. The Benedictine Augustin Schelle, a follower of the Enlightenment philosophers Kant and Wolff, even used statistical data to prove the usefulness of celibacy. He rejected the criticism of the French Enlightener Montesquieu, according to whom celibacy—in a time of many religious vocations—diminished the growth potential of the population. Schelle responded by demonstrating that monasteries and the vow of celibacy did not diminish, but rather stabilized, the population. Dioceses and monasteries allowed men and women who could not afford to sustain a family to support themselves in a useful, religious way. If celibacy were abolished, the number of poor people would increase because the land would be inadequate to feed the sudden increase in population. While Catholic monks advocated celibacy as a means of population control, secular Enlighteners propagated unlimited population growth.[31] An Austrian clergymen also translated an essay by Nicholas Bergier, who commented that in ancient Rome one could hardly find seven virgins who would devote their lives to be priestesses of Vesta despite their luxurious lifestyle, while one word of Jesus Christ "motivated an uncountable mass of people in all areas of the world to live in celibacy."[32] The former Jesuit Benedict Stattler of Bavaria also defended celibacy. Every society needs, he taught, a class of people, namely priests, that works only for the advancement of Christian morals and spirituality. Stattler too emphasized that a priest's function as spiritual father and educator would be seriously compromised if he had to care for a family. To be a father and husband is a vocation by its own right, one that would take time away from being the father of a big parish: "To live both vocations with the same necessary perfection would be a burden, which most could not shoulder."[33]

The debate over celibacy became more radical after the French Revolution. Beginning in the fall of 1791, priests were legally allowed to get married in France, and a law of 1793 forbade criticism of this new practice, punishable by deportation. When Christianity was officially abolished as the state religion on November 7, about three thousand priests married to prove they were "enlightened" and healed from "fanatic Catholicism"; many, however, were merely attempting to save their necks from the guillotine. It was a marvelous deed of forgiveness that the pope graciously reintegrated many of these priests back into the French church after Napoleon signed a concordat with the Holy See in 1801; the only condition was that the priest had to be separated from his former wife.[34]

Biblical Studies and Historical Criticism

Already in the fifteenth century, Renaissance humanists had begun to examine the Bible using the tools of history and philology. In the sixteenth century, Catholics—especially Jesuits—championed exegesis and produced works of lasting importance. Soon, however, despite the support of the Council of Trent, oriental language research (Hebrew, Aramaic, Arabic, Syriac, etc.) began to be neglected by Catholic theologians, and Catholicism fell behind Protestants in biblical expertise. Nevertheless, especially in the late seventeenth and eighteenth centuries, the Catholic Church could boast of remarkable Bible scholars, men who embodied Enlightenment thought without sacrificing fidelity to their faith. The most important Catholic exegete was undoubtedly Richard Simon, who developed an original hermeneutic for interpreting Scripture in the last decades of the seventeenth century. Even today conservative Catholics label him a "heretic" or "Spinozist," usually because they fail to read his writings and instead rely on the judgment of Simon's conservative critics. Simon was a French priest, a member of the Oratory, who saw a major threat to religion in Spinoza's reading of Scripture using reason alone. In response, he argued that one had to read the Bible with the rule of faith—that is, guided by tradition and the living church community. Simon, however, made enemies when he publicly ridiculed those who read Scripture allegorically. Simon instead focused on the literal meaning of the text. The interpretation of a verse was acceptable to Simon if it suited the text and did not contradict the teachings of the church, even when it deviated from the consensus of the early Church Fathers. He also devised a new understanding of the inspiration of Scripture in order to defend the faith against Spinoza. Simon claimed that the human authors of the Bible were instruments of inspiration, but that they made mistakes when they used their own reason, attempted to explain images, ordered the narratives, or abbreviated sources. However, he made clear that Scripture never errs when it comes to the truths about salvation. Simon even went so far as to question the Mosaic authorship of the first five books of the Hebrew Bible; that Moses wrote the Pentateuch was universally affirmed at that time, and so Simon's novel opinion led to the censorship of his books. But his views on inspiration were eventually adopted (without credit) by the Second Vatican Council.[35]

Inspired by Simon's work, the Catholic French court physician Jean Astruc began to conduct literary-critical analysis of the Old Testament. He had accepted the idea that the book of Genesis lacked integrity, as demonstrated by Hobbes and Spinoza, but he did not share the common disbelief in Moses's authorship. Instead he argued that Moses had compiled a series of sources. One of Astruc's main criteria for dividing up the biblical sources was the use of different divine names, Jehovah and Elohim. This was the beginning of a process of discerning several redactions of the biblical texts, a project that has continued ever since. The Oratorian Charles Francois Houbigant followed Astruc's principles and, in 1753, published a four-volume edition of the Old Testament that reconstructed the text with the help of the Samaritan Pentateuch. Around the same time, the Clementine Society of Paris, founded in 1744 by the Capuchins, was working to generate interest among Catholic clergy in oriental languages such as Aramaic, Coptic, Syriac, and Arabic, though their efforts were interrupted by the French Revolution before they could be widely implemented.[36]

In Germany, Catholic exegetes were heavily influenced by their Protestant peers and increasingly tried to read Scripture as literature, abandoning the traditional allegorical reading of the Bible. This, however, created conflict with church authorities. The most prominent incident involved Johann Lorenz Isenbiehl of the University of Mainz. In his 1778 book on the prophecy of Isaiah 7:14, he insisted that the verse did not indicate the future birth of the Messiah, not even allegorically.[37] Johann Jahn, a Norbertine professor of exegesis at the University of Vienna, was

similarly engaged with the historical-critical method. He came to the conclusion that the Old Testament books of Job, Jonah, and Tobit were not
historical accounts but educational poems, and that the New Testament
healings of demonic possessions could be explained by modern medicine.
Jahn also had an idiosyncratic view of inspiration: in his eyes, the authors
of the Bible wrote according to their own imagination and experience,
while divine inspiration only served to prevent these authors from writing
anything erroneous.[38]

In Scotland, Alexander Geddes worked ceaselessly on a new translation of the Bible and argued that the first five books of Moses were neither
strictly historical nor mere fiction; in his eyes they were myths. This did
not mean that Geddes doubted the veracity of the accounts but merely their
factuality: as myths they were true, but they were not historically true. The
account of Adam's fall, for example, had to be read as the mythic account
of the painful condition of human life. Geddes also proposed a radically
new understanding of progressive revelation: he believed that many divine
truths had been communicated in a way that accommodated the needs of
the ancient Israelites given the state of their culture and knowledge, and
that over time a more progressive understanding of these truths could
be expected. Geddes's favorite example was slavery. The condoning of
slavery in the Bible could be explained by the primitive culture in which
the Israelites lived. In his time, however, slavery could no longer be condoned. Geddes's critics wondered, though, how far such accommodation
could go. Was Jesus's talk about the eternal flames of hell just an accommodation to his listeners? Should such language now be abandoned?[39]
Geddes's theory made Catholic leaders worry about a potential loss of
faith. As a consequence, eighteenth- and nineteenth-century popes and
bishops warned Catholic exegetes against regarding historical criticism as
the only way of reading Scripture rather than as a tool that complements
traditional reading, backed up by the wisdom of the early Church Fathers
and the teaching tradition of the church. Other Catholics, such as Leander
van Ess, inspired by Pietism and the Evangelical Revival, attempted to
establish regular Bible reading among the Catholic laity. Such attempts to
disseminate the Bible among the laity, however, had only limited success.
The Council of Trent had insisted that vernacular translations contain a
commentary in order to prevent private and potentially heretical interpretations. This turned well-done translations into multi-volume works that
were not only too expensive for the average reader but also impractical for
devotional reading. Moreover, evangelical revivals at the beginning of the

nineteenth century made Bible reading again suspicious in the eyes of church authorities. As a result, not much progress was achieved in this area until the twentieth century.[40]

State-Sponsored Reforms: Portugal

State governments were often the main sponsors of Enlightenment reforms. The kingdom of Portugal is a good example. The common view that rational thought and Enlightenment were weak in Catholic Portugal does not reflect reality. Especially after 1750, Portugal underwent a period of reform. Not only was the curriculum of the venerable University of Coimbra completely overhauled and replaced with a new state-run education system, but the power of the Inquisition was curtailed, and slavery was abolished (although not in the colonies). All these changes were intimately connected with the powerful minister of Portugal, the Marquis de Pombal. Historians have wondered whether the Marquis de Pombal was actually a genuine church reformer, despite some of his anti-clerical actions, especially against the Jesuits; after all, in 1759 under Pombal's leadership Portugal became the first state to officially suppress the Jesuits. Some have argued that much of his ecclesiastical policy was in fact only a radicalized version of what Catholic Enlighteners had already suggested, while others insist that his only motivation was to increase the king's power.[41] It is impossible to come to a final verdict on this question, partly because the Marquis left hardly any notes about his own personal faith. One of the few documented pieces of evidence is Pombal's appreciation of the German erudite Benedictine Martin Gerbert, who was no Enlightener but who was inspired by the Tridentine Reform. Pombal praised the way Gerbert based all theology on Scripture and tradition, criticizing only his strong support of the papal office. While radical in many areas, in questions of doctrine Pombal seems to have embraced a fairly traditional theology.[42]

Medical doctors had a major influence on Portuguese Enlightenment culture. Under the protection of Pombal, they imported the works of European Enlightenment authors. But religious orders also participated in the dissemination of Enlightenment thought. Portuguese Oratorians were at the forefront of these efforts. Like the Jesuits, their order had been founded during the Counter-Reformation, but they had an entirely different community structure. Every house was independent, rules were minimal, and members were given maximum freedom to develop their talents. Many oratories opened schools, and thus they threatened to undermine not only the Jesuit monopoly on education but the entire Jesuit enterprise, precisely because Oratorian schools followed a modern curriculum that integrated the latest in science and philosophy and stressed the vernacular over Latin. Drawn to this updated pedagogy, parents began to withdraw their children from Jesuit schools, which were increasingly being seen by some as outdated.[43]

In a 1746 book, the Capuchin Luis Antonio Verney launched a major attack on Jesuit schools. Although the Inquisition seized Verney's book immediately, his ideas spread secretly and influenced Pombal. Verney, a follower of Francis Bacon, advocated a "modern theology" that was based on history and Scripture but also open to new impulses, including Protestant ones. The friar even saw something positive in the Reformation. After all, it had forced Catholics to reform their church and to better articulate their faith. Such a view was radically new at the time; officially, the Reformation was considered a wound to the church and could therefore have only negative implications. Verney, on the other hand, even upheld the value of reading heretical writers, which especially shocked the Portuguese Inquisitors. The Capuchin tried to express a nuanced position: he reasoned that the church only rejected the heretical interpretation of Scripture and dogma but not the philosophical or philological methods of heretics. If the methods proved to unearth new insights, one could and should adopt them without fear. Pombal was deeply impressed by Verney's suggestion that the Portuguese Inquisition be placed under state control in order to ensure that human rights and dignity were no longer violated, and he implemented this proposal in 1769. Verney was convinced that neither church nor state should prosecute dissenters, or even radical Enlighteners, because "the observation has been made that the devil is most afraid of countries where philosophy, medicine, law and theology are properly taught."[44] Education, not persecution, was the key to eradicating ignorance, superstition, and theological mistakes.

Miguel da Anuciação of Coimbra was among the Portuguese bishops who supported Enlightened Catholicism. He advocated a liturgical renewal that retrieved ancient traditions, reformed ritual exuberance, and founded a Liturgical Academy. There, young priests would be formed in a new, less Baroque, and more rational form of worship that centered on the essentials of the faith: the Eucharist and a personal connection to Christ. Despite his sympathies for the Catholic Enlightenment, however, Bishop

Miguel strongly resisted the attempts of the state to subjugate the church. He is an important example of how it was possible to be both enlightened and obedient to the Holy See. Another such example is Bishop Manuel do Cenaculo. He encouraged his clergy to abandon prejudices and superstitious practices and educated them in modern theology and philosophy. He said that he did not want his priests to be a "fugitive light, but instead a light of good consistency; ... [their education] should be like live coals, on which to roast and melt away all the dark matter, smoke and shadows of ignorance and error."[45] Clergy were ready to face the challenges in their own parishes only after a thorough education, one in which the challenges of the modern world were taken seriously. Cenaculo thought that priests should no longer live in their own Catholic subculture but partake of Enlightenment culture, thus bringing their enlightened faith to the marketplace of ideas.

Verney and the Oratorian Antonio Pereira de Figuredo found themselves in conflict with Rome because they supported Pombal's vision of an independent Portuguese church under the king's authority, similar to the arrangement in France. As early as 1761, Pereira published his theses about the Portuguese king's right to tax clergy without papal approval and potentially to reclaim all church property for the crown. This ideology of regalism, in which the king had universal authority over the church, was influenced by German Febronianism, and it included the claim that the crown could freely appoint bishops. It was an attempt to revive the ancient understanding of bishops as having full jurisdiction by the power of their own office, with the primacy of the pope understood in merely honorific terms, such that the church would no longer be a "government of despotism, of domination and of might, but a government of modesty, of service and humility."[46]

But regalism tended to blindly succumb to even the most "unpalatable" wishes of the state. In their desire to reform the church, Catholic Enlighteners like Verney and Pereira naively entrusted the sovereign with all power, believing that the king would, like a medieval ruler, benevolently seek the church's welfare. Yet times had changed. The eighteenth-century state had assumed total control of welfare and was, unlike earlier times, no longer interested in a symbiotic coexistence of church and state. The church was instead to become a subdivision of the state. Only the official alliance of throne and altar kept the state from crushing the identity of the church completely. Yet when this alliance broke, as it did in France, then state policy could very easily become brutally anti-clerical or even anti-religious. The greatest damage caused by regalism, however, was the rift it caused in the church in Portugal and wherever else it was practiced, be it in Spain, France, or Germany: supporters of the papacy stood against national church reformers, each steadfastly denouncing the other party as heretical or dangerous to the survival of the faith. This mutual distrust weakened the church as it battled outside enemies, and it made the church vulnerable to movements that sought the rejection of all religion, especially in the decades after the French Revolution of 1789.[47]

Catholic Enlightenment and the Abandonment of the Baroque Lifestyle: Spain

The reign of Charles III from 1759 to 1788 was marked by a sincere interest in the reform of Catholicism. The king was personally pious, and he believed that the unenlightened faith of his people—who lived, according to him, in intellectual darkness and superstition—was a major reason for Spain's decline in morality and economic strength. The unreformed ancient faith was seen as a stumbling block for Spain's arrival in modernity. After all, according to the king's reasoning, the traditional Catholic view that one should not strive for financial success, but rather merely for self-subsistence and contentment, was poison for the development of the economy. To overcome this, the king and his ministers, especially from the 1760s on, sought to place the Spanish church completely under government control. Diocesan seminaries were put under the control of reform-minded priests, curricula were rewritten, and competitive exams were introduced to find the best qualified priests for the most distinguished parishes.[48]

The Jesuit order, whose central authorities were located in Rome and which boasted about its devout obedience to the pope, did not fit into this plan. Since it could not be controlled, it was considered dangerous. When riots broke out in Madrid over enlightenment reforms, the government, especially minister Pedro Campomanes, charged that the Jesuits were behind them. In fact, recently discovered evidence seems to confirm that the order was indeed embroiled in the incident.[49] Consequently, all Jesuits were identified as enemies of the state and were therefore expelled from Spain in 1767. Afterward, Spanish Catholic reformers who were influenced by Renaissance humanism, Catholic Enlightenment, and Jansenism took charge. Moral integrity, practicality, and simplicity in worship, as well as the rejection of philosophical theology, were all on their agenda. Spanish Jansenism included a number of spiritual movements with sometimes conflicting goals, held together only by a strong appeal to the revival of pastoral care and the preservation of national traditions.[50] Due to reformers' influence at court, ostentatious Baroque forms of piety, such as public self-flagellations of hooded penitents and excessive processions, were banned. The reformers also believed that Catholics had to be taught that the most important religious ritual was the Eucharist, and to be persuaded against the veneration of the saints or pilgrimages. Catholics should learn, they said, to see the Mass as the culmination of their prayer life and therefore to disregard peripheral forms of devotion. The government also lifted bans on vernacular translations of the Bible and encouraged the public to read Scripture.[51] It is important to note that the reform programs of state officials and Catholic Enlighteners were often identical, differing only in motive. While state reformers aimed at the improvement of the political economy, Catholic Enlighteners intended primarily to purify the faith and only secondarily to profit the state. Nevertheless, all these reforms meant bidding farewell to the "sensory road to salvation," which had been a goal since the Council of Trent, even though the council hadn't explicitly said so. Spain's Baroque churches are in fact a reminder of the opposite: artwork and sensory experience were believed to lead to an encounter with God. Catholic Enlightenment reformers, however, detested this supposed demonstration of God's magnificence and the rituals that accompanied it. Hastily and without sensitivity, long-standing prayer traditions were abolished. Instead of slowly changing rituals that were dear to the faithful, they were proscribed overnight. From one day to the next, the traditional way of mourning a dead family member had to change dramatically: no more hired mourners, no decorated coffin. In Mexico, the dances of the Amerindian tribes were forbidden, even though one of the first missionaries had declared that candles, incense, vestments, and music were essential to "uplift the souls of the Indians and move them toward the things of God."[52] Moreover, the reformers misunderstood that in addition to engaging the senses, religious rituals had sociological importance. Funerals were attended by hundreds of people and thus reinforced the faith of all participants. By overemphasizing the individual through strict Enlightenment regulations, the corporate identity of Spanish Catholicism was substantially weakened. This was one of the most striking, unintended effects of the enlightened reforms in Spain but was generally true wherever radical reforms were imposed.

Unlike in other European countries, however, the reforms in Spain did not attempt to bring about a secular form of Enlightenment—as described by Montesquieu or Voltaire—but rather aspired to the ideals of Renaissance humanism, with the ultimate goal of moving toward even greater collaboration between church and state. Thus, most reforms were not anti-clerical in nature, except for the expulsion of the Jesuits. The driving idea behind the reforms was the attempt to mold the clergy into civil servants who would support educational and governmental reforms, so that the church would become a force for societal progress. The reformers only embraced some of the ideas of "mainstream" Enlighteners such as John Locke, Montesquieu, Newton, and even Hume. Only concepts that did not threaten the religious identity of the country were accepted. Therefore, toleration for other faiths was not on anybody's agenda.

The most prominent Spanish Enlightener was a Benedictine monk, Benito Feijoo. He was convinced that Catholic thought had to come to terms with the discoveries of science, and that the biggest obstacles to such progress were outdated philosophies and the Catholic "ghetto mentality" that regarded Protestant and Jewish thought as dangerous. According to Feijoo, echoing Aquinas and the masters of scholasticism, truth was truth regardless of its origin. Only by following truth—which requires a skeptical attitude toward one's own ideas as well as the ideas of others—can one hope to overcome ignorance and superstition. Yet many conservative Catholics abhorred Feijoo's skeptical approach to inquiry. How could he advocate such skepticism as healthy? Was not Descartes, the father of skepticism, to be blamed for the decayed state of religion? In fact, Feijoo did not think so. In his eyes, it was superstition and anti-intellectualism that had brought down religion, together with the scientists' exaggerated belief that they did not need religion. If the men of science had been more skeptical of their own achievements and had not extrapolated their findings to the realm of metaphysics, there would be no conflict between religion and science. Feijoo advocated a humble science and a humble theology at a time when humility as a virtue had lost its value.[53]

Don Pablo de Olavide is the most curious case of a Spanish American Enlightener. Born in Lima, Peru, he left for Spain in 1751, studied in Italy and France, and became acquainted with Enlightenment authors. Giacomo Casanova, who met him in Madrid, described him as a man who worked zealously to eradicate religious prejudices. By 1766, he was a high-ranking administrator in southern Spain, where he advocated reform. He suggested that the local universities abandon scholastic philosophy and instead introduce sciences and new philosophical currents. Moreover, he supported radically curtailing clerical privileges, which he thought were impeding the reform of education. Nonetheless, Olavide was unhappy with the intellectual ghetto of the Spanish church and the unwillingness among church officials to support new ways of thinking that would benefit the poor. But he was not an enemy of the church as such. He saw himself as a radical Catholic Enlightener. He detested ostentatious religious ceremonies and emphasized the importance of an interior spiritual life. He expressed the importance of practiced charity once to a gathering of noblemen: "Gentlemen, you would do far better assisting your neighbor to use this money to develop agriculture and increase the value of your properties and thus give sustenance to the poor who are perishing; that would be a good devotion."[54]

Olavide also befriended the German Catholic maverick Kaspar Thürrigl, who sought to cultivate and populate the Sierra Morena, a three-hundred-mile-long mountainous unpopulated region in southwestern Spain. Thürrigl promised to attract six thousand hardworking German families to the area. The contract he signed with the Spanish Crown stipulated that he was only allowed to bring Catholics to the country, since Protestants were not tolerated. By 1768 about four thousand settlers had arrived. Now, however, it became obvious that many were Lutherans who had lied in their papers. When Spanish officials found out, they threatened to deport the immigrants and to forbid new settlers to enter the country. Thürrigl and Olavide, however, were both tolerant, and they had no problems with Protestants living in the community. They ultimately managed to keep the settlers from deportation. Nevertheless, some German monks, who ministered to the settlers, began to complain to the Spanish court about Olavide's liberalism, and he was branded a heretic. In 1774 the Spanish Inquisition began investigating him and Thürrigl for propagating religious indifferentism, doubting religious miracles, and restricting religious processions. While Thürrigl was acquitted, Olavide was sentenced to eight years in a monastery prison, perpetual banishment from Madrid and Lima, and the loss of his nobility and possessions. The enemies of the Enlightenment had won a decisive victory. The actions of the Inquisition stunned Europe. It seemed unbelievable that a reformer like Olavide had fallen victim to a group of fanatical monks and that the Spanish Crown would allow such a perversion of the law to occur.

In 1780, after several years of forced indoctrination in the monastery, Olavide was able to escape to France, where he survived the Revolution by withdrawing to a remote rural estate. Witnessing the terrors of the Revolution, he became convinced that only a poor training in the Catholic faith could have made the French so susceptible to Enlightenment propaganda. Arrested by the new government in April 1794, he must have feared execution, and he began writing his memoirs. Released in 1797, he returned to Spain. The government there allowed his reentry because, in his recently published memoirs, Olavide recanted his earlier positions. He reported that his imprisonment in the monastery and the horrors of the Revolution caused him to change his mind. He now proclaimed that religion was the only power that helped men to love each other, to correct abuses, and to create a good society. The philosophers he had earlier admired, especially Voltaire, he now despised for trying to eradicate religion and to deprive people of its consolation.[55] Yet Olavide still advocated a Catholic Enlightenment, especially when it came to catechesis. He was convinced that many Spaniards became critics of religion because they had never been properly educated about the beauty of the Catholic faith and its life-affirming message: "What is religion other than the accomplishment ... of what a human being is seeking for his own happiness and perfection? ... Among all philosophical systems ... only Christianity justifies and proves the ardent desire of the human heart to be happy and immortal."[56] Still, he was convinced that the current proscription of other faiths would not save the Catholic creed in Spain. Instead, laypeople should face the challenge of growing in their faith throughout their lives and spreading it among themselves. Olavide astutely realized that faith had become an "option" alongside the "secular option" of indifference or atheism. As long as theologians did not understand this, and until they produced a catechism that addressed this change in mentality, there was no hope for a religious revival.[57]

Olavide's trial poorly served the cause of the anti-Enlightenment. It was used by radical Enlighteners to demonstrate the backwardness of Spain and of Catholicism, and within Spain the trial intimidated even the moderate voices of reform into utter silence. Radical ideas, such as the belief in a democratic reorganization of the church—which would finally be disseminated through the decrees of the Italian Synod of Pistoia—did not gain ground until the end of the eighteenth century. This "democratic Jansenism," which circulated in the 1790s at the University of Salamanca, influenced the future leaders of Spain, who would come to draft the famous liberal constitution of 1812.[58]

A Diversity of Catholic Enlightenments: Italy

The Enlightenment in Italy was quite diverse, not only because the country was not yet unified, but also because a more radical Catholic Enlightenment, exemplified by Fernando Galiani and Giambattista Vico, existed alongside a Catholic Enlightenment that was mainly influenced by the spirit of the Council of Trent and strong currents of Jansenism. Overlooked by most historians, the Italian Catholic Enlightenment demonstrated a remarkable flowering of diverse opinions and proved how internationally connected these thinkers were.

Next to radical Catholic Enlighteners we can identify a second group, which we could call an "Enlightenment in a Tridentine Mode," exemplified by Ludovico Muratori. He was, like so many other Catholic Enlighteners, a devout priest; he was also a good friend of Pope Benedict XIV and an esteemed scholar. Immensely interested in history, philosophy, the sciences, and theology, Muratori aimed at synthesizing the scholarship of the French Maurists, who specialized in historiography, German philosophy, and Italian science. For years he worked at the famous Ambrosiana Library in Milan and acquired all the tools a historian needed: knowledge of philology, paleography, diplomatic theory, and historiographical method. Moreover, he fell so much in love with books that he became a librarian, a position he kept throughout his life. He published extensively on medieval Italian history, and even today his works stand out for their diligent and unbiased presentation of the past. This was a remarkable achievement, especially since the polemical use of history in order to defend the church was still widespread at that time. Instead, Muratori suggested a "sound critical" approach that did not ameliorate the past but presented history in all its thorny and embarrassing details. He combined his quest for historical truth with the search for a sound philosophy that could illuminate his faith and his scholarly endeavors. This led him to an appreciation of English empiricism, the works of Leibniz and Wolff, but also the more critical thinkers such as Pierre Bayle. Yet he was never wedded to any one tradition or school but instead was an eclectic thinker.

Reason and logic could, in his eyes, never be enemies of faith but are necessary to fully understand the Christian religion. Muratori advocated this position in a book that became a bible for all Catholic Enlighteners: *On the Moderation of Our Cleverness in Religious Matters* (1714). In it he highlighted how important sincere academic investigations are to an intelligible, rationally defensible faith, but he also made clear that when it came to dogmatically defined truths of faith or morality, or to the undefined doctrines that had always been held by believers, human cleverness and innovation must find their limits. In interpreting the Bible, Muratori embraced the new methods of criticism and supported the use of archaeology and history. One did not have to follow the biblical interpretations of the Church Fathers, he insisted, if they did not pertain to the common faith. As a consequence, he encouraged scholars to distinguish the immutable and essential elements of faith from those that were man-made and thus reformable. For Catholic Enlighteners, Muratori's book was liberating. Finally, someone had outlined a path of relative liberty through which one could reformulate the faith in less scholastic ways and bring it into dialogue with modern scholarship. Last, the book called for a change of heart in the Roman Curia regarding censorship: officials should give authors a chance to explain their reasoning first, and the curia should apply a hermeneutic of generosity rather than always reading the works of Catholic Enlighteners with suspicion of heresy. Muratori's open-mindedness and his impeccable scholarship soon made him well known in Protestant circles as well. He corresponded with leading intellectuals regardless of their religious affiliations and thus contributed to the rise of a more irenic, perhaps even ecumenical, stance among Catholics. Despite his sympathies for some Jansenist ideas, such as a simpler liturgical life without excessive veneration for Mary, a more collegial understanding of the office of bishops, and the reading of Scripture in the vernacular, he remained a close personal friend of Pope Benedict XIV, who defended the erudite librarian against a number of attempts to silence him.[59]

In Italy, Newtonian science was received with great enthusiasm from the earliest years of the eighteenth century. This fresh focus on the sciences, however, led to a new kind of theologizing, called physico-theology. Drawing on the most recent findings of physics, theologians redefined God's attributes. For example, one theologian attempted to deduce the existence of an intelligent and benevolent creator-god from the breathtaking design of the universe. The problem with such reasoning, which originated in England, was that it did not concede much ground to revelation and tradition. Yet the goal of connecting science, religion, and morality, and of overcoming confessional boundaries through such an approach, was attractive. Celestino Galiani was the most brilliant exponent of Italian physico-theology. A Celestine monk, he and his circle had admired Galileo despite the appearance of his works in the *Index of Forbidden Books*. Galiani's friend, the priest and famous mathematician Antonio Conti, validated the importance of scientific discoveries for a new worldview, in which the "anatomical, botanical, chemical ... conspire to demonstrate that where one discovers order in the parts and in the whole, there is a single intelligence and not many, if the whole and the parts are in accord in a harmonious system."[60] In short, the sciences had brought to light a side of God that had hitherto been neglected, namely, his place as creator of the most harmonious system imaginable. Consequently, the Protestant philosophy of men such as Gottfried Wilhelm Leibniz, which stressed the harmony of the best of all possible worlds, or of Christian Wolff, which emphasized the connectedness of all things, were greeted with enthusiasm in these circles. Accounts of the newest scientific and philosophical endeavors were merged with Roman Catholic tradition to create an eclectic blend of theology. It was not to everybody's taste, but it was open-minded and answered the most pressing contemporary questions.

Celestino's nephew Fernando Galiani followed a different path. He had received minor orders but lived a rather libertine lifestyle. Even so, Galiani never abandoned his faith and made some remarkable contributions to Catholic Enlightenment literature. He was a friend of Diderot (who despised religion) and he frequented the Parisian salons, but he was nevertheless a philosophical maverick. One could never entirely know which side of a conversation he would support. Galiani was an ardent proponent of liberalism; in 1752 he said: "Liberty is such a precious gift from heaven that princes must never take any part of it from anyone, or restrict its use, except for the most serious causes and necessities."[61] His high reverence for freedom led him not only to declare property sacrosanct but also to insist on economic liberty. This went hand in hand with his belief in political liberty, since only free agents would act responsibly for their own sustenance. Twenty years before Adam Smith's *Wealth of Nations* (1776), Galiani had already defended economic liberalism; the fact that he was Catholic and wrote in Italian, however, diminished his impact. Possessed of a pessimistic personality, he distrusted altruism and humanitarianism, and he came to believe (anticipating Karl Marx) that humans only act to further their own economic interest. Religiously, Ferdinando was somewhere between orthodoxy and nihilism, closer to deism, although he definitely received Catholic last rites on his deathbed.[62] Galiani is perhaps most famous for one of his disputes with Diderot. In a Parisian salon the two debated the existence of God and the authenticity of the Christian revelation in front of an excited audience. After dinner, Galiani sat down in a chair, holding his wig in one hand and leaving the other free for gesticulation:

> Let us suppose ... that he among you who is most convinced that the world is a work of chance is playing dice, not in a gambling house but in the most honorable home in Paris, and that his opponent gets seven twice, three times, four times, and keeps on constantly. After the game lasts a while, my friend Diderot, who is losing his money, will not hesitate to say: "The dice are loaded, I am among cutthroats!" "Ah, Philosopher, what are you saying!" Because ten or twelve throws have left the dice box in such a way as to make you lose six francs, you believe firmly in an artificial combination, in a well-organized swindle, and on seeing in this universe so prodigious a number of combinations, a thousand and thousand more difficult and more complicated and more lasting, and more useful, you do not suspect that the dice of nature are also loaded and that there is up there a great thief who makes a game out of catching you.[63]

For the average Catholic it was, of course, blasphemous to call God "a thief" or a "rascal"—yet by shocking his listeners, many of whom had become indifferent to a belief in God, he made them think, attracted laughter, and earned intellectual respect. Cynically, he nevertheless also often mocked the faith, doubted the immortality of the soul, and gave in to a pessimistic fatalism. Galiani even had no problem calling the earliest humans "monkeys"—a hundred years before Darwin.

Giambattista Vico is regarded by some as the only first-rate eighteenth-century thinker who never wavered in his Catholic faith. In his groundbreaking book *New Science* (1725), Vico rejected the idea that humanity was thrown into history without divine care and assistance, and he instead demonstrated that religion was the driving force behind human history. For him it was religion that made humans out of beasts, mainly by taming emotions. A truly atheist culture was, therefore, impossible in his eyes. Most important, Vico rejected the notion that mechanistic philosophies could explain human affairs.[64] According to him, the human mind could only obtain secure knowledge about things that had been created by the human mind. Since mathematics or physics were products of the human mind, one could not reduce human affairs to mathematical laws, as Descartes and others had proposed. Humans could learn much more by studying themselves than by observing nature. By demonstrating that human self-introspection is valuable, Vico opened a path to more serious reflection on human emotions, motives, and purposes. He applied this insight to history and thus arrived at the idea of a collective or social consciousness of mankind that could be traced over time. Humans know what they are, what a plan is, and what other people's plans are. This amounts to a knowledge of "why" and it is superior to simply knowing "that," having a mere knowledge of facts. Because all humans share the same capabilities and are connected through God's creative spirit, all human affairs are discoverable by humans and thus can be the object of research.[65]

Vico's most revolutionary notions include the idea that civilizations follow historical laws of rise and decay and his theory about the connectedness of all human experience. Although he sometimes got in trouble with the Inquisition, Vico's influential friends in the Roman Curia successfully defended his system as a genuinely Christian philosophy. They stressed that Vico had demonstrated humanity's guidance by divine providence through history. The divine providence that guides cultures to achieve progress in Vico's system was, however, different from Baroque theology: according to Vico, providence guided humans through natural causes and not through miracles or divine intervention. Another, more heterodox aspect of Vico's philosophy was his conviction that there are no timeless moral values. Yet one of Vico's most astute interpreters has argued that perhaps the Neapolitan genius did not completely grasp the consequences of every theory he proposed; in any case, Vico was a profound Catholic of the Enlightenment who does not fit into any simple category.[66]

Conclusion

Despite substantial differences between the cultural and political contexts in which Catholic Enlighteners lived and worked, it seems that a few common themes emerge that connect them all. Catholic Enlighteners had a sincere wish for a reform of the church. What the mission of the church should be, however, was fiercely debated. Should the church focus on temporal and social welfare or on the supernatural aspects of the faith? Should it be under the control of the state or function independently? All of the Enlighteners maintained some continuity with the Catholic tradition; none of them completely rejected past doctors of the church, doctrines, or councils. In fact, even the most critical voices of the Catholic Enlightenment, such as Feijoo, relied to a great extent on the achievements of medieval scholastic philosophy but rejected its early modern offshoots. Another common feature is their desire to search through the opinions and scientific discoveries of their day to integrate what was true, good, and beautiful into their theologies. In particular, the zeal of post-Tridentine reform ideas figure prominently among Catholic Enlighteners.

However, are the desire for reform and the intellectual mining of contemporaneous culture specific to the Catholic Enlightenment? By no means. We can find them in practically every Catholic reform movement and in particular in reform movements of modernity. Thus, it seems justified to label the Catholic Enlightenment a reform movement that had its roots in the late medieval reform movement and the Tridentine Reform.

The Catholic Learning Curve

TOLERATION AND TOLERANCE

THE ENLIGHTENMENT'S CONTRIBUTIONS to religious toleration and tolerance are well known. But most would probably not count the Catholic Church among its champions. Yet some Catholic thinkers and politicians, predominantly in Europe, were important advocates of tolerance and toleration. Before we go any further, some clarification of terms is in order: Tolerance is the inner, personal act of respecting others' beliefs. Toleration, however, is a legal phenomenon. It can either mean a civil toleration of religions or an ecclesiastical toleration of church critics. Tolerance could mean either a personal tolerance or a theological tolerance. Only the latter was really controversial because it could lead to the idea that different denominations or religions are equally valid.

Toleration as a Necessary Evil

One has to go back a few hundred years before the Enlightenment to understand fully the problem toleration posed for Catholics. Through the Middle Ages, religion was no private matter. It influenced every aspect of everyday life. It gave coherence to a people before "nations" and central governments existed. Religious dissenters were considered a threat to society and non-Catholics as worshippers of false Gods. There could only be one true religion. Judaism was (more or less) tolerated because it proved the trustworthiness of the Bible, but other Christian churches, each with a distinct truth claim, were inconceivable. Then came the Reformation. The unity of Western Christendom was suddenly shattered. Soon there were many Christian churches, each claiming to be "the one, true church of Jesus Christ." Most European rulers believed each territory should be united by faith and thus violently suppressed opposing creeds.

How did the Catholic Church respond? According to canon law, every Catholic king was obliged to actively take measures against "heretics." The religious wars in France and Germany, however, did not produce a clear winner. One proposed solution was for each government to choose a religion and oblige its subjects to practice it, with toleration of other creeds at the government's discretion. In principle, all kinds of religions could be tolerated as long as no harm came to the state.[1] Nevertheless, in the eighteenth century most Catholic bishops still viewed the toleration of other religions as a necessary evil. Most Catholic thinkers did not ask "How can I be more respectful toward other faiths?" but rather, "Is it really *necessary* to tolerate other faiths?"[2]

Related to the issue of toleration was the problem of conscience. The imperative to follow one's conscience had long been a core Catholic teaching. But what if one's conscience led to false conclusions? Then it was ignorant of the truth. If nothing could be done to change that, then one had an "invincibly ignorant conscience." Eighteenth-century Catholics increasingly began to apply this belief to Protestantism. According to Catholic Enlighteners, a Protestant could be excused for not recognizing the truth of Catholicism: if one grew up Protestant, one's conscience was formed from the earliest days accordingly, and one could not expect to overcome it. The belief that Protestantism was true was therefore not a condemnable heresy but invincible ignorance. Such a view was, although it sounds counterintuitive for us today, Catholics' *first* step toward accepting other beliefs. Catholic theologians stopped labeling Protestants heretics, decreasing tensions between them. If Protestants were no longer heretics, then the obligation of canon law to wage "holy war" against them was no longer binding and one could find ways to foster peaceful coexistence. Catholic Enlighteners even began calling members of other Christian churches "shadow" Catholics insofar as they participated in the graces of the Catholic Church without their knowing; for example, by continuing the sacraments and following the teachings of the Bible, they kept some elements of Catholicism alive. The more such elements a church possessed, the greater its participation in Catholic truth. This led the Italian Jansenist Bishop Ricci (in 1787) and the Irish Augustinian Father Alexander Kenny (in 1789) to call Protestants "our dear separated brethren," alluding to their imperfect participation in the Catholic Church.[3] The ecumenical theologian Beda Mayr even argued that Catholics should be willing to compromise on all traditions that were not doctrinally fixed if such a move brought "the separated brethren back."[4] The phrase was also frequently used by the romantic convert Friedrich von Stolberg and was eventually adopted by the Second Vatican Council in its decree on ecumenism, *Unitatis Redintegratio* (1964), as the official description for non-Catholic Christians—yet without any reference to the Catholic Enlightenment.[5]

The French Idea of Toleration, or Why It Did Not Originate with Voltaire

Centuries before Enlightenment thinkers wrote pamphlets about the necessity of toleration, it was widely practiced in post-Reformation Europe. Yet only over the last few decades have historians successfully dismantled the myth of the sudden arrival of toleration in the eighteenth century. Social historians were especially influential in bringing this change about: they demonstrated that toleration was found not just among the educated elite but among people of all classes who lived in religiously mixed communities. This toleration came in a variety of forms, but all of them included the "peaceful coexistence with others who adhered to a different religion."[6] By developing rules for a stable coexistence, conflict was contained and physical violence avoided. Wherever the will or necessity for such coexistence did not exist, intolerance and violence could flourish. Looking at the landscape of Early Modern Europe one can identify a number of regions in which such religious toleration developed long before the eighteenth century but was nevertheless enriched by the Enlightenment. Yet toleration in Catholic countries owed its existence predominantly to the efforts of Catholic sovereigns, theologians, and laymen, and only in a few instances to enlightened bishops.

France had suffered from particularly acute religious intolerance. The clash between the French crown and Calvinist reformers, the Huguenots, in the sixteenth century is well known for its length, cruelty, and the vast number of lives it cost. Peace was achieved by a toleration edict, but less than a hundred years later in 1685, King Louis XIV revoked it, setting off another wave of anti-Huguenot persecution. Catholics were not much bothered by this. The popes applauded it. No church leader or theologian advocated the moral urge to fight for toleration, because Huguenots were seen as a threat to the state church. Yet, a generation later, a small group of

fanatic Catholic Jansenists were able to sway public opinion in favor of toleration, though their actions dangerously undermined state and church.[7]

Jansenists were traditionalists. They strongly believed that the Council
of Trent had perverted the truth of Catholicism. According to Pascal,
Arnauld, and other Jansenist thinkers, the official Catholicism of 1600
was no longer the Catholicism of the first five centuries. This could especially be seen from how much the council deviated from the teachings of
the most important Church Father, St. Augustine. In a 1,300-page treatise Cornelius Jansen argued that the Church Fathers had believed that
humans were unable to do any good without the grace of God. Moreover,
he insisted (following Augustine) that one could never know whether
one would enter heaven because it was uncertain whether one had the
grace to persevere to the end of life. Jansen also taught double predestination: according to him and his followers it was clear that God had chosen
from the beginning of the world all those he wanted to save, and those
he reprobated to hell. All these ideas had been rejected by the Council
of Trent, which equated them with Protestant errors. The council had
even stated that one was "free" to accept or reject God's call, while for
Jansen this was a figment of theological imagination. He claimed that
such reasoning made God a politician hoping to persuade his creatures,
rather than an all-powerful creator. The greatest critics of Janenism, the
Jesuits, argued that freedom was such a high good that God would never
destroy it. Moreover, God would never predestine a soul to hell. Every creature would receive the necessary grace to receive salvation; if that person
declined the offer, it was personal responsibility that paved the way to hell
and not God's eternal will.[8]

While the Jansenists placed rigorous demands on humanity, the
Jesuits were realists. This became clear in conflicts over the sacrament
of confession. The Jansenists taught that because sin destroyed loving
friendship with God, one must be truly sorry in order to receive absolution. The Jesuits realized that this asked too much of most people. They
were aware that many Catholics just did not know what it meant to love
God or how to do it; thus, one could not make it a prerequisite for receiving the sacrament. Moreover, withholding absolution, as the Jansenists
demanded, only deprived sinners of sacramental grace and might motivate them to turn their backs on a church that failed to help them in an
hour of need. The Jesuits therefore successfully argued that the minimum requirement for receiving absolution was sorrow for one's sins, even
if the motivation was only fear of God's judgment. The Jansenists were

not convinced. They insisted that their conscience demanded opposition to the papal condemnation of Jansen's teachings. Consequently, they also rejected state attempts to discipline them as interference with the sacred realm of conscience. Gradually, this discussion undermined the French state-church and Jansenism challenged the king's claim to absolute obedience. The transformation of Jansenism from a small sectarian group into a set of beliefs that attracted people of various societal and intellectual backgrounds had brought about a powerful threat to the government.[9]

When, in 1692, the Jansenist priest Pasquier Quesnel published a book of moral reflections on the New Testament, Louis XIV asked the pope to issue a decree condemning Jansenism. Pope Clement XI published it under the title *Unigenitus* in 1713. In the eyes of most historians it cracked the foundations of the French monarchy. The king demanded that the decree, which branded Jansenism as heretical, be recognized as law. This, however, enraged the local parliaments, who believed the king was overstepping his boundaries. In their eyes the king already had enough power; he did not need to use force against conscientious dissenters like the Jansenists. Moreover, the law aligned the king with the pope, whom the French regarded overwhelmingly as a tyrant. The parliaments felt that they were expected to ratify a decree by a foreign despot and thus surrender the freedom of the French Catholic Church to the papal see. Many resisted the king's wishes and even claimed that the new law violated the constitutional principles on which France was built. Meanwhile, the Jansenists began appealing to the public for support. They launched an enormously successful clandestine journal, the *Ecclesiastical News*, which brought a steady stream of Jansenist news and opinion pieces to the attention of a wide audience. For almost eight decades, the *News* successfully evaded government attempts to identify its printers or to dismantle its distribution network. It was a "masterly vehicle of propaganda," in which the Jansenists could openly question the rights of the king.[10] This provided the foundation for the radical questioning of the monarchy altogether just a few decades later, during the Revolution. Such criticism merged with Enlightenment ideas, most notably those in Rousseau's *Social Contract* (1762), and from this, a strange group of bedfellows coalesced, people who, for very different reasons, opposed the newly emerging royal tryranny: noblemen, who were offended by royalist demands and papal laws; clergy and simple believers, who adored Jansenist piety and rejected the structures of the state church; and secular Enlighteners, for whom toleration was a core philosophical principle.[11]

In the 1730s, a series of miracles was reported to have occurred in Jansenist graveyards, which made matters more difficult. Although the supporters of Jansenism believed the miracles confirmed their beliefs, the church and the government refused to acknowledge that any miracles had occurred. This, however, led to more reports of miraculous events and created a major embarassment for the king and the bishops. Both gained reputations as tyrants who resisted even God himself. A satirical placard found at one miracle site sums it up: "God Take Note, by Royal Command, Miracles in This Place Banned." Then, in the 1750s a number of anti-Jansenist Catholic clergymen spread the practice (already sporadically in use) of withholding the sacrament of extreme unction from Jansenists. This sent shock waves through the country, as it meant that the church would let a Jansenist Catholic go to hell rather than administer the sacrament. Many considered this a clear abuse of the spiritual powers of priests and consequently sued in court, often successfully. Such behavior, however, changed the mood of the people. If there was still a majority that supported the anti-Jansenists measures, these events swung the pendulum in favor of the persecuted.

In 1749–1750, thirty riots broke out in Paris alone, and the despotic measures taken against the Jansenists were a major motivation for them. Beginning in 1749, the church decreed, all suspected Jansenists who could not provide a certificate declaring that they had confessed their sins to a non-Jansenist priest were to be refused extreme unction. The first victim, Charles Coffin, was a famous intellectual and former rector of a university. It was a publicity disaster for the church, especially because four thousand people attended the funeral, which became a demonstration against the oppressive Catholic hierarchy. The resistance grew to such intensity that in 1752 the parliament of Paris even forbade the clergy from withholding the sacrament, against the express will of the archbishop. The next year the king managed to silence the parliament but only at the price of open opposition, which in the end served him ill, as he had to concede in the ensuing power struggle to permit the Paris parliament to decide important issues of church governance. Parliament thus became the "voice of the nation," not just the guarantor of old liberties, charged with ensuring that the king, who had lost prestige and influence, ruled justly. Apart from the fact that this anticipated a representative government as it developed in the Revolution of 1789, this policy shift allowed for greater toleration of Jansenism and a better control of what was perceived as "abuse of spiritual powers" by the clergy. Priests who still refused the sacraments were exiled or forced to resign from their parishes; even the archbishop of Paris was unseated. It was in this intellectual and public climate that the Enlighteners like Voltaire could speak up against the "infamy" of the Catholic Church.

In the ensuing decade, Jansenists tackled their next enemy, the Jesuits. The order maintained considerable influence in France and, due to its allegiance to the pope, symbolized Roman intolerance. In pamphlets, which often sold more than ten thousand copies, Jansenists ridiculed their opponents until the Parisian parliament finally expelled the order in 1762. This was a stunning victory for French modernizers. Yet secular Enlighteners, who were also no kindred spirits of the Jesuits, had not contributed much to this defeat of Catholic "intolerance" in France. To save face, they began a publicity campaign. It centered on the case of the Protestant Jean Calas, who had been executed for murdering his son to prevent his conversion to Catholicism. But Calas had only confessed under torture and Voltaire was able to demonstrate that the son had committed suicide. His 1764 *Treatise on Tolerance* charged the state with judicial murder, but saved his fiercest ire for the Catholic Church: because the church embraced unrestricted intolerance and religious fanaticism, innocent Protestant citizens could be accused of heinous crimes and suffer injustice. Yet, "to put it plainly, Voltaire could hardly fail to attract significant support for his campaign" as he was riding on the wave Jansenism had created over the past few decades.[12] Nevertheless, Voltaire and his comrades were successful in claiming victory: the Enlighteners were able to convince later generations that they and not a religious, intra-Catholic controversy had won the day for tolerance.[13] The Jansenism controversy also had a downside. It polarized French ecclesial thought, demoralized priests, and ultimately radicalized the Enlightenment, which redefined itself as anti-clerical or even anti-Christian; in the French Revolution this reorientation of the Enlightenment would exact bitter revenge.[14]

Germany and Austria—Laboratories for Religious Toleration

Among historians of Early Modern Europe, the Dutch Republic enjoys the privilege of being seen as the most important center of religious toleration. This is certainly correct if one looks at the intellectual debate about toleration and the development of individual liberties.

Yet the biggest, most religiously diverse "nation" of the time was the Holy Roman Empire, which comprised roughly what is today Germany, Austria, Belgium, Luxembourg, the Czech Republic, and parts of northern Italy. Moreover, since it was a loose union of sovereign states it stands out as a laboratory in which different approaches to religious toleration were tested. The empire had not only been the hotbed for the Reformation but also the region where new ways of coexistence were found. The Peace of Westphalia of 1648, which ended the Thirty Years War, not only brought peace to a region that had lost about a third of its inhabitants on the battlefield or to plague, but it also institutionalized religious toleration for three mainstream Christian denominations, namely, Lutherans, Reformed/Calvinist Christians, and Catholics. Subsequently, the most elaborate discussion of toleration developed in Central Europe.[15]

The Bavarian Jesuit and canon law professor Vitus Pichler articulated the default position of most Catholics when he described tolerance as a weakness. Toleration was allowed only if it was a lesser evil than "holy war."[16] In this spirit, religious dissenters were arrested and executed in many Catholic areas—as late as 1747 in Lucerne, Switzerland. Yet resistance to this position grew when people came to see other denominations as sincere seekers of truth and no longer as "devils." In the 1780s the Swiss priest Bernhard Ludwig Göldlin publicly denounced the hunting of heretics and argued that a properly understood Catholic faith did not have to condemn other beliefs; Catholicism could be tolerant.[17] Of course, a considerable number of Catholics did not share Göldlin's beliefs and sought the prosecution of dissenters. This became clear in 1775, when the Peruvian-born Enlightener and royal administrator Pablo de Olavide denied a German friar permission to build a monastery among the German settlers in Spain. The disgruntled priest charged him with heretical views and collaboration with the "enemies of faith," especially Enlighteners such as Voltaire and Diderot. Olavide stood trial and was sentenced in October 1778 to eight years of house arrest in a monastery. While for enlightened Catholics the episode was shocking, the Bavarian Dominican Thomas Aquin Jost publicly rejoiced and hoped that soon more Enlighteners would be hunted down and preferably executed: "It would be justified to burn the atheist Vanini in Toulouse at the stake. It would have been justified to condemn the free-thinker Lyschzinius in Poland to the fire. It would have been justified to throw the corpse of the dead atheist Florentinus Rugger ... into a manure hole."[18]

Yet the number of hardliners like Jost was on the decline. Instead, a strong opposition to religious persecution and discriminaton formed, particularly in Austria under Emperor Joseph II of the Habsburg dynasty, an enlightened man who did not have any sympathy for democracy or equality but possessed a strong sense of justice and human dignity. His realm was by no means limited to the Alpine region of modern Austria but comprised also the Czech Republic, Slovakia, Hungary, parts of Northern Italy, Bulgaria, Moldavia, and some southern regions of Poland. It was a multi-lingual and multi-religious empire. His views had been shaped by a number of Catholic Enlighteners. Under the protection of Joseph II a new view of the church arose, called Josephinism, according to which the church served the state. The sovereign had every right to interfere with the life of the church or to impose reforms on it. In his dominion, the emperor forced the church not only to accept a number of more or less impractical reforms, which soon stopped after his death, but also to face the reality that Catholicism could no longer be defended by force. He passed laws that allowed Protestants to build churches for the first time since the Reformation and allowed Jews to live more freely.[19] Catholicism was suddenly no longer the protected sole church of the realm and no longer had the public sphere to itself. Now, Protestant bell towers and cemeteries were permitted, and Protestant processions filled city plazas.

Early in the reign of Joseph II, it was not at all clear that the Catholics who supported toleration would prevail. They did because the most prominent voice of resistance, the conservative provincial diets, controlled by the clergy, had already been stripped of their importance by Joseph's mother, Empress Maria Theresa. In France, by contrast, similar entities successfully fought against the toleration of Protestants until 1787.[20] Maria Theresa's reforms had prepared the way for her son's by creating a central government, which meant that religious uniformity was no longer required for political cohesion. While his mother was a staunch Catholic who would not waver in prosecuting dissenters, Joseph II came to the realization that religious unity in the Habsburg empire had been a fiction all along. While certainly almost everybody in Vienna was Catholic, at the outskirts of the empire, in Transylvania, Bulgaria, and Romania, no such uniformity had ever existed. Catholics, Greek and Serbian Orthodox, Lutherans, Pietists, Unitarians, and other groups lived together in small villages, usually without any conflict over religious questions. Moreover, enlightened economists had learned that Protestants and other religious groups had a positive influence on the work ethos of the Austrians. One such economist was Joseph von Sonnenfels, whose parents had converted from Judaism to Catholicism and who from 1763 to 1791 held a university chair in economics in Vienna. Sonnenfels had enormous personal influence on the sovereign. He openly argued that the state should restrict itself to the oversight of external religious *behavior* and should exclude private religious *beliefs* from the state's agenda. Religion was for Sonnenfels always a means for the state to make citizens fulfill their duties. Since every religion that acknowledges God as legislator and judge can serve this purpose, such religions should be legally acknowledged and tolerated. Nevertheless, he excluded any toleration for atheists or freethinkers. Another outspoken critic of Catholic intolerance was the jurist Heinrich Watteroth. His 1781 pamphlet aggressively requested full equality of all citizens regardless of religion. A freemason and a Catholic, he was convinced that only toleration could bring about peace and prosperity for all. Joseph II's private tutor, Christian August Beck, had taught him to respect the dignity and inviolability of individual conscience in religious matters. Beck successfully influenced Joseph II to stop deporting Protestants from Styria to Transylvania. This episode, along with the end of deportations of Moravian Protestants, demonstrated that the Habsburg government no longer sought to achieve religious unity by means of force.[21]

As in France, where the religious conflict between Jansenists and Jesuits pushed public opinion to favor toleration, an event and not an idea paved the way for the toleration laws of Joseph II. In 1777 Jesuit missionaries began preaching about the truth of Catholicism in Moravian villages, which were believed to be secretly (and illegally) Protestant. The priests announced from the pulpit that the empress had declared freedom of religion. Of course this was a lie, but the Jesuits thought this was the only way to find out how many "secret" Protestants lived in the villages. The promised freedom filled the hitherto anonymous Protestants with so much enthusiasm and confidence that thousands openly confessed the belief they had carefully hidden for generations. The local government, however, omitted the story about the Jesuits and instead reported to the empress that thousands of subjects had "suddenly apostasized," that is, forfeited their membership in the Catholic Church. The enraged empress immediately required the punishment of the leaders of such "seditious" activities. Her son Joseph, however, requested religious freedom for the Protestants. According to him toleration would also be economically prudent because adherents of different religions would not be forced to emigrate and could instead work for the industrial progress of the realm. He wrote to his mother:

> There must be either complete freedom of worship, or you must expatriate everyone who doesn't believe as you do.... By what authority? ... So long as the state is served, the laws of nature and society observed, your Supreme Being in no way dishonored but respected and adored, what ground have you for interference?[22]

Chancellor Kaunitz finally explained to Maria Theresa that the reason for the mass "apostasy" lay in the decayed state of the Moravian Church, which had been practically untouched by the reforms of Trent. He had hit a nerve. After all, the empress was considered (after the Spanish king) the most important Catholic ruler in the world—how could she admit that "her" church was in a state of disarray? She acted immediately. Several reform decrees were promulgated and new dioceses erected. Most interesting, she appointed a theological reform commission consisting of the enlightened priest Leopold Hay—the brother-in-law of Joseph von Sonnenfels—and two other reform-minded Catholics. On November 14, 1777, she also agreed to tolerate tacitly the Moravian Protestants, though she maintained the official discriminatory laws that excluded non-Catholics from holding public offices, owning land, and participating in certain crafts and trades.[23]

The theological commission was supposed to return the Protestants of Moravia to the Catholic faith by making the Moravian church more attractive. This included a better education of the faithful about their faith, but also a re-education of the priests in the region. The clergy were instructed to let go of any fanaticism and polemics when approaching Protestants or dissenters and instead to abide in charity and clemency. The formerly secret Protestants, however, had no intention of giving Catholicism a second chance. Instead, they were encouraged by alleged miracles that occurred in their midst, which they interpreted as verification of their beliefs. In the spring of 1780, Hay suggested that Maria Theresa allow Protestants to worship publicly, a permission that would have allowed them to build their own churches; until then, communities had to come together for worship in semi-secret houses. The cardinal-archbishop of Vienna was vehemently opposed to such a plan and successfully convinced the empress to declare that a Catholic monarch could never allow such "evil."

When Joseph II assumed the sole sovereignty of the realm in November 1780, he executed his plans to reform Catholicism, both out of political calculation and religious conviction. He quickly granted the principal non-Catholic denominations legal toleration in all the provinces of the monarchy. The toleration laws were supposed to make "dissident" subjects "happier" and thus less likely to emigrate; on the other hand they should attract Protestants from other, less tolerant Catholic countries to settle in the Habsburg domains and thus bring their working power and investments under his rule. By March 1781 heresy was no longer a civil offense. On May 22 of that same year Hungarian Protestants were freed from taking Catholic oaths and the obligation to attend Catholic ceremonies. The most important toleration edict, however, was passed on October 13, 1781. It included a number of provisions granting new freedoms in all provinces: the permission for non-Catholics (Lutherans, Calvinists, and Orthodox) to worship publicly (with restrictions), to build prayer houses in cities with at least one hundred families, to employ religious ministers, and to open confessional schools. Moreover, the discriminatory laws that had banned non-Catholics from certain trades or crafts or from the ownership of land were lifted. Catholics, on the other hand, were admonished to treat members of other churches with love, respect, and gentleness. Joseph II called it a new "true Christian toleration." It was popularized by priests who were sympathetic to the Enlightenment and Jansenism, such as Mark Anton Wittola (1736–1797). For the opponents of toleration, especially Cardinal Migazzi of Vienna, non-Catholics were insufferable "criminals" who threatened the existence of church and state. Wittola answered such fanaticism by pointing out that toleratation, including that of atheists, was a Catholic and Christian virtue. Wittola's works are good examples of the public atmosphere that Joseph II's reforms created. It was no longer enough for the emperor to decree a law. The population had to become "more enlightened"—it had to be educated. This is the reason so many historians have given short shrift to the Austrian Enlightenment, arguing that its toleration laws did not go far enough. That may be true, but what the laws sought was not top-down change but a fertilization of society with new ideas so that toleration could advance to tolerance. That is why so many writers worked ceaselessly for the propagation of the emperor's ideas and did not engage in sophisticated academic discourses. The goal was to reach a wide audience, not a few already "enlightened" professors. Count Johann Fekete of Galantha, a Hungarian correspondent of Voltaire, wrote aptly: "Were these books more profound and better written, they would not have been read with the same intensity and also not so well understood by commoners."[24]

A good example of the changes Josephinism wrought can be seen in the diocese of Königgrätz, Bohemia. Bishop Leopold Hay, champion of a tolerant Catholicism, admonished his clergy in a pastoral letter of November 20, 1781, to stop calling other churches or religions "false." Delivery of controversial and polemical homilies, as well as searching for heretical books, had to end. Most important, however, he ordered believers to quit harrassing Protestants and disturbing their religious services and to abstain from all "unwise" proselytizing. The latter was common, for example, when priests harrassed dying Protestants and terrified them with stories about hell which they could only avoid by becoming Catholic. The priests were now ordered not only to stop such practices but also to disregard the traditional ecclesiastical law that forbade every non-Catholic a burial in a Catholic cemetery. Lutherans and Reformed Christians could now be buried alongside their Catholic brethren as long as they did not yet have their own cemeteries. Last but not least, the clergy was told to disseminate the principles of toleration to the faithful and thus to gain the population's support for the new law. Hay's pastoral letter greatly impressed the Protestant world and was reprinted in numerous non-Catholic journals; the pope and Roman Curia, however, were silently disapproving of the bold bishop.[25]

The most nuanced reflection on what toleration could mean for Catholic thought, titled *On Ecclesiastic and Civil Toleration* (1783), was written in northern Italy, in the Habsburg territory of Tuscany. Its author, Pietro Tamburini, was a Jansenist and thus interested in arguing for the toleration of his own views. The most controversial Jansenist views were those that questioned the current governance of the church; Jansenists favored strong local churches and supremacy of a council of all bishops over the pope. Tamburini made clear that the church should tolerate "heretics" out of love of peace and unity, and advised the church to minimize dogmatic decisions as much as possible, since irrevocable statements would create schisms. He also argued that Jansenism should be fully tolerated *within* the Catholic Church and no longer be branded "heretical." In order to bring about such "ecclesial toleration," the church had to learn to give up any attempt at coercion, whether exile or incarceration, because such force was antithetical to the true spirit of Christ. Catholic governments, on the other hand, should tolerate other religions for the sake of the common welfare and should have only limited influence over the church. Although

Tamburini could also envision a separation of church and state, according to him it was preferable that the sovereign protect the established religion (which was for him Catholicism) and suppress other religions *if* their doctrines threatened to overthrow common virtues or the sanctity of laws. Coercion, however, and violent suppression or forced emigration were only warranted if one could expect a religious group to become a security threat. A follower of such a group would then be a "civil sinner" and consequently a disturber of public and religious peace. The papacy, of course, condemned such liberal views. Pope Pius VI even visited Vienna in 1782 to attempt to convince the emperor to repudiate some of his laws. Yet he failed. For many European states, the new Habsburg laws served as an inspiration for their own toleration edicts, for example, in Hamburg (1785) and France (1787). Even the Englishman Edmund Burke was impressed by what had been achieved in Vienna. One of the most oppressive and conservative Catholic regimes in Europe had been transformed almost overnight into one of the most tolerant.[26]

Heretics, Misunderstood Catholics, and Deists in Bohemia

The 1781 toleration edicts were a quantum leap into modernity, but many problems of religious diversity remained unsolved. One of them pertained to Christian groups in Bohemia, where only Lutherans, Calvinists, and Greek Orthodox were officially allowed (restricted) public worship, a privilege denied to other dissenter groups, especially the Utraquists or Hussites. The issue was touchy because only two hundred years earlier bloody wars had been fought over the religious unity of Bohemia, and the scars remained. Yet despite this violent past, reform-minded Catholic Enlighteners were able to come up with a plan for religious pacification. They began regarding the formerly hunted heretics, Utraquists (also called Hussites), as "secretly Catholic." What they meant was that the Utraquist demand that the Eucharist should be administered in both kinds—namely, bread and wine—was not heretical but could easily be reconciled with Catholic belief (as it is today). This totally forgotten episode can be credited as one of the earliest instances of true ecumenism. The Catholic Enlighteners did not expect the Utraquists to forsake their religious views but rather argued that Catholics had misunderstood them. It was somewhat ironic that it was a Jesuit, the philologist

Josef Dobrovsky, who most outspokenly defended the Hussites and condemned the Counter-Reformation—which the popes had launched (with the help of the Jesuits) against the churches of the Reformation—as a manifestation of intolerance and ignorance. Likewise, Johann Karl Count Herberstein, the Bishop of Laibach, maintained a tolerant policy toward the Hussites. Yet again it was the Roman Curia that could not accept such a view because it insinuated that the popes of the past had made a mistake and that doctrine could change. Pope Pius VI even publicly condemned the bishop's pastoral letter on toleration in 1787. In it, Herberstein had said nothing offensive. He only defended the new toleration policy of Joseph II and stated that toleration of other beliefs was a test of love and virtue:

> Our ... prayer, our virtous lives and our religion—if it is purified from all superstition—will ... convince our opponents of the truth of our doctrine.... If their religion educates good, faithful, calm and industrious citizens, if it contributes to the common welfare and to its exterior happiness, it is civilly good and the monarch is legitimate in accepting these faithful people in his realm ... and granting them security and protection in exercising their religion.[27]

The Bohemian abbot Otto Steinbach von Kranichstein defended religious toleration in a fine historical study published in 1785. According to him every person had the natural right "to worship the Supreme Being, or the ineffable Creator, according to his innermost conviction." Similarly, the Jesuit Ignaz Popp regarded Jan Hus, whom the Council of Constance had burned as a heretic in 1415, as a basically orthodox Catholic theologian who had been misinterpreted by popes and narrow-minded Catholic theologians. The Piarist Mikulas Voigt even declared that the Protestant Reformers could not claim Hus as one of theirs because he was utterly Catholic. Caspar Royko, professor of church history in Prague, boldly professed that Catholics should *not* regard Protestants as enemies but as brethren. None of this sounds remarkable to twenty-first-century readers, but it was revolutionary at the time. To state as did Royko that most religious violence of the sixteenth century was the result of Catholic fanaticism and intolerance or that a universally acknowledged Protestant reformer and condemned heretic was really a good Catholic was a confession of guilt and error that the church only publicly acknowleged more than two hundred years later. After 1789, however, any hopes for a reunion of Utraquist and Catholic churches were shut down by the papacy, for whom the Catholic Enlightenment was by then a dangerous mix of historical relativism and suspiciously progressive doctrine.[28]

Yet there was one group that made even the Austrian government uncomfortable. It was a small community of Moravians, which even the tolerant bishop Hay described as "deists." For an educated eighteenth-century person the term "deist" evoked Voltaire and his friends, people who mocked established religion and instead argued for the belief in a rational God who governs the universe without the need of any supernatural revelation. Likewise, it was reported that these Moravian farmers believed in a God who revealed himself mostly in nature. They denied the Trinity but prayed the Our Father and endorsed the belief that virtue would be remunerated while vice would be punished in the afterlife. This group also rejected the office of the priesthood and instead insisted that God "lived in their souls." This triggered in bishop Hay the memory of the so-called Israelites, a group that had preached similar doctrines thirty years earlier but was brutally persecuted and its leaders executed. Hay reckoned that this had only affirmed their faith, which he saw now resurfacing among the Moravians. He was convinced that only education could help to bring these men and women back to the Catholic creed. In an official letter to the emperor he even invoked the ideas of toleration of the French Enlightener Montesquieu. If all other measures were unsuccesful, he recommended that Joseph II exile the leaders of the new "sect." Joseph, however, was made anxious by the Moravians. He viewed them as a subversive group that could instigate a revolution or overthrow the moral foundations of the empire. He decided to forcibly exile dozens of Moravian families to Siebenbürgen and Galicia, but promised that anyone who embraced the Catholic faith could return. It had been one of the emperor's hardest decisions, and now he felt embarrassed because he was forced to act intolerantly.

In the newspapers, some writers publicly ridiculed the emperor, but most supported him. Yet it was again a Catholic Enlightener, the ex-monk Peter Adolph Winkopp, who most fervently demanded the full toleration of the Moravian deists. In his book *History of the Bohemian Deists* (1785), Winkopp argued that toleration and tolerance should never be dependent on the will of the sovereign but should be deduced from the principles of natural law: just like the right to property is essential for one's temporal happiness, there also exist rights inherent in every person that are essential for one's *spiritual* happiness. If humans establish a nation for the sake of their temporal welfare, then the spiritual welfare is naturally excluded from the state's prerogatives. Nevertheless, the state must support the individual's religious conscience. "Nobody can prescribe," he reasoned, for a human being "what she is allowed to eat or drink. Likewise a human being has the authority and right to follow her own judgment regarding the satisfaction of the needs of the soul and the refinement of his thinking through the knowledge of God."[29] Yet Winkopp went a step further. Not only must one follow one's conscience in religious matters but the state cannot have any interest nor does it have any legitimacy in judging the truth of such beliefs, because they are *private* matters. The state must be completely neutral toward one's privately held beliefs and must protect the right of each citizen to hold them. If each citizen, for the sake of her spiritual happiness, searches for truth, then citizens must be able to freely exchange their views about that search. Freedom of public speech and press are the consequences. The ex-monk also questioned the axiom of the Habsburg government that belief in the Christian creed or some other historical revelation of God (e.g., the Bible) is the necessary prerequisite of toleration. Such historical revelation could not have a stronger effect on morals than natural religion, or the duties one can grasp with reason alone:

> The God who commands a Christian to obey a worldly authority, commands a deist to do the same through reason. And I dare say that because the deist is even more convinced of the divinity of the book of reason, he is more profoundly penetrated by such divinity than the Christian of the divinity of Holy Scripture.... Such penetration will be more effective than that of a Christian.... The true deist can never be intolerant, can never persecute others who think differently or believe differently than he does.[30]

Winkopp thus argued that the Moravian deists deserved toleration. According to him, atheists and freethinkers should also be tolerated if they supported the common good. In fact, he even thought that religion was neither the only nor the best foundation for a state. Winkopp therefore emerges as one of the most radical Catholic voices in favor of religious liberty—and despite that, he remained in good standing with the church.[31]

Poland—Europe's Largest Catholic State

Poland, like the German states, was a hotbed of religious dispute. While today Poland is closely associated with Catholicism, in the sixteenth century, when the country was in a union with Lithuania, it was fragmented.

The nobility was divided among the Reformed/Calvinist, Latin Catholic, and Russian Orthodox creeds. After 1573, every elected king therefore had to swear to uphold religious peace. Yet, by the middle of the eighteenth century, all but a hundred noble families were Catholic, and the commonwealth of Poland-Lithuania, as it was officially called, was the largest Catholic state in Europe. Most non-Catholic families had been stripped of their political rights, especially the right to serve in parliament, although non-Catholics still made up about 18 percent of the population (before the first partition of Poland in 1772). This changed in 1764, when the Russian empress Catherine the Great demanded greater tolerance for non-Catholics, mostly for the sake of Russian Orthodox noble families. Parliament refused her demand, only relenting after Russian agents kidnapped several high-ranking aristocrats and two bishops. The newly elected king, Stanisław Poniatowski, who had come to power only because of Catherine's support, was met with distrust because of the Russian violation of Polish sovereignty. In 1768 an opposition movement began a war against the king and Russian influence. The uprising led to partition, in which Prussia, Russia, and Austria seized about a third of the commonwealth. Anti-Russian sentiment diminished only when Catherine backed down from her requests for greater rights for non-Catholic noblemen. In fact, no non-Catholic nobleman was elected to the parliament until 1784. Catholic hegemony was only challenged during the Great *Sejm*, the great session of parliament, between 1788 and 1792.

While the majority of bishops and clergy initially tried to defend their privileges, soon a substantial minority realized it could not win against public opinion that the church should pay taxes and undertake other reforms. In September 1790 the parliament, in the midst of discussions about a new form of government, also tackled the question of toleration. The proposed law declared—for the first time in Polish history—that Catholicism was the "dominant" religion of the land and suggested that apostasy from it was a criminal offense and should be punishable by death. This made non-Catholics fear that Poland would return to the unhappy days in which Protestants were expected "not only to suffer, but calmly offer up their necks under the sword of fanaticism." The king resisted, arguing instead that the different Polish faiths should learn to live together without insulting each other. The law was passed nonetheless, but without specifying *how* apostasy should be punished. The next law promised all inhabitants of the Commonwealth "peace in confession and rites, guaranteeing that no clerical or lay authority shall be able to persecute anybody for reasons of confession or rites." Apart from granting religious toleration, this law also admonished religious ministers to refrain from harrassing believers of different faiths and thus to act in the spirit of reconciliation. King Stanisław made it clear that such toleration did not only extend to the established churches but also to new religions that might spring up in the future, as long as they did not disturb public order. Some bishops were appalled by this liberalism, especially because it allowed Unitarians to express their beliefs in public, preaching about their denial of the Trinity and the divinity of Jesus. These laws made it into the new Polish constitution of May 3, 1791. It was drafted by, among others, the fearless proponent of Catholic Enlightenment ideals, the priest Hugo Kołłątaj. The final text read:

> The dominant religion of the nation is and shall be the holy Roman Catholic faith with all its rights. Conversion from the dominant faith to any other confession ... is forbidden under penalties for apostasy. Given, however, that the same holy faith commands us to love our neighbors, therefore we owe peace in faith, and the protection of the government to all people, of whatever confession, and so we guarantee the freedom of all rites and religions in the Polish territories, according to the laws of the country.[32]

Poland went much further than Austria had. Its new constitution did not specify which religions were tolerated and did not restrict public worship. Since the constitution superseded *all* old laws, there were no "laws of the country" that could limit it. Freedom of religion was, with the exception of apostasy, *without limits*. The Polish clergy was in full support of this "Revolution," which unlike in France did not take an anti-Christian turn.

Yet, one problem loomed as a major challenge for Polish toleration. While many Ukrainian Orthodox were joined with the Roman pope in the so-called Uniate Church, a substantial minority remained Orthodox and vowed obedience to the patriarch of Moscow. At a time in Polish history when political pressure from Russia was immense, one needed the backing of *all* citizens, including the Orthodox. In order to bring this about, Catholic Enlighteners planned to set up a Polish hierarchy of Orthodox bishops, who were independent from Moscow and only spiritually linked to the patriarch in Constantinople. The pope, however, was adamantly opposed to such plans. He feared the arrangement would weaken the Catholic Uniate church, and thus his own flock. After all, he had no authority over the Orthodox faithful. Also, the Polish Catholic bishops were not very supportive. It was again Hugo Kołłątaj who undertook the challenge to persuade the ecclesiastical leaders. In a plea to Archbishop Cieciszowski of Kiev, he argued that the fatherland should be a "good mother to all," and that the Orthodox would much faster become "Poles" who backed the constitution and the king, rather than the Russian empress, if their faith was taken seriously. No Orthodox bishops were allowed to live in Poland, so how could the Orthodox feel free? If the government did not allow an Orthodox hierarchy, it would sooner or later lose the support of this faith group and ultimately the entire Ukraine to Russia. Stanisław Soltyk, a Catholic layman, tried to rally support in the parliament for toleration. God himself should look after human consciences, he said, "but let us, in the spirit of Christian mildness, persecute no opinion, but with justice, exemplary lives, the virtues proper to our ruling faith, draw them towards the sweet relations of unity." Only if the Orthodox were treated fairly could they one day join the Catholic Church and support their country against foreign invaders, including the Russians:

> Most Serene Estates! Liberty is our greatest secret against any foreign usurpation, it is the strongest defensive wall against neighbors' invasions, let people speak in different languages, let there be differences between them as regards religion. Freedom, when well understood, justice, given strictly to everyone, will unite them most swiftly, and will teach one sentiment, the same expressions of their own liberties.[33]

The Polish bishops vehemently rejected the proposal. Archbishop Cieciszowski didn't even see why the Orthodox needed their own bishops. Their requests, he felt, were disproportionate to their needs. Bishop Skarszewski claimed that if an Orthodox hierarchy was permitted, Catholicism would no longer be the "dominant" religion the new constituition declared it to be. Such toleration went too far for him. Instead he understood by toleration the traditional Catholic position, shared by the pope, that one grudgingly refrained from persecuting others and allowed them some limited space for their religious needs. The religious Enlightenment, however, won this battle. The bill that allowed Orthodox bishops passed in May 1792 by 123 to 13 votes. A contemporary saw in this immense majority a proof that Poland was "progressing." Nevertheless, the measure came too late. Only a few months afterward, Russian armies invaded the commonwealth, resulting in the second partition of Poland, which was soon followed by the demise of Poland as a sovereign nation in 1795.[34]

What is most fascinating about the rise of toleration in Poland is the dramatic changes the country made in just a few years: the Catholic Enlighteners and the king no longer believed that religion was the "glue" that kept the nation together and that consequently all dissidents had to be persecuted or at least kept in check; but belief in the values of the new constitution—above all, liberty and justice for all—now fulfilled this purpose. Instead of viewing religious dissenters as potential traitors, especially as conspirators with either the Russians or the Germans, the enlightened state was able to rally their support by recognizing their religious rights. By granting religious freedom with few limitations, Poland showed that it had become one of the most modern states in the world. Secular values everybody could share replaced hotly debated religious beliefs as the foundation of society. In the short time the Polish constituition was in force no religious conflicts erupted. One can only wonder how religious coexistence would have developed had the Polish experiment been allowed to continue.

The Idle Bystander: The Papacy

In the eighteenth century the papacy had lost most of its political power, and its government, the curia, was universally believed to be hopelessly closed-minded. As a result, the papacy suffered tremendously from the Jansenism affair. Enlighteners could not help but see in it an intellectually immovable remnant of the Middle Ages that was unwilling to conform or even to learn from the challenges modern society posed—in particular, religious diversity. While throughout Europe the bells of toleration began to ring, the Papal States made no strides toward improving conditions for non-Catholics.

When Pope Benedict XIV was elected in 1740 it looked as if the reformers had finally reached the highest office of the church. But such hopes were soon dashed. Benedict was a timid reformer. For almost every enlightened step forward, he took a step back. By 1750 he had begun backing a more repressive Catholicism; the short, moderately liberal spring was over.

Even though he is often portrayed as an "enlightened pope," he was certainly no friend of toleration. The diplomatic negotiations surrounding Silesia serve as a good example of his stance that religious intolerance was indispensable. The region had originally belonged to the Catholic Habsburgs, but since 1740 it had been occupied by the Prussians, whose king, Frederick the Great, was (at least officially) a Protestant. The conflict arose because the king wanted the right to appoint a successor (*coadjutor*) for the ailing archbishop of Breslau. It was the first time since the Reformation that a Protestant king had requested such a right. The pope was outraged and refused. After all, only Catholic kings could have such influence over appointments and only as a privilege given by the Holy See, not as a "right." But Frederick was unimpressed by the pope's protest, informing him and the to-be-replaced Cardinal Sinzendorf that "The Holy Spirit and I have decided together that prelate Schaffgotsch will be elected coadjutor bishop of Breslau and that those electors among the Cathedral vicars who resist our decree will be regarded as supporters of the Viennese court and of the devil. Whoever resists the Holy Spirit deserves ... damnation." When the Sinzendorf finally gave up his protest, he deeply offended his old friend Benedict XIV, but he alienated him even more with a pastoral letter of August 28, 1742. Only months after bloody battles in which the Austrians had lost control over their province, the cardinal now admonished all Catholics not only to acknowledge their new Protestant king but also to be tolerant and civil toward their new, immigrating Protestant brethren. Nobody should call them "heretics" any longer or make jokes about their forms of worship. Instead, all Silesians should live in peaceful harmony under the will of the new king.[35] For the pope, such an embrace of toleration was wrong because Catholics were in the overwhelming majority, but he also regarded the cardinal's words as naïve. Benedict feared that Catholics could not compete with the educational institutions that Protestant churches were now building in a region that had been overwhelmingly Catholic. Catholic tolerance could motivate Catholics to send their children to Protestant schools, which might increase the number of conversions. The pope was afraid that Catholics could not compete in a free religious "market"—at least not yet.

It should therefore not surprise us that he also put some of the most important works of Enlightenment writers on the *Index of Forbidden Books*. The list included works of mockery by Voltaire but also the famous *Spirit of the Laws* by Montesquieu, which articulated the idea of a separation of powers. The pope feared that reading such books would confuse

Catholics, especially those who did not have a solid faith, and encourage them to abandon their religion. Any Catholic caught reading books on this list (which later also included Kant's *Critique of Pure Reason* and Dumas's *The Three Musketeers*) without special permission would be punished with excommunication.[36]

Pope Benedict's view of toleration is clearest with respect to the Jews. Nowhere in Europe were Jews really welcome; they were at best a tolerated minority. At least in the Papal States they were never persecuted or subject to violent outbursts on a massive scale. Catholic Poland, however, was known for its anti-Judaism despite the fact that it housed Europe's largest Jewish community, about 750,000 people. In particular, rumors about rabbis who sacrificed Christian children in ritual murder caused violent mobs to burn down Jewish ghettos or to demand the death penalty for the accused. After a series of trials that had terrorized the Jewish community, the Jews of Volynia, backed by the Carmelite monks of the city, who called the accusations superstitions and legends, asked the pope in 1758, briefly before his death, for help. He sent his best man, Cardinal Ganganelli, who would later reign as Pope Clement XIV, to investigate the Polish cases. His report is a particularly astounding piece of eighteenth-century Catholic thought because it refuted the accusations and showed that the ritual murder charges were invented out of ignorance of Judaism and motivated by anti-Jewish hatred.[37] However, the cardinal did *not* question the veracity of the reports about two murdered children in Trent (1475) and Bozen/ Rinn (1462), because the church had already approved the veneration of these two "martyrs."[38] Doubting them would have been tantamount to admitting that the previously approved veneration had been mistaken and that the church had erred. The "martyrdom" and veneration of Andrew of Rinn, today proven (as have all such accounts of ritual murders) to be forged by anti-Jewish agitators, had even been approved by Pope Benedict XIV in 1755. In his decree the aging pontiff even predicted future ritual murders and thus "ended up endorsing the most ferocious accusation thrown at the Jews: that of being child killers, through the claimed practice of ritual murder," as historian Marina Caffiero aptly summarizes.[39]

The Jews of Rome were confined to a ghetto. Wearing a yellow badge was prescribed by law and guaranteed that one was recognizable as a Jew. Leaving the guarded and walled ghetto was only possible at certain times. Since no Jew was allowed to own real estate, the 12,000 Jews living in Rome had to rent houses from Christian landlords. Although they were not allowed to work in most "honorable" professions, Jews paid high taxes, which in return eased the tax burden on Christians. Every sabbath, Jews were required to hear a Christian sermon or pay a small fine. The purpose of these sermons was the conversion of the Jews. A substantial number of them indeed converted in order to live a much freer life and to receive a sizable initial payment from the papal court. But other conversions were not free. Children who were baptized secretly by Christian midwives against the will of their parents were considered Catholics who had a right to grow up with their new faith. As a consequence they were taken from their homes and placed in special institutions, where the "orphans" received religious instruction.

Although Benedict XIV forbade Catholic midwives to deliver in the ghetto, another issue was a greater threat to the Jewish community: the practice of "offering" someone to the Catholic faith. Under normal circumstances, Christian parents "offer" their child to the church for baptism. However, in the context of Judaism it usually meant that one family member, who had converted to Christianity, would offer a child even against the will of his or her parents. Most often it was one parent who had converted and thus "offered" the child. However, anyone who had the child in his "possession" could do so. In a number of cases it was grandparents or even distantly related uncles. Originally, the church had not accepted the offerings of grandparents or uncles, but Benedict XIV, himself a trained canon lawyer, recognized the practice. Since even unrelated persons could offer a child and thus end the parent-child relationship, the intimidations of the fishmongers, who had their stalls right outside the gate of the ghetto and who were famous for their anti-Jewish prejudice, were not without force: they continously threatened Jewish mothers with stealing their children and offering them to the church. If the children escaped from the religious "orphanage" they could not just return to the ghetto, since no Jew was allowed to hide an "offered" person or try to persuade such a person not to get baptized. If a person who prepared for baptism in one of the so-called catechumen houses changed her mind and fled, she was punished with up to five years in prison and the confiscation of all her goods. Since the will of a child's father was considered legally decisive, Benedict XIV also ruled that "when a Jewish mother becomes a Christian and offers her son to baptism, contradicting the father who remains in Hebraism, for the favor of the faith the woman can be said to become a man, and the mother to become the father."[40]

The Jewish community did not stand idly by when Catholics forcibly baptized Jewish children. In 1755 the conflict between the Jews and the pope reached its peak when two little girls, both not yet at the age of reason (that is, seven years of age), were kidnapped from their widowed mother by their uncle and offered for baptism. Jewish lawyers wrote a sophisticated plea to the pope in which they insisted that the mother's natural and civil rights trumped the religious fervor of the uncle. "Given that it is certain that the widowed mother has full natural power over the daughter, and that the uncle is indisputably not furnished with any right over his nephews and nieces," the papacy had in the past always rejected such offerings unless they were also acceptable to the mother. Yet Benedict, relying on his earlier writings, responded that if children stated that they were open to baptism, they had to be held in the orphanage until they reached the age of reason and could decide whether to be baptized. They should not be returned to the parents, who would most likely dissuade the children from converting. The "favor of faith" trumped the rights of the mother, because the supernatural "treasure" such children would receive through baptism was far superior to anything a parent could naturally offer. The rights of the mother, the pope insisted in this case, should be restricted to the first years of a child's life, to nurturing and weaning. For Jewish mothers the principle that their pure maternal love was the best guardian for their children was not applicable. The pope thus made clear that he rejected modern judicial thought about the natural rights of parents and instead claimed a superior role in defining them.[41]

Things changed a bit under Benedict's successor. In 1762 a young Jewish couple in Rome conceived their third child. The couple was unaware that the paternal grandmother, who wished to convert, had offered her three granddaughters, two toddlers and one still unborn, for baptism. The two girls were taken by force from their parents. The rector of the catechumen house insisted that he also had custody over the fetus, but that the mother could remain in the ghetto. The Jewish community protested vehemently, arguing that the precedent set under Benedict XIV went against all law known to mankind. Rome's Jews appealed to the patron saint of theology, St. Thomas Aquinas, who had argued against the offering without parental consent. The argument backfired. The responsible officer of the curia not only defended Pope Benedict's decree but also made clear that the pontiffs were the supreme and absolute rulers of the Papal States, who just like any other ruler could extend or limit parental oversight and parental rights. Yet, even for Monsignor Veterani, who was certainly no friend of the Jews, the claim that the unborn fetus could be offered went too far. He dissented from the opinion of his colleague and instead argued that because the fetus was intimately connected with its mother, the grandmother had no authority or power over it. Nor did church law, since the unborn were according to him not fully formed "persons," and the church had no right over the womb of a woman. Ultimately, the pope decided to reject the offer of baptism. Yet the two older girls had to remain in the orphanage to "explore" their desire to be baptized until they reached the age of reason. Only the baby, after it was delivered, was returned to its parents. In December 1763 Clement XIII signed a rescript, "sharply ordering the couple to abstain from further appeals and to accept destiny."[42] Likewise, his successor, Pope Clement XIV (the former Cardinal Ganganelli) allowed "offerings" and did not see any need to give Jews *equal* civil rights. While many cardinals, bishops, and academic theologians could maintain social contacts with Protestants at the end of the eighteenth century, such normal civility or tolerant behavior was still unthinkable with regard to Jews. As late as 1781 the Bishop of Ferrara, Cardinal Mattei, admonished Catholics never to "eat, drink, play, stay the night, sing, go to a funeral with Jews," never to allow Christian employment in a Jewish household (especially not as a wet nurse), not to let a Jewish doctor into one's house, and never to give Jews honorable titles in legal documents.[43]

Not much changed over the next few decades, in fact, not until the end of the Papal States itself in 1870–1871. Although Jews had officially been "Roman citizens," they lacked crucial rights and were forced to live within the walls of a ghetto. Perhaps their fate was better than in other Catholic countries of the time, but not nearly as good as in the Dutch Republic or the short-lived "new" Poland of 1793.

Conclusion

The advances toward greater toleration of religious minorities in Catholic states were achieved by Catholic sovereigns or pressure from the public. Often the rulers were influenced by Enlightenment thought; but long before the secular Enlightenment, many areas had already achieved peaceful coexistence—for example, by strictly insisting on the private aspect of an individual's religion, by instititionalizing parity, or by developing segregated confessional subcultures.[44] Thus, toleration was often a confluence of both older experiences and new thought. Yet civil toleration in Catholic countries never did entail full equality. Bishops and popes were adamantly invested in defending old privileges and saw in any concessions to other communities of faith nothing better than a "necessary evil." Consequently, nothing changed in the Papal States. Protestants were unwelcome there, and Jews had sharply curtailed rights.[45] All advances of Catholic kings and theologians in civil toleration and theological tolerance were achieved against the will and intervention of the Roman Curia. Yet, by eliminating the powers of national churches to use force and violence against dissenters or other beliefs, governments made Catholicism more acceptable. The Romantic revival at the beginning of the nineteenth century could build on this fact and focus on the attractive sides of the faith, or as François-René Chateaubriand called it in 1802, on "the genius of Catholic Christianity."[46]

3

Feminism, Freedom, Faith

CATHOLIC WOMEN AND THE ENLIGHTENMENT

WOMEN'S EXPERIENCE OF Enlightenment Catholicism varied significantly depending not only on social class but also on geographical context. New opportunities became available to women, but they still faced many restrictions and struggles. It was France that produced the most prominent and productive women writers of the eighteenth century. Catholicism flourished in France, although only the clergy, not the crown, had adopted the reforms of the Council of Trent, such as better catechization of the faithful and better education for the priests, even though they implemented them with astounding slowness.[1] French Catholic life was spiritually strong, likely thanks to its competition with Huguenot Protestants, and had produced Catholic reformers and mystics such as Vincent de Paul, Francis de Sales, and Cardinal Pierre de Berulle. Much earlier than in France, the effects of the council were felt in Spain and Italy. Soon, Tridentine zeal also spread to the overseas colonies of the European powers, opening up global discussions about the role of women in society and in the church.

Spanish Voices Defending Women's Equality

In Early Modernity, the education of women was not a priority in Catholic countries. This changed when the church realized that lack of education among its followers made it difficult to implement the reforms of Trent. One of the most outspoken supporters of women's education in the age of reason was the Spanish monk Benito Feijoo, a writer whose popularity was rivaled in Spain only by Cervantes. His book, *Defense of Women*, was published in 1726 and thus sixty years earlier than the works of Jeremy Bentham, the Marquis de Condorcet, and others who are usually hailed as early advocates for women's rights.

Feijoo's treatise shocked the traditional Spanish elites. A woman was expected to be docile and in charge of only domestic affairs. The theological rationale behind this view was that women were viewed as direct descendants of Eve and thus prone to being sinful, gullible, and both morally and intellectually weak. Although such preconceptions were undermined by the successful reign of Isabel of Spain, or the overwhelming visionary power of St. Theresa of Avila, the dominant gender prejudices remained.

Feijoo believed that not only were such prejudices wrong but that they were holding back progress. Blind adherence to tradition prohibited dialogue with modern thought, especially in the field of science, which might call into doubt deeply held prejudices. Feijoo, however, suggested that a true scholar had to be aware of his prejudices and ready to give them up if they proved to be irrational.

Feijoo's starting point was to question the standard prejudice that women were deficient and weak, that is, that they were merely "imperfect" men. His analysis of anti-women writers revealed their misogynist hypocrisy: many condemned women publicly but privately adored them. Moreover, the monk demonstrated that many "female vices" existed only because of the non-virtuous behavior of their male spouses. A wife who was not taken care of would naturally become disgruntled and unhappy—but this was her husband's fault, Feijoo argued. He even attempted a new reading of the biblical account of the Fall of Adam and Eve. While most understood the narrative to be an account of how weak Eve was when tempted, and how seductive she was in seducing the otherwise strong Adam to sin, Feijoo gave the story quite a different spin. According to him, Adam had been the weaker of the two. After all, it took the devil himself, the master of all deception and cunning, to fool Eve, but only a human to tempt Adam. That women should be subservient to their husbands was therefore not the result of their alleged physical or intellectual inadequacy, but rather the penalty for Eve's role in the Fall. Such subordination made sense to Feijoo, since both spouses, equal in dignity and endowed with talents, could not act as heads of the household. The husband should fill this position but should always remember the biblical rationale for his role.

The Benedictine also challenged the idea that women could not comprehend complex thought. Most books that claimed this, he clarified, were written by men. If they had been written by women, men would be considered feeble. Additionally, he demonstrated that one could not expect women to be scholars when they were not allowed to study, when they were treated as if they were merely destined for domestic servitude. Such bold questioning of gender roles did not go unchallenged. Most critics feared that Feijoo wanted to prove women's superiority over men. Some critics also had personal reasons to be angry with him: one complained that after his wife read Feijoo's treatise, she transformed from an obedient wife into an unruly woman who neglected her domestic responsibilities and instead demanded proper education. Only decades later when a number of institutional Enlightenment reforms were put in place did the Spanish government see in Feijoo's writings an important catalyst for improvement in women's education. After all, the argument ran, if the whole population received education, and not merely 50 percent of it, the transformation and reform of Spanish society would happen much faster and would be much more substantial.[2]

The writer Josefa Amar followed in Feijoo's footsteps. Her *Discourse in Defense of the Talent of Women* (1786) is a remarkable manifesto in favor of full equality. Intellectually and morally, she stated, women were equal to men and should therefore have access to institutions of higher learning and learned societies, such as the newly founded Spanish Economic Society.[3] Amar stated with confidence and irony: "When God gave the world over to the disputes of men, he foresaw that there would be endless points of disagreement among them, upon which they would never be able to agree. One of these seems to have been the debate over women's intelligence."[4] She not only argued for justice for women but also for a reform of religion in the spirit of the Italian reformer Ludovico Muratori, and thus showed herself to be a true Catholic Enlightener. She claimed that devotion had to go beyond external rituals and instead transform one's personality by virtue and grace:

> Real devotion and virtue consist not in the exterior of visiting numerous churches and reciting many orations, a vice more common to women than to men. ... [W]hat is more important is to cement in them that true and solid virtue consists in practicing good and abhorring bad, in controlling one's passions, in mortifying one's appetites, in practicing charity, and above all in complying with one's obligations.[5]

Amar also boldly reinterpreted the story of the Fall. She had obviously read Feijoo's work, but she saw something new in the biblical account. Eve is portrayed as a woman with talent and curiosity. She gives in to temptation out of curiosity, out of her desire to know more. Adam, on the other hand, sins out of arrogance and simplemindedness. Amar did not recognize many fundamental differences between the sexes. She lamented that women were everywhere un-free. The Christian West objectified women, claimed intellectual superiority over them, and denied their capacity for rational thought and an independent life of the mind. Amar was convinced that women would be much happier if they could follow their intellectual pursuits in public. Thus, she concluded, women, who were inherently equal, should be allowed to join academic societies and not be pushed into separate academies for women.

In 1790, Amar published a more specialized treatise on women's education in which she developed a concept of "female happiness." Women can and should be actively involved in the public sphere, she reasoned, without disrupting society. Without challenging the traditional view that women should also keep a harmonious marital home, she argued for the right of women to gain a proper education. Such education, however—and here Amar differed from most other writers—should not just be intellectual but also bodily and "moral." It must be aimed at making women comfortable with and in their own bodies. Nature, as intended by the creator, should guide morality. Pregnancy and the education of children should be as natural as possible, she stated. Like many Enlightenment writers, she also defended—against broad resistance, as we will see—breastfeeding, however, not by referring to Rousseau, who was also a staunch defender of the practice, or to a secular ideology of instilling nationalism by mother's milk, but by appealing to her own Catholic faith:

> The obligation for women to breastfeed their children is a natural right. The very Creator, who in his wise providence has made it so that woman can conceive and give birth, has also given her the means and the instruments to nourish her offspring without distinguishing on this point the least difference between a woman of low rank and the most illustrious and respected lady.[6]

In Feijoo and Amar, the Spanish Catholic Enlightenment produced two extraordinary proponents of women's rights. Moreover, both also challenged traditional theological interpretations of Scripture, which regarded women as inferior to men and as inherently more sinful. Until today, however, their contribution to modern thought has remained widely disregarded.

Women as Scientists and Theologians: Caterina Bassi and Maria Agnesi

Two examples of women whose academic achievements bolstered Amar's arguments are Laura Bassi and Maria Agnesi. Laura Caterina Bassi was only the second woman to receive a university degree at a European university, and the first to receive a chair, namely, for experimental physics in Bologna.[7] She began her academic career in the 1740s, studying Newton and researching problems associated with gravity. From the 1760s onward, supported by her husband, she focused on electricity, but in her scholarly career she produced only four small works. Her fame derived not from these publications but from her aura as the first woman university teacher in a field dominated by men, from her wide network of correspondents, among whom one can find physicists, philosophers, and writers, and from the fact that—in addition to her academic pursuits—she was a loving wife and mother of eight children.

Bassi's career was possible because Italian society developed a new openness toward female education in the eighteenth century. This openness was the fruit of the Italian Enlightenment, which revived Renaissance ideals of women's education. In France and Germany, on the other hand, such ideals had never flourished and were largely forgotten. Bassi's career consequently dazzled the Germans and the French, for whom women could never be equal members of the academy. Trained by a private tutor, Bassi gave her first disputation in 1732 to an invited audience. Among the listeners was the new Archbishop of Bologna, Prospero Lambertini, who eight years later would be elected pope and take the name Benedict XIV. He persuaded Bassi to speak in public and participate in the important scholarly debates of her day. The university professors were so taken by her presentations that they conferred upon her the degree of doctor of philosophy. The senate of Bologna offered her a permanent university position as professor of philosophy but restricted her public speaking and instead emphasized her role at ceremonial events. Only in 1739 was the proscription on public lectures lifted. Everybody expected her to remain a chaste virgin, dedicated to science and God, just like some of her

Renaissance heroines, but Bassi broke with this traditional role when she got married in 1738. Her husband Guiseppe Veratti was a physics professor, and Bassi's interests moved gradually toward physics also.[8]

Maria Gaetana Agnesi was the female voice of the Catholic Enlightenment. She became famous as a mathematician and developed her own philosophy of religion. By the age of thirty she had published her first disputation in philosophy and had become a minor celebrity in Italy. Yet she devoted her studies increasingly to mathematics and published an important work on calculus in 1748 that was even translated into English and French. Two years later she was offered a lectureship position at Bologna, where she could have worked with Bassi, but she rejected the offer in order to stay with her father.

For Agnesi, science and religion did not exclude each other but instead were two different spheres of truth that were both created by God. Thus, neither could contradict the other. The more natural knowledge one gained, the more one would know about God's creation. With the help of Newton, Bacon, Malebranche, and other modern philosophers and scientists, she hoped to reform the educational system of her day and make Catholicism an intellectually competitive force in the eighteenth century. Following the classic Catholic understanding of nature as creation, she was convinced that the contemplation of nature was never "mere" science but always the search for God. In her posthumous manuscript *The Mystical Heaven,* she explains that true contemplation will move from concrete objects to abstract truths, and that such a process of elevation was based on the complete surrender of intellect and will. Rational pursuits and mystical contemplation were not in competition, but cooperated. Historian Massimo Mazzotti has shown how her emphasis on the "capacity of attention" best captures this intersection of the spiritual and scientific worlds. By this term she meant that to master a discipline, one has to focus all of one's energies. Specifically, in order to comprehend higher mathematics, one has to sharpen one's intellect by eliminating disorderly thoughts and images. Mathematics becomes thus the preparatory school for proper devotion, which—as her fellow Italian Muratori had pointed out—should be focused on the mysteries of God.[9] Agnesi is also remarkable because at the height of her career, she withdrew from her intellectual activities. The death of her father, who had prepared her for an academic life and who might have pushed her more into the spotlight than she had wished, caused her to recalibrate her life. She now devoted herself to charitable works, taking care of orphans, prostitutes, the elderly, and the sick. She supposedly explained once:

> Man always acts to achieve goals; the goal of the Christian is the glory of God. I hope my studies have brought glory to God, as they were useful to others, and derived from obedience, because that was my father's will. Now I have found better ways and means to serve God, and to be useful to others.[10]

Bassi and Agnesi are two examples of Catholic women scientists of the Enlightenment. Nevertheless, their international reputation and acceptance makes them stand out among their peers. Both demonstrated to the male-dominated academic community the important role women can play in scientific discovery. In the grand narrative of women's scholarship, both are often referenced, but their profound religious commitment, which drove their scholarship, is hardly ever appropriately acknowledged.

Freedom to Marry versus Authoritarian Fatherhood

Despite the clear directives of the Council of Trent about the freedom of spousal choice, one should not suppose that every Catholic obeyed Catholic teaching. Although the church condemned "probationary" marriages (that is, sexual relations before the exchange of vows to test mutual fertility) and other lax practices, only at the end of the eighteenth century—in some regions only in the nineteenth—were such guidelines fully accepted. Around the middle of the eighteenth century, a significant number of European and overseas regions demonstrated a more laissez-faire attitude toward marriage.

A well-researched example is the Island of Malta, between the African and Sicilian coasts. Although Malta was one of the most Catholic states in the early modern world, governed by the Knights of St. John, one can frequently find at the end of the eighteenth century Maltese individuals condoning "carnal commerce" as not sinful, or accepting fornication as a "relief" of natural urges. Malta was home to many "secret" marriages, in which the couple exchanged their vows without the assistance of a priest. This is evidence that some Catholics understood marriage as a private matter and rejected the church's authority over it. Such privatization was advocated especially when parents did not give their consent, or when one of the partners desired to break a binding engagement. Yet the sacredness of marriage itself was not denied, and it seems that Catholics knew very well that it was the exchange of their vows, and not the priest's blessing, that fulfilled the sacrament.

Clandestine marriages could be the way out of a prior promise to marry. In 1779 a twenty-year-old Maltese hairdresser named Salvatore di Marco left his fiancée for Eugenia Busuttil. Yet the fiancée's mother and brother sued to force him to fulfill his prior commitment. Instead, he made an "ingenious" move and appeared with his lover in the confessional of a parish priest. The groom simply said in the presence of the priest "This is my wife!" while his bride responded with "This is my husband!" The marriage was valid because the exchange of vows was done in front of a witness, but it was illegal because the church had not sanctioned it. Both were put under house arrest but allowed to leave soon afterward as a happily married couple. Yet it seems that this more casual attitude toward marriage was more advantageous to men, since they were able to abandon their earlier, possibly pregnant, lovers without being held morally or financially responsible.

While the church does not recognize divorce when there is a valid marriage, since a valid marriage is indissoluble, it does allow for annulments in which a judge decides that a marriage never existed. Catholics often got out of relationships this way, especially if one of the spouses had betrayed the other or had concealed an important fact such as debt or impotence. In Malta as elsewhere, however, husbands sometimes escaped marital bonds by enlisting in foreign armies and thus thrusting their wives into economic misery. Without a breadwinner, wives often had to prostitute themselves or bribe witnesses who would testify that their spouse had died abroad so that they could remarry.[11]

Often historians have celebrated the Enlightenment for increasing the freedom of lovers to marry according to their own will, but this trend was not universal. In fact, the eighteenth century also saw an increase in patriarchal influence over marriage decisions. A good example can be found in Mexico. In this thoroughly Catholic country, arranged marriages, over which neither bridegroom nor bride had a say, had been rejected at least since the sixteenth century. The Spanish motherland also shared this view. Recent studies have shown that it was in Spain and Mexico that the freedom of individuals to choose their spouses have prevailed for the longest time, and that these countries resisted the universal trend to give the father of the household more authority. While parents certainly arranged meetings with potential spouses and gave their children guidance, patriarchal force was rejected in Mexico and Spain. The church itself reinforced this trend. The Council of Trent had reaffirmed that the two spouses had to decide freely to marry, and Spanish clergy disseminated this doctrine through catechisms and homilies throughout the sixteenth and seventeenth centuries. Certainly it was also mentioned that the Catechism of Trent admonished children not to marry against the will of their parents, but it was obviously also admitted that a parent's permission was not essential. In most Protestant areas of Europe, however, parents maintained a veto power over their offspring's marital choices and often arranged marriages, even against the wills of their sons and daughters. This was also customary in France, where the kings refused to accept the decrees of the Council of Trent. Instead, they declared, contradicting universal church law, that marriages against the will of the parents or the royal government were invalid.

Why did the idea that love was the primary motive for marriage enjoy such support in the Spanish-speaking world? As unlikely as it might seem, it was the enthusiastic reception of the teachings of St. Thomas Aquinas by Spanish theologians and philosophers that made the difference. The Spanish scholastics, echoing Aquinas, emphasized the importance of mutual love for the marital bond and stated that the spouses had to find in freedom God's will for them. These ideas had penetrated society to such an extent that state institutions also protected marriages from parental interference. This calls into question the idea that the patriarchal family was superseded by the ideal of an egalitarian family, or that community life was replaced by individualism. What major historians of family have described as the epitome of the modern family—namely, freedom of choice in marriage—"occurred in what historians have considered the archetype of the traditional social order—sixteenth century Spanish society, under an authoritarian religion," that is, Catholicism.[12] Thus modern historians are faced with what many would consider a paradox: freedom over one's life decisions and traditional religious authority could coexist in harmony, as the examples of Spain and Mexico prove.

A similar insistence on individual choice can be found in ecclesiastical norms about entering monasteries. Canon law gave women and men the opportunity to gain release from their monastic vows if they could prove that they were forced by their parents or others to enter a monastic community. Anne Jacobsen Schutte has shown that it was again the Council of Trent's insistence on freedom of choice that protected and saved women from a lifestyle they had not chosen and liberated them from paternal tyranny.[13]

Until the 1690s, local priests were also quite lenient in condoning premarital sex because it was usually connected to the promise of marriage and because the ancient Spanish code of honor ensured that a man kept his word. During the eighteenth century, however, men increasingly chose not to accept this ancient code as binding. Honor declined in favor of socioeconomic values. In this context, fathers sought the authority not only to protect the sexual integrity of their daughters but also seek financially stable futures for them.[14] At the same time, the idea of "love" changed.[15] While for earlier generations romantic love always entailed a promise of responsibility and the belief in a greater divine plan, eighteenth-century love seems to have mutated into an unstable emotion. After the honor code atrophied and after "love" became an excuse to condone sexual adventurousness, the pretexts for not keeping a promise of marriage had become trivial—many men claimed sudden immaturity or insanity. Women bore the scars of these cultural changes. In France a similar trend was perceivable, yet only in certain regions. In Nantes, for example, the proportion of young women who gave birth sooner than nine months after their weddings rose from 63 percent in 1726 to almost 90 percent in 1787.[16] Some men did not marry their partners at all, and when the promise of marriage was broken, the offspring were effectively abandoned to an uncertain future. If the child was handed over to a foundling home, the result was almost certainly death. Thus it cannot surprise us that parents wanted to prevent such scenarios with a renewed influence on the contractual side of marriage. The pendulum had again swung, and now the will of God was once more in the hands of concerned parents.

Sex, Birth Control, Abortion, and Breastfeeding

Enlightenment thought influenced almost all aspects of everyday life. Governments implemented reforms that affected midwifery, agriculture, worship, and education, while "public intellectuals" argued in journals and pamphlets about other steps toward perfecting society and church. While it is indisputable that some reforms helped women—for example, better access to education—other ideas diminished their opportunities.

On average, half the children born in the eighteenth century died before they were ten.[17] The number of children born out of wedlock, who were labeled "illegitimate," was also quite high. Especially at the beginning of the century, the church attempted to lower the number of illegitimate births by emphasizing virginity for girls and church-sponsored weddings. For a long time, the clergy had tolerated the tradition of entering marriage only after conceiving a child despite the fact that officially the church rejected premarital sex as sinful. With the Tridentine Reforms, such toleration quickly receded. While such actions might sound "repressive" to modern ears, in context they were not. The problem women faced was that the promises of men to marry them if they became pregnant were no longer kept as dutifully as in the previous century. The consequences were devastating for many. As the numbers of illegitimate children skyrocketed, so did the number of women whose reputations were—in the eyes of the contemporaries—once and for all ruined, and who had only a slim chance of ever getting married. Men did not acknowledge their illegitimate children as they had in the seventeenth century and left the financial burden entirely to their abused partner. To blame the Catholic Church for the actions of these men is to reverse the cause and effect. That this went hand in hand with an unfortunate stigmatization of women and their illegitimate children by some clergy is, however, true. While illegitimate children in Spain and Portugal were not discriminated against at all, in Germany, priests often wrote negative comments about such children in the baptismal records.[18] The marginalization of unwed mothers alienated them from their families, which in the past had taken care of illegitimate offspring. As a consequence, many mothers had to abandon their children to foundling homes, where the majority died due to negligence and malnourishment.[19] Between 1750 and 1799, child mortality in the Dublin foundling home was a shocking 89 percent. "Witnesses at mid-century described infants' bodies being 'stored' in vast coffins under the stairs, and then buried thirty-five at a time; the hospital is said to have reeked of death."[20]

Catholics of the eighteenth century also attempted to limit their fertility by practicing birth control, mostly before they entered marriage.[21] The most common way of avoiding pregnancy was to interrupt the sexual act. Some Catholic moral theologians of the time condoned *coitus interruptus*, but at the end of the century most Catholic moralists rejected it, and one can find accounts of priests from Malta to the Black Forest consistently admonishing their parishioners against the practice.[22] According to the patron saint of moral theology, Alphonsus of Liguori, interrupted marital discourse was only permissible to avoid death, for example, if the house was on fire.[23]

Early term abortions sometimes occurred because a small—and over the century, decreasing—number of Catholic theologians believed the fetus would only gain his or her soul, and thus the status of a person, after quickening. In 1661 about six hundred Parisian women confessed to their priests that they had undergone an abortion before quickening.[24] In the eighteenth century, however, the ancient idea that the fetus would gain its soul only a few months after conception was put to rest. Its demise began when in 1708 the feast of the Immaculate Conception of Mary the Mother of God was inserted into the official liturgical calendar. Pope Clement XI decreed that the feast had to be nine months prior to the birthday of Mary and thus on December 8. Only because Mary was a full human person from the first moment of her being she had been endowed with grace and thus preserved from all original sin. This decision influenced how theologians looked at human conception. If Mary was a human person with a soul from conception on, then it was likely that all human life began at conception. A few decades afterward, scientific evidence buttressed this theological argument. In the 1740s, medical doctors began to describe a fetus as a "little child." The Italian physician Giovanni Bianchi had introduced the differentiation between embryo and fetus, and his insights were spread among theologians in a book titled *Sacred Embryology* by the Jesuit Francesco Cangiamila. Additionally, Jansenists, who were pessimistic about the possibility of obtaining salvation and who did not think that an unbaptized fetus could be saved, forced the church to act: women were instructed to be careful so that no spontaneous miscarriages happened and priests were admonished to baptize the child of a deceased mother through caesarian section. The endorsement of Cangiamila's work by Pope Benedict XIV made it widely influential, and at the end of the century, Enlighteners and Catholics defended unborn life together: for the secular Enlighteners the fetus was an unborn and valuable citizen who had to be protected, while for the church it was a human person created in the image of God who had the right to life.[25] Nevertheless, it was Catholic Enlighteners like Franz X. Mezler, a professor of medicine at the University of Vienna and a devout Catholic, who insisted that short-lived, deformed babies should also be baptized. His rationale was simple: a woman can only give life to another human, regardless of its form or shape. He continued: "Moreover, the sacraments are there for humans, not humans for the sacraments—this is a principle of reason and of Christian charity. It would be loveless heartlessness to expose such a questionable creature to the danger of losing its eternal bliss and to kill its body and soul."[26]

Early modern Catholic parents sometimes deliberately caused the death of their children by neglect, usually from the fifth child onward. Such practice was euphemistically called "himmeln" (to bring into heaven) in German, just as an abortionist was called an "angel maker." Catholic as well as secular Enlighteners attempted to eradicate such child neglect and taught the masses about their duties as parents. In Malta, the local bishop reminded his flock in 1788 that if pregnant mothers refrained from taking food or did heavy work with the intention to cause a miscarriage they were actively pursuing murder. Yet the church did not only admonish by words. Parish priests were instructed to provide financial help to girls who sought abortions so that they could safely carry children to term.[27] In the French colonies one could consider contraception and abortion as tacit expressions of resistance of the slave population against their oppressors. The French Lazarists taught the slaves of Bourbon (today Réunion) to be open to conceiving children and that contraception was only allowed within the sacred ties of matrimony. The average childbirth rate among slave women, who were baptized Catholics, was an astonishing 2.3 compared to a 5.6 average among the French colonials. A 1785 document reveals the reason for this: "The principal cause is that most of these women destroy the fruit of their womb, not wanting to bring into the world children as unhappy as themselves."[28]

In some areas of Germany, Catholic women had many more children than their Protestant peers, who practiced birth control more widely. Even more interesting, while Protestants had fewer or no children in economically difficult times, Catholics tended to have more.[29] Childbirth itself was of course risky, mainly because of infections. Wet-nursing, the practice of giving one's child to a professional nurse for breastfeeding, was not everywhere the standard practice. Many women disliked it and preferred nurses who lived in their own household, but often their husbands urged them to give the offspring to a wet nurse because in some areas it was taboo to have sex with a nursing woman; likewise, sex was believed to spoil the quality of the milk and could thus endanger the child. By outsourcing the activity to a wet nurse, the husband could again claim his marital "rights" and feel sure that his child received good milk. In France and Germany the use of wet nurses was encouraged to increase the likelihood of more pregnancies. In Lyons, about 75 percent of the female population employed such nurses, and in Paris at the eve of the Revolution, the figure was about 98 percent.[30] Since women who worked as wet nurses were usually poorer, and since breastfeeding was common and accepted among the rural population, many more children were born to middle- and upper-class families than to poor ones, at least in France. By privileging big families, the French government subsidized this child care industry until the dawn of the nineteenth century.[31] Yet, when wet nurses were not paid—for example, during the demanding years of the Revolution in France—they often stopped feeding the babies, so that in 1792 the infant death rate at the Montpellier hospital, which had ceased paying wet nurses, was 80 percent. Catholic moral theologians usually condoned wet nursing, but some condemned the practice as a mother's refusal of maternal duties. In most cases, however, the husband's right to intercourse trumped the right of the child, and according to these theologians, the wife should give her child to a nurse if her husband insisted on regular intercourse. She could justifiably reject her husband's advances only if she was unable to pay the nurse, some Jesuits argued, so as to protect her milk supply.[32]

One of the first European proponents of breastfeeding one's own children was Marie-Angelique Le Rebours. In her 1767 book on nursing she informed her readers that nursing was medically proven to reduce fertility. By nursing their own offspring, women would gain more control over their bodies, their own lives, and of course reproduction. This in turn gave rise to a new concept: "maternalism," the notion "that motherhood was an extraordinarily powerful force that needed to be unleashed on the world at large."[33] For the Enlightener Jean-Jacques Rousseau, breastfeeding was essential to ensure the proper development of the child, since the "whole moral order stands or falls on whether or not mothers nurse their children."[34] Thus, breastfeeding became a political act, and during the Revolutionary period it became the symbol of nationalism: the mother's milk that a child receives induces the love of one's own country. This contrasted sharply with the view of Catholic Enlighteners such as Josefa Amar, for whom breastfeeding was part of the divine order of things and who rejected any attempt to politicize this intimate act of motherhood.

In the eighteenth century the importance of female midwives slowly decreased. Midwives and Catholic priests, however, worked well together, especially in the countryside; this close relationship was expressed, for example, in the ritual in which the midwife brought the delivered child to church for baptism. Theologians increasingly insisted, however, that midwives stop baptizing newborns right after birth unless the baby was in danger. If there was a danger of death during delivery, even intra-uterine baptism was possible: the midwives were instructed to inject a sponge with water into the mother's uterus and recite the baptismal formula.

In 1742, a Cistercian monk named Antonio José Rodríguez began publishing his four-volume work *New Aspects on Medical-Moral Theology*. His enlightened theology became quite influential and even led to a change in Spanish law: in 1749, following Rodríguez's advice, the king of Spain decreed that a post-mortem caesarian section must be undertaken on a woman if there was the slightest chance that she could be pregnant so that if a fetus was present, it could be baptized, should it still be alive.

Even as the medical knowledge of theologians and doctors increased, midwives still had no reliable access to it. Instead of receiving proper schooling, they were increasingly ridiculed and marginalized. In 1784 a Spanish priest, who obviously had read modern medicine and had absorbed the Enlightenment ideals of progress, exclaimed that midwifery was "despicable, and not uncommonly [practiced by] ... sinful and inebriated women."[35] Faced with such attitudes, it was the enlightened Spanish Benedictine Benito Feijoo who most vehemently argued from a Catholic perspective against male dominance over the delivery room. The virtue and intimacy of women was violated by male midwives, he insisted. Instead, he pleaded for a better education of midwives:

> Yet if it would be possible to undertake measures for women to be well trained in this art, men should be entirely excused of this trade. And would it be possible to take these measures? Doubtlessly. Some distinguished practitioners could be recruited through generous awards to efficiently teach several capable women, who thereupon would teach others, and so on. The trade is sufficiently lucrative such that enough impoverished women would be eager to learn it.[36]

Yet Feijoo's Catholic pro-woman stance was rejected from the start, and physicians, surgeons, and secular Enlightenment thinkers successfully campaigned to establish the physical and medical incompetence of women and their subservience to male surgeons.

Madame Leprince

The Enlightenment's, especially Rousseau's, new ideal of the "mother" as the most important teacher of a child and the key to a new society, helped create a political emphasis on the role of mothers, called "maternalism," as noted above. Mothers were, for Rousseau, responsible for molding their children into virtuous citizens, but by emphasizing this role he actually restricted women to the domestic sphere and increased the gender opposition of "woman" and "man."

For the last several decades historians have assumed that this division had increased due to the economic changes that set in midway through the industrialization of the eighteenth century. In the seventeenth century, the household was the predominant site of economy. It was largely non-commercial and non-competitive, and also a moral community. The primary goal of households was simply to maintain their self-sufficiency and integrity, not to accumulate more wealth. In this older hierarchical system, the father of the household held the primary position of authority, though women participated in the workforce equally. In the eighteenth century, capitalist market forces put pressure on the household as an economic unit and forced married men to find better, industrial work outside the home. With their new, higher income they purchased a "desired consumption good: patriarchy" and slowly forced women out of the labor force.[37] Yet a dramatic decline of women's participation in the labor force did not occur until the middle decades of the nineteenth century.[38]

Even if economic reasons cannot explain the gender divisions that developed during the eighteenth century, "by 1800," summarizes historian Keith Thomas, "gender divisions had sharpened, particularly among the middling and upper classes. ... The sexual division of labor became more rigid; and so did the assumption that men and women embodied complementary human qualities which justified that division and called for different forms of personal fulfillment."[39] Enlightenment ideas about economic growth in a commercial economy created the context in which the population increasingly disregarded the old value system of the household, so that gender roles were renegotiated and ultimately became stereotypes.[40] A good example of such disregard is the idea of many secular Enlighteners that women bear children not for their families, but "for the nation." Children were thus increasingly seen as guarantors of the state's welfare through their labor and not as members of a family.[41] Although some secular Enlighteners and their followers tried to overcome the gender dichotomies, the majority saw womanhood as "a life of servitude, hardship and self-sacrifice."[42]

Women were increasingly restricted to the domestic sphere, which the Enlighteners romanticized as the "dream" of every "patriotic" woman, while men were expected to become pillars of economic productivity. As a result, a cult of domesticity developed in which women were portrayed as economically dependent upon their husbands, and in which a woman's main duty was to create—in submission to her husband—a harmonious home and family life.[43] In some areas, however, this cult of domesticity helped women to articulate their own preferences. One could, in this setting, find other women with similar interests and form small networks of mutual intellectual exchange. For some, domestic space became a place of self-determination and new forms of female creativity found expression. Some scholars even speak of a "domestic revolution" in the eighteenth century, one that would be echoed in early feminist ideas. Especially in Catholic countries, the home was seen as both a residence and refuge where Christian virtues could be exercised, and which stood in contrast to a world full of temptations.[44] One Catholic writer in particular stands out for clearly expressing this new self-understanding of women in the domestic/maternalist culture, namely, Madame Leprince.

Voltaire's statement that Jeanne Marie Leprince de Meaumont would only write "little catechisms for young ladies"[45] was typical of male writers who felt challenged by a successful female competitor. She is of course universally known as the author of the most famous version of the story *The Beauty and the Beast*. She stood up for expanding women's opportunities and for fostering girls' self-esteem through education. Her experience as a governess in England in the 1740s convinced her that British women were widely oppressed. Back in France, she began writing her first book—one of seventy—in order to contribute to the end of such oppression. In the four volumes of the *Young Misses' Magazine* of 1756—which was translated into most European languages—she articulated her vision for the education of young girls. Long before Rousseau and other modern pedagogues, she sought to adapt education to the needs of children rather than trying to adapt children to a prefabricated education. She published novels, treatises on education in general, and texts on the education of boys. Especially famous is her utopian novel *The New Clarissa* (1767), in which she dramatizes her vision of self-determined women who are in full control of their lives.[46]

Leprince had a new—some would say proto-feminist—view of women, and she worked to make that vision a reality. In eighteenth-century society men expected women to act according to emotions and thus to act irrationally, without proper recourse to reason. "Educated" women were those who were able to express the appropriate emotions according to societal standards, almost like a machine. For Leprince, such a view was deeply offensive. Women were not mindless machines who ran according to pre-defined emotional settings, she insisted, but peers to men.[47] Although she did not question a wife's obedience to her husband, she believed it had limits:

> I have already told you, your obedience to him must be limited by that [sic] you owe to God: I trust they will never be at variance; but the means of keeping within those limits, without alienating his affection, is to convince him daily and in the most trifling occurrences, that you have no greater pleasure than that of obeying him. . . . When you are under the necessity of thinking or acting contrary to [your husband], never wound him by a flat contradiction; rather seem at first to acquiesce, then mildly remonstrate with him, and by arguments convince him that the plan he is going to adopt, though good, is subject to inconvenience; suggest some other means of accomplishing his wishes; in short, contrive, if possible, such expedients as will make him believe he is following his own inclinations, while he is guided by yours.[48]

This statement is part of a theological trend. While the rise of capitalism gave the husband more economic and practical influence, the church increasingly questioned his ability to lead his family morally. This was a fundamental shift from the attitude one hundred years earlier, when manuals of moral theology gave the husband the right and privilege to correct his wife's behavior and the responsibility to form a virtuous family. Now theologians had completely reversed their stance. Among the many changes, perhaps most important was that men were no longer permitted to physically punish their wives. In the age of reason, the church relied almost entirely on wives to correct their husbands and to sanctify their families. Men had lost the moral authority to supervise their spouses. This finding, until now completely overlooked or underappreciated by historians, also helps to explain why so many missionaries, for example, in North America, relied on newly baptized women as lay ministers.[49]

Leprince's works were revolutionary in two additional ways. She proposed that girls should be educated independently of any relationship with men. They should learn how to read, to think, to write, and to calculate regardless of their future marital status. To think of a woman's education independent of any practical use in marriage was an utterly new idea. For Leprince, however, it was the most natural thing in the world, since nobody taught a man math with his future wife in mind![50] While for many Enlighteners such as Rousseau, the wife ultimately existed only for the husband's enrichment, we encounter in Leprince's vision of marriage two equal partners who contribute to one another's mutual fulfillment through dialogue and tender love.

Her profound knowledge of Catholic theology and the Bible becomes especially apparent in *The Americans* (1770), a grandiose six-volume dialogue about the encounter of young American natives with world religions. These volumes demonstrate Leprince's commitment to mutual understanding between religions, but also her steadfast Catholic faith. As a Catholic Enlightener, Leprince rejected both religious radicalism and indifferentism and instead argued for a tolerant yet fervent religious life. Literary scholar Peggy Schaller stated that her "religion was one of hopeful persuasion by a clear respect for the opinion of others."[51] Nothing expresses her theology more succinctly than a quotation from her novel *Civan—King of Bongo* (1754), in which she makes clear that it is not preaching but good examples that convince others: "Let them know by your example that there is a religion that purifies behavior and brings happiness to those who practice it; but remember that God wants hearts that give themselves willingly."[52]

Women as Breeders and the Invention of "Love"

One of the most widely repeated accusations against Catholicism is that it turns women into birthing machines and expects couples to have as many children as possible. Neither of these claims is true. In fact, it is the Enlightenment that can be charged with having turned women into "breeders."

France was perhaps most notorious for enacting laws that tried to encourage families to have more children. Fathers of twelve or more living children could receive from King Louis XIV special tax privileges, even a pension. The push for massive population growth, which was never successful, came about through bad demography. False statistics seemed to prove that the population was declining, and officials warned that dystopian nightmares would befall *la grand nation* if the trend continued. However, another Enlightenment fixation stood behind such policies, namely, that a nation should strive to grow its economy. A growing economy, which also brought an increasing need for labor, was possible only if there were more children. Moreover, the higher the population, the higher would be the tax revenue. Therefore, a woman was encouraged to give birth to as many children as possible, "for the sake of the nation." One of the first critics of such population measures, long before the famous Thomas Malthus, was a Catholic: the Freiburg professor of cameralism and policing, Franz Joseph Bob. Bob demonstrated the dangers of excessive population growth, and thus he pointed favorably toward the policies of certain Catholic German territories where no efforts were being made to increase the population, and where instead there were actually impediments to marriage and a prohibition of emigration. These measures helped to keep their population steady, he said. Additionally, he exposed the high costs of population programs in Italy and Spain and their utter failure.[53]

The average French woman in 1700, who married at twenty-five, gave birth to five or six infants. About 25 percent of women had nine or ten children baptized, while only 11 percent had families of twelve or more. From the middle of the century to the Revolution of 1789, the number of families of ten or more children shrank by half. In 1789, the average French woman bore only four children. In the age of Enlightenment, population-growth propaganda was widespread and especially supported by the Enlightenment philosophers, who believed (falsely) that France's population was on the decline. Montesquieu, for example, was quite insistent that it was the role of a woman to bear children and not to have personal ambitions. Although later in life he articulated a preference for the idea that marriage was more about companionship, he and most of his philosopher friends viewed limitations on human and marital fertility as an offense against nature. Even the radical Enlightener Diderot did not approve of contraception or family planning, but instead praised the big family with ten or more children as the positive antithesis to the "overly refined, luxury-loving and depopulating present."[54] This Enlightenment view of marriage as a means for population growth, solely concentrated on procreation, seems to be a secularized version of the pessimistic view Jansenists had of marriage: it was necessary as an outlet for the sexual drive and for begetting children, but was hardly ever mentioned as the locus of mutual companionship.

The church encouraged couples to have children, but it always despised the secular population growth agenda. It did so because, as a seventeenth-century Jesuit said, "marriage not only gives heaven a husband and wife ... it makes them trees of life in the center of the earthly paradise of the church, producing fruits worthy of the eyes, hands, and mouth of God."[55] Rather than encouraging couples to have as many children as possible, the church taught spouses to leave such things to God, to practice occasional abstinence, and to celebrate anniversaries with common prayer; through each of these practices, the church encouraged growth in intimacy and companionship. The French historian Agnes Walch has discovered that this view of marriage had its roots in both the Renaissance and the Council of Trent, but of course it also had ancient roots. While the Renaissance of the fifteenth century, especially in Italy, rekindled the idea of chivalry, the council insisted, against Protestant attacks, that marriage was a sacrament. As such, it was a means of God's grace, which the spouses administered mutually for the life of their marriage. With Trent, Catholic theology had (re)discovered the more profound spiritual aspects of marital relationships—this was one of the most remarkable shifts in modern Catholic theology. The *Catechism of the Council of Trent* (1566), published to popularize the teachings of the council, taught a radically new view of matrimony without contradicting the perennial teaching of its sacramental nature. Whereas older Augustinian views centered on marriage as necessary to overcome the constant temptation of fleshly desires, Trent taught something much more positive. It insisted that the first motive for marriage was companionship, "encouraged by the hope of mutual assistance in bearing more easily the discomforts of life and the infirmities of old age," and only secondarily about the wish for children and after that the taming of sexual lust.[56] The *Catechism* even explicitly stated that "by the grace of this sacrament husband and wife are joined in the bonds of mutual love, cherish affection one towards the other ..."[57] and that both together should try to find God's will and follow it. The Jesuit Thomas Sanchez even acknowledged the importance of tender care for each other, of hugs and kisses, to reinforce each other's love.[58]

This emphasis on mutual love was motivated by the council's zeal for a reform of Catholic life down to its most basic unit, the family. The *Catechism* portrays spouses as soul mates who accomplish their mutual

sanctification by living and praying together. This union of love is compared to that of Christ and his church. Such a spiritually renewed family
was supposed to inspire the entire church and to disseminate the message of reform. This understanding of marriage was popularized further
by St. Francis de Sales's bestselling *Introduction to the Devout Life* (1609),
which specifically advised married couples lovingly to fulfill their duties.
More and more, authors followed de Sales and wrote books about how
to achieve good marriages. Most of them made clear that it was not pas-
sionate desire that held a marriage together but tender love. Also in the
seventeenth century, Catholic laypeople became involved in marriage
counseling. Historian Lesley H. Walker has argued that the advent of the
"Enlightenment mother" cannot be understood without the preceding
efforts of the Catholic Reform to stress that mothers were entrusted with
instilling virtues in their children and family.[59]

Yet many contemporaries did not share the belief that the spiritual
union of spouses was achievable. The more Jansenism spread, with its
pessimistic view of the depravity of human nature, the more the sacramental view of marriage darkened. Pressured by Jansenism, by the 1680s
the optimistic view had receded in favor of a more rigorist view of marriage that again emphasized procreation instead of mutual companionship as the main motive for marriage in official church documents and
in theological discussion.[60] In the eighteenth century even the works of
St. Francis de Sales were purged of their Renaissance optimism regarding marital companionship, and the clergy lost interest in the married
couple because the battle with anti-religious Enlighteners shifted the
church's priorities. Only at the end of the eighteenth century did Catholic
Enlightenment thinkers respond to such a one-sided view by reviving
Trent's ideal of marital piety: the goal of a virtuous life together ordered
toward the achievement of salvation through each other's assistance.[61]
Women writers especially championed these ideals. Indeed, Madame
Leprince was among the first to articulate mutual love as a tamed passion and to argue that reasonable emotion was the duty of spouses, in a
catechism she wrote for young girls:

> The sacred bonds of wedlock make it the couple's strict duty to love
> one another. . . .. Give this love substance by basing it on virtue. If it
> had not reason other than beauty, charms and youth . . . it would
> soon pass, as they do; but if it is tied to the qualities of the heart and
> soul, it will stand the test of time.[62]

Leprince stands in the tradition of a Catholic theological trend that began with the Catholic Reform, especially in the teachings of St. Ignatius of Loyola, the founder of the Jesuits, who stressed the individual vocation. For him, as for most Catholic Enlighteners, it was clear that marriage was a vocation to a special state of life. If this was true, then it was appropriate to discern whether God wanted one to enter such a union. The practice for such discernment came from St. Ignatius's *Spiritual Exercises*. In the eighteenth century, such discernment methods became widespread among Catholic laypeople due to their increased literacy. Moreover, the Pietists, a Protestant revival movement, stressed such discernment and individual conversions, and their books were read by Catholics who were interested in religious revival. This cohered with the Enlightenment's own emphasis on individual choices, so that we should not be surprised to see all three influences—that of Ignatius, Pietism, and Enlightenment—intertwined in Catholic writers, such as Leprince, who see marriage as a vocation.

Another pre-Tridentine view of marriage was that it was actually dangerous. Because it is a "particular relationship," it can become selfish, causing the couple to turn inward and forget their broader social obligations to kinfolk and family. This view was rejected by another Catholic Enlightener, Stephanie Felicite de Genlis. Her novels and pamphlets, which were widely read and even reached a broad audience in France, England, and Germany, argued against the views of both advocates of the negative Jansenist view and also the views of secular Enlighteners. In her 1785 *Moral Catechism* she first describes marriage in quite traditional terms as a contract between two spouses. Yet, for a fulfilling marriage, she adds, such a contract has to be founded on love, and love on virtue. De Genlis makes clear what she means by this: love is the opposite of dominance and power plays, and it is not just a virtue but a sentiment of the heart.[63] Only after the Revolution did de Genlis change her mind on romantic love, arguing that friendship formed the foundation of a lasting marriage.[64]

Proto-Feminism in New Religious Orders

Historians have pointed out that women tended to excel in work that defends corporate, ethnic, or religious demands "in the face of real or imagined external attack, undoubtedly because they sense that this is an area where they are likely to be given an unusual amount of creative scope."[65] The Catholic Reform, which began in the late fifteenth century before the Council of Trent, with its zeal to reform the ecclesial landscape and transform society from within, and thus to save souls, provided especially appealing opportunities for women. Hence, it cannot surprise us that from the sixteenth to the eighteenth century, dozens of new female religious orders came into existence.[66]

The Catholic Reform unintentionally created the possibility of an active apostolate of women, as historian Susan E. Dinan rightly put it. This might be surprising, since historians have shown how the Council of Trent restricted the vocational choices of women to cloistered religious orders. Nevertheless, it enticed countless women to work with zeal for the Tridentine reform, and this new apostolic energy was put to good use. Women participated especially in charitable confraternities (such as the Ursulines), which were in the course of the late sixteenth and seventeenth centuries transformed into religious congregations. Charismatic women also founded such confraternities for specific challenges such as taking care of unattended orphans or sick people, educating girls, and helping the poor. A number of these new forms of female religious life were created in France, where the decrees of Trent were only received in 1615. The best example is St. Louise de Marillac's Daughters of Charity, which she had founded in conjunction with St. Vincent de Paul. The enormous success of this confraternity, which also allowed poor women to become members because no dowry was expected, persuaded the French bishops to rethink the assumption that enclosure in a cloister was the only option for women. Due to Marillac's and de Paul's excellent networking in France and Rome, the growing confraternity, which had a regular cycle of work and common prayer, was approved by the pope in 1646. The community circumvented the control of local bishops by being directly placed under the authority of the male Vincentian order. The Daughters of Charity was not a confraternity but a new type of religious life for women, who were not cloistered and actively served the poor and marginalized.[67]

During the first half of the eighteenth century a "second Tridentine Reform" went into full swing, giving women even more opportunities to work for the good of the Church. Pope Benedict XIV approved the Institute of the Blessed Virgin in 1749 as a women's religious congregation. The importance of this decision can be appreciated only against its historical background: the Englishwoman Mary Ward had actually founded the order in 1610, and it was intended to be a mirror image of the Jesuits. She focused on a female religious life that was active in the world, especially through education, rather than an enclosed life in the cloister. Moreover, she refused to accept any interference by local bishops, which significantly complicated her efforts to get the church's official approval for her Institute; in fact, the order was suppressed during her lifetime and only a hundred years later revived in different form. While Pope Benedict's decree *Quamvis Justo* still held in principle that bishops should oversee religious institutions, it also gave women's communities like the Mary Ward Sisters or the Daughters of Charity the status of a religious community, protected against episcopal interference. Thus, if sisters wanted to work outside the cloister, they could do so while at the same time being acknowledged as fully professed sisters (not "nuns," as this term was reserved for enclosed orders whose members take solemn vows in a cloistered community). This development also had a significant impact on female monasteries of older orders, which occasionally lacked discipline and had become places of laxity, and sometimes even lasciviousness. Ecclesiastics now worked to bring about a spiritual renewal of their communities and often tightened existing rules about the cloister.[68]

Many historians have called the Council of Trent's tightening of the cloister—the enclosure behind monastery walls—a reactionary move against the liberties of women's monasteries. Yet these historians overlook the fact that even the great female reformer St. Theresa of Avila herself, among others, viewed the cloister not as a prison but rather as protection against distractions from the world; according to her, the cloister liberated women, allowing them to spend their time in contemplative prayer. That others viewed the enclosure as oppressive, especially if they were not used to this way of life, is beyond doubt, but the question of how much contact monks and nuns should have with the world was as old as the monasteries themselves. Trent envisioned a renewal of female contemplative religious life and considered the cloister the best way to secure that. However, the council's regulations were frequently ignored by female superiors. Some resisted the imposition of the new lifestyle—especially those orders that had never had a strict cloister—and instead maintained a flexible form of enclosure. Contemplative communities without any field of practical work in the world were not entirely shut off from society but still entertained connections to it and remained places of intellectual creativity. Even Pope Benedict XIV, who had tightened the enclosure for Cistercian nuns in 1742, encountered sharp criticism from female religious. After all, for many it meant a change of their traditional lifestyle in contradiction of their vows, which constituted a legally binding contract. Theologians soon found a solution. They argued that one should not understand the papal command literally but adapt it to local traditions; otherwise it would make the life of monasteries impossible. Nuns insisted that their contacts with the world were also necessary to keep in contact with those who provided money and protection, and especially in order to attract young women interested in a religious vocation.[69] The main argument, however, was that each order, or even each community, had a special charisma or vocation: one saw interaction with the world as important, another did not. The pope's view on this question had apparently shifted seven years later when he permitted the establishment of the Mary Ward sisters, and this shift seems to suggest that he learned to better appreciate such a variety of vocations.

In some communities, however, a serious religious life was no longer on the agenda; they looked more like single-sex luxury condominiums than like monasteries. Some allowed themselves (relatively) lavish indulgences, such as coffee or chocolate, and even vacations in spas, as long as they were prescribed by their physicians.[70] Those that only accepted women of noble birth were especially prone to such amusements. In these places, a "cell," as the room of a nun is traditionally called, was an apartment consisting of three or four rooms, some with a sunroof and a patio. Often, noble nuns had permission to keep pets, to play musical instruments, to host dances in the cloister, to receive visitors, and to avoid fasting.[71] Of forty-eight female monasteries that existed in Mexico in 1756, thirty-six practiced such a "relaxed observance." These were clear signs of decadence. If a female superior tried to make changes, she faced fierce opposition. In Oberwerth, Germany, such an increase in discipline turned an already disgruntled nun into an assassin, who attempted to poison the entire convent.[72] Increased zeal also brought the community of the Conceptionist nuns of San Miguel de Allende in Mexico almost to its end. From 1759 to 1772 the nuns debated whether to embrace tighter discipline and more religious fervor. The younger nuns wanted to answer the critics of the Enlightenment world by giving up their opulent lifestyle. They therefore chose to live in simplicity and austerity, without personal servants or maids. The tension between the reformist young nuns and the older ones almost tore the community apart. This example is just one of many in which female monasteries responded to negative sociopolitical discourse about their lifestyle and attempted to demonstrate their service to the church.[73]

One of the most common misconceptions about women's religious life is that sisters or nuns passively accepted every command of ecclesiastical leaders or state powers. Instead, many nuns demonstrated brave self-confidence if they felt that their rights had been violated. In 1748 the nuns of Torcy in France, for example, disobeyed the archbishop's decree to dissolve their community, and in 1745 the nuns of Malnou resisted the king's command to merge with another monastery. The most famous instances of female resistance and independence, however, are the Carmelite nuns of Compiègne, who for their silent resistance to the French Revolution were beheaded, and the Jansenist nuns of Port Royal, who against royal and papal pressure remained steadfast supporters of Cornelius Jansen. One can get a sense of the extent to which women religious exercised resistance by considering the actions of the Franciscan nuns of Beauvais, who refused to accept the papal bull *Unigenitus* (1713), which had condemned Jansenism. When the archbishop tried to remove the prioress and harshly reminded her that it was the king's wish, she responded that "the king is not above God ... and the power of the king does not extend over our souls."[74] A Benedictine nun exclaimed that her conscience demanded disobedience: "There is a time to keep silent and a time when one must speak up. .... Today silence is no longer permitted."[75] The Jansenists are sometimes portrayed as self-centered fanatics, but this depiction mischaracterizes them. Instead, they stood for an ascetic church, one free from luxury, and championed a renaissance of biblical spirituality. The Jansenist theologian Quesnel advised nuns to stand up to "those persons, who would wish to take advantage of their authority which the quality of priest and confessor gives them in order to weaken you: you should no longer listen to them nor respond to them."[76] He also argued that Holy Scripture had been abused by men, but not women, and gave women—against tradition—the right to engage in regular Bible reading.[77] Yet Jansenist nuns were not just admonished; as a consequence of their rebellious behavior, they were also exiled, refused the sacraments, and harassed by spiritual guides and priests. Communities were split up and monasteries were destroyed. Outraged by such persecution, some of them publicly appealed to parliament, engaged barristers, or published pamphlets. Among supporters, the nuns were seen as humble martyrs for a just cause who were resisting human tyranny. While the nuns were described as exemplifying stereotypically male virtues, bishops, popes, and the king were compared to despotic women.[78] Such language motivated twentieth-century literary scholars to identify a surge of "Jansenist feminism" in France—one of the earliest appeals to the public in favor of women's rights.[79]

Many of the new orders were founded to meet the need for female education.[80] The Ursulines, especially, became known for their work in this field. In the first third of the eighteenth century the sisters also reached New Orleans, where they began teaching girls and thus radically improving female literacy. This helped the women of New Orleans to gain more independence from their husbands and thus to achieve greater equality.[81] In heavily Protestant areas such as North America, sisters like the New Orleans Ursulines were more or less "ideological outlaws." The sisters rejected the notion that a woman should be subservient to her husband, which Protestant society expected, and thus they demonstrated that self-determined roles for women outside gender stereotypes existed. The Ursulines proved that women could realize relative autonomy, gain financial independence, and pursue ambitious projects without paternalist "support"; therefore, they were a thorn in the flesh of the narrow culture of domesticity around them.[82] The sizes of monastic schools varied considerably. Some sisters, such as those serving in New Orleans, had only a handful of boarders (often across the racial and social spectrum).[83] Others—for example, the Monasterio de la Concepción in Lima, Peru—had 251 nuns and 790 other females in residence in 1700, some of them employees and private servants, but most of them students. Many nuns there received young girls as maids. The nun-teachers educated their servants in practical things, but also in literature and in religious matters. In return, the girls were expected to provide lifelong service to the nun-teacher. This sounds at first like a one-sided bargain, but one must not forget that many, if not most, of these girls had no families and never would have had any chance to receive a proper education. Moreover, the work of a private servant within a female monastery was not harsh, consisting mostly of household duties. The nuns considered themselves mothers to these girls, who often came to them at a young age. This, however, troubled the bishops, who feared that women who had such motherly authority over others could not be submissive brides of Christ and thus would not be obedient to the church. They tried several times to ban children from the cloister—without much success.[84]

Monastery education came under attack in the eighteenth century. Pedagogues and anti-clerical Enlighteners doubted that a secluded convent was the best place to educate young girls and transform them into "natural women." How could a girl learn to live in the world from women who had decided to abandon it? The cloister was regarded as harmful for the delicate souls of the young girls because it enticed them to seek amusement and debauchery after their graduation from the austere convent education.[85] If convent education was really that bad, why were so many cities eager to have teaching convents settle within their walls? Why did so many middle- and upper-class families generously donate to the nuns' teaching enterprise for their daughters, and why did these convents always have sufficient vocations? Moreover, if the schools were so bad, why was female literacy so much higher in areas with convent schools than in areas without them? Certainly, the nuns had limitations as teachers, but this is true of every teacher and every institution. The schools were effective in providing basic education, but of course they were not schools where one learned critical thinking; neither were most universities at that time. Ridiculing the nuns' educational attempts also completely disregards the fact that these cloistered (or un-cloistered) women were often themselves well-educated intellectuals.[86] One only has to compare the number of active female writers in the German monasteries between 1600 and 1700—there were 271—with the number of active female writers in England in the same time period—231 women.[87] This clearly demonstrates, despite differences in the quality and scope of writing, that women religious constituted a literary world of their own, one that deserves serious scholarly attention.

Conclusion

Eighteenth-century women were a vital part of the Catholic engagement with the Enlightenment culture. Against conventional wisdom, Catholic theologians spoke out in defense of women's rights, whether in fields like science and education or in women's choice of marital partners. While some secular Enlightenment reforms brought women greater freedom—to accept inheritance, to file for a divorce—they also degraded women, seeing them as "breeders" for the sake of the nation and diminishing their role to that of pleasing wife and mother. The Catholic Church, by contrast, emphasized the mutual love and tenderness of spouses, and female Catholic proto-feminists were leading the way in claiming equal rights, especially in the area of education. Catholic theology also underwent a substantial shift when it abandoned the husband as the moral center of the family and instead began focusing on the mother.

Catholic women engaged in scientific pursuits and other occupations transcended conventional gender expectations and roles. Women's religious life in cloisters and convents must be taken seriously as contributing to eighteenth-century intellectual culture and progress. Against much resistance, sisters and nuns created new spaces of activity hitherto unavailable to them and championed the necessity of female education. Women writers like Josepha Amar supported a natural relationship of women to their bodies and even went so far as to anticipate ideas of the modern feminist movement, while Madame Leprince and Madame de Genlis addressed the need of mutual spousal friendship in marriage and thus the end of female oppression.

Yet, overall scholarship on Catholic Enlightenment women is still underdeveloped. The lack of literature on this subject is striking and poses the question of why such a big part of women's history has hitherto been left unexplored.

4

Catholic Enlightenment in the Americas, China, and India

AFTER THE REFORMATION and the Council of Trent, a new fervor for missions set the Catholic Church ablaze. Missionaries went to all corners of the world, but in most cases they traveled under the protection of European colonial powers. In the Middle East, however, they relied on good relations with the local, non-Christian governments. The Catholic Enlightenment flourished in the Americas, China, and India. Yet the Enlightenment also had negative effects on these locations, especially South America.

Latin America's Enlightenment: From Brazil to Mexico

Conventional wisdom holds not only that the Portuguese and Spanish rejected the ideas of reform and Enlightenment but that their colonies were especially impenetrable to European Enlightenment thought. However, the opposite is true. Latin Americans not only often attended European universities and brought back with them the ideas they learned in lecture halls, coffee salons, and masonry lodges, but book traders regularly imported even censored books. In addition, Latin American universities were open to Enlightenment ideas. They replaced old curricula, introduced experimental sciences, added the works of John Locke or Benjamin Franklin to their required reading lists—all without any anti-clerical agenda, because the main propagators of this reform were clergy or committed Catholic laypersons. In Argentina, the Jesuits and Franciscans, still holding a monopoly in education, introduced the modern thinkers to their students, starting in the 1750s. John Locke's empiricism was welcome because it was thought to be easily compatible with Christian doctrine: if all knowledge derived from the senses, then sinful behavior and wrong ideas about God could be explained as a result of people incorrectly interpreting their sensory data. Consequently, a properly articulated revelation from God in the form of Holy Scripture was necessary, and theology was essential to correctly interpret it. Other aspects of Locke's philosophy that could be used to undermine the faith or the predominant role of Catholicism, such as his thoughts on toleration, were more or less passed over.

In 1786 the Jesuit scientist François Jacquier, a friend of Voltaire and an orthodox Catholic, became the standard author of Argentinian textbooks on philosophy. This demonstrated an openness to scientific discovery that led a remarkable number of Latin American priests to successfully engage with aerostatics, botany, and geography. Among the most famous is Bartolomeu de Gusmão from Portuguese Brazil, who experimented with air pressure and who is credited as the inventor of the aerostat; he had to flee from the Portuguese Inquisition to Spain in order to continue working on his airship. Most clergy, it seems, did not find anything objectionable to the use of new science, philosophy, political theory, or even the fermentation of theology by all three, but only rejected ideas that threatened substantive parts of their faith. This open-minded yet eclectic Latin American Catholic Enlightenment produced a number of extraordinary thinkers.[1]

Colonial fantasies saw in South America and Africa inferior continents that awaited European "civilization." Usually, the Spanish and Portuguese colonists and explorers, and in particular Catholic missionaries, are charged with such a view. While missionaries of the sixteenth century sometimes did have an inferior view of the Amerindian culture and population, the idea of a generally "inferior" South America did not originate until the eighteenth century. It was an invention of the Enlightenment. Men such as the German philosopher Georg W. F. Hegel stated with conviction that the Aztec culture had to collapse when it was "touched" by the European "spirit" of culture, and indulged in the fantasy that Amerindians were sexually disinterested whereas the conquistadors were full of virile power.[2] Although the Catholic Enlightenment shared much of the Eurocentric sentiment of superiority, it seems to have appreciated Amerindian culture much more than its secular counterparts.

Jesuits engaged enthusiastically with new philosophies and were sometimes sought-after correspondents of leading Enlighteners such as

Leibniz or Wolff. Long before the European Enlightenment reached their shores, the Jesuits of South America contributed to a better understanding of Amerindian cultures and to the natives' welfare. The failure to take their work seriously as contributions to the Enlightenment republic of letters is not only a sign of latent anti-Catholicism but also of an arrogant and condescending Eurocentrism.

It might surprise some that among such Catholic Enlighteners is the Jesuit Joseph Francisco Gumilla, because in his natural history *The Orinoco Enlightened* (1741–1745) he often talks about the "natural wonders" along the Orinoco River. How could someone who emphasizes wonder belong to the Enlightenment, with its emphasis on rational comprehension? The answer is simple, yet complex. At the time, descriptions of nature and expressions of wonder did not fall into different categories; both had their place in natural history. Moreover, wonder was considered the summit of knowledge; rationality could comprehend only so much. This echoes the traditional distinction in Catholic theology between *scientia*, the knowledge of apparent causes, and *sapientia*, or wisdom, the higher and supernatural form of knowledge. Famous for such limitation of knowledge is the German philosopher Immanuel Kant, but a generation before him Ludovico Muratori, the Italian champion of Catholic Enlightenment, had offered similar ideas. According to him, in the moment of awe and wonder the mind comprehends its own limits and begins praising "the author of nature, that intellect, and infinite power that knows, and can do so many things superior to ours."[3] Gumilla also followed Muratori, who since 1708 had publicly insisted that experiential understanding was the supreme path to new knowledge, as well as his Spanish countryman Benito Feijoo, who combined Christian philosophy and scientific skepticism.

In many ways Gumilla's description of South America's second biggest river, which flows through present-day Colombia and Venezuela, blends scientific description with a view of spiritual progress. This made it necessary to correct the mistakes of ancient church authorities on scientific questions. Gumilla, as well as other Jesuits, however, applied a rhetorical tactic to put at ease the minds of timid conservatives, who feared that heretical innovations were being introduced. The Jesuits described their explorations and achievements in modern science as an organic development of ancient thought. Often they had to bend the ancient authors' intentions quite a bit to achieve this goal, but the strategy helped them to escape the charge that they were "dangerous modernizers." Because historians have not generally understood this rhetorical strategy, much of

Jesuit scientific discourse was completely passed over.[4] Gumilla's missionary attentiveness and contribution to the scientific world should not be
excluded from Enlightenment history because it also had spiritual moti-
vations. After all, other explorers were driven by commercial or political
motives, yet we still regard their texts as part of the Enlightenment. By
revisiting missionary literature such as that of Gumilla, it becomes clear
that science was not only consolidated in North but also in South America.
This corrects a standard stereotype and gives Latin America its place in
the history of scientific progress.

Even more important than Gumilla was the Mexican-born Jesuit
Francisco Javier Clavigero. Clavigero powerfully refuted the notion that
Catholics condescendingly looked down on South American culture. After
being exiled, in the 1760s, from Spanish Mexico to Italy, he encountered
shocking prejudices about America. One Jesuit recalled in a letter that his
Italian barber asked him if Amerindian women were at all comparable to
European women and if the sun was similar to the sun that he saw in Italy.
Yet, not just commoners but also academics espoused such ideas and even
publicly celebrated their pseudo-knowledge. Armchair scholars wrote treatises contemptuous of American culture that deeply disgusted Clavigero.
While such sentiment led some Jesuits to propose Spanish America's independence from the motherland, it motivated Clavigero to set the scholarly
record straight in a four-volume history of ancient Mexico.[5] This book was
inspired by emerging Mexican nationalism and the desire to show the
world that the European settlers in America ("creoles") had not "deteriorated" to the level of the Amerindians. While he was convinced of Spanish
superiority, he did not ridicule Amerindian culture: much to the contrary,
he included in his work the most sympathetic accounts of Amerindian culture one can find among Enlightenment writers. Clavigero even included
a chapter in which the Jesuit demonstrated that syphilis did not originate
in the Americas, as Europeans claimed, but was a thoroughly European
import to the colonies. Instead of denigrating ancient Mexican culture,
he compared it to the Greek civilization that had been subjugated by the
Turks; in the case of Mexico, the Spaniards were the oppressors.

It is important to note that the armchair anti-Americans were all
famous Enlighteners. They were enraged by the traditional description
of America as a paradisiac colony inhabited by noble "savages" because
such an account seemed to buttress Jean-Jacques Rousseau's claim that
society was a degenerating force and that the Amerindians who lived in
the most "primitive and least cultured" society were the happiest human

beings. If Rousseau was right, then the scientific and cultural progress of the Enlightenment was nothing short of a disaster. Thus, in order to prove Rousseau wrong, French naturalist George-Louis Buffon and other scholars attempted to destroy the image of the noble savage. Buffon conceived in the 1750s the "scientific" theory—without having ever set foot on American soil—that Amerindians were a debased, deteriorated race and that even American nature had waned. He unleashed an unprecedented polemic against America among French, British, German, and Spanish scholars, who consequently portrayed a whole continent as "inhabited by degenerate, hopeless natives." Thus, the "black legend" of America was born. The most outspoken defender of America and its colonist population was Clavigero, supported by the ex-Benedictine Antoine-Joseph Pernety, the Ecuadorean Jesuit Juan de Velasco, Bishop Jose Granados y Galvez, and other Catholic clergymen.[6]

Some of Clavigero's enemies claimed that the many swamps in South America were a clear sign that America had recently emerged from the flood of Noah's time and was therefore much younger than Europe and less developed. The inhabitants were more ignorant, and all animals disproportioned and deficient. The Dutch philosopher Cornelius de Pauw went even further when he described Amerindians as almost animals—physically weak and lacking capacities for rational thinking, learning, morals, and religion. It was such accounts that justified the inhumane treatment of Amerindians by colonial powers. Instead, Clavigero defended Indians as strong, chaste, and clever. Clavigero saw no difference between the Mexican mind and that of a European and thus sharply rejected de Pauw's racism. Moreover, he found the assertion that the Incas and Aztecs were barbarians ridiculous. After a careful description of both civilizations, he made clear that both were civilized people with a developed concept of a supreme being, an organized government, laws, and even a monetary system. Most remarkable is perhaps his defense of Amerindian languages. While de Pauw thought Amerindian expressions were animal-like, Clavigero demonstrated that although they lacked equivalents for European philosophical terms such as "substance" or "metaphysics," they contained enough abstract terms to enable the missionaries to preach about the mysteries of their religion.

The Jesuit even defended ancient Aztec laws against European colonialist views. Buffon and de Paw, but also the famous Abbé Raynal and Scottish Enlightener William Robertson, found them cruel and inhumane but were reminded by Clavigero that some European laws had been just as bloodthirsty and cruel, especially among the ancient Romans and Greeks. Even Aztec religion was not dismissed by the Jesuit as superstitious and barbaric. He instead insisted that it deserved thorough research, free from emotion and personal bias, because "the religion of the Mexicans was less superstitious, less indecent, less immature, and less irrational than the religions of the most civilized nations of ancient Europe."[7] Bloody sacrifices among Aztecs had clear parallels in Greek, Roman, Israelite, and other cultures. Even in ancient Spanish temples human sacrifices were performed—probably many more than in America, he claimed. The Mexicans simply did what all the other nations of antiquity did. By reminding European scholars of their own past, Clavigero turned the tables and forced his peers to face their own colonialist arguments. Even the gruesome behavior of the conquistadors was not condoned by Clavigero, who condemned their atrocities.[8] This does not mean that Clavigero accepted all of Amerindian culture or embraced it; he despised much American native culture and stressed the differences between creoles and Amerindians, but he nevertheless spoke up in defense of American culture when "enlightened" Europe despised it.

In the footsteps of Clavigero stands Jose Antonio de Alzate y Ramirez, a Mexican priest and scientist. By using some of the most superb Enlightenment inventions, namely, gazettes and journals, he worked more than any other scholar of his time to counter the negative views of European Enlighteners of Latin America and exposed their factual errors. He refuted repeatedly in his journal the claim that the Spanish conquest of America was easy because of the weakness of the Amerindians, stressing that the *conquistadores* were supported by allied tribes. The widely believed horror stories about human sacrifices were, according to Alzate, exaggerated and taken out of context. Moreover, by pointing to archaeological discoveries he demonstrated that ancient Mesoamericans had known basic laws of mechanics, were well versed in geometry, and were advanced in the knowledge of astronomy. Alzate also maintained, like other Catholic Enlighteners, a wide network of correspondents and was fully immersed in the scientific community of his time. He worked on botany, economy, geography, and history. His academic mastery was finally honored when he was made a corresponding member of the French Academy of Sciences in 1771, the first such honor ever awarded to an American.[9]

Until the middle of the eighteenth century the Jesuits in Paraguay ran about thirty so-called reductions, collective farming communities, which together included about 100,000 Amerindians.[10] Every adult Indian had to work two to three days a week for the community. From the products of this work all common expenses were paid. The houses belonged to the community. Private property was allowed but restricted to smaller items. The Jesuits were responsible for the administration of the reductions. The missionaries not only feared the intrusion of slave hunters and infection with dangerous diseases but also the moral corruption of the Indians by the settlers. But the Jesuits were able to keep foreigners and Spanish settlers from entering their territories. This seclusion, although it protected the Amerindian tribes, prompted the distrust of governmental and ecclesial authorities. Political leaders and bishops likewise resented their exclusion and the disregard of their authority. The end to this experiment came about through Enlightenment politics of economic growth. Portugal was demographically weak and could not provide its overseas colonies with enough workers. Pombal, head of the Portuguese government, therefore decided that it would be best to integrate the Amerindians into society and thus end the protectionist policies of the reductions. Indians should be encouraged to enter mixed marriages with European settlers and have many children in order to increase the labor force. This plan clashed with the Jesuit goal of protecting the integrity of Amerindian culture. The tribes resisted—even by military force—but were defeated. The Jesuits, however, were blamed for the resistance and expelled from Portuguese and Spanish colonies in 1767. As a consequence, much of the cultural heritage of the Tupi-Guarani tribes was lost not because of missionary zeal but because of "enlightened" policies of economic growth and colonial exploitation.[11]

Numerous other examples of Catholic Enlighteners from Latin America could be given, but they are passed over in the established narrative of Enlightenment history.

North American Catholicism

None other than the superior of the American missionaries, John Carroll, stated in 1784 that Catholicism in his homeland had "undergone a revolution, if possible, more extraordinary, than our political one." He not only meant the free practice of the Catholic faith—unheard of before the Revolution—but also the ideas that had taken hold of the American Catholic experience. Three of these ideas seem to be associated with the Catholic Enlightenment. The first was trusteeism, which meant that church property was administered not by the bishop or any clergy but by

parish trustees, who were laymen. The second was a democratic arrangement of the church, including even the election of a bishop. The third was
the ease with which American Catholics adapted to the new political situation after the Declaration of Independence, and their support for religious
tolerance and liberty.

Catholicism in the thirteen colonies was different from Catholicism in
other British possessions in North America. While the British tolerated
Catholicism in their Canadian territories, such liberal toleration did not
extend to the lower thirteen colonies. In many colonies Catholics were
regarded, just as in England, as foreign spies or enemies who were subservient to "tyrannical popes." This sentiment was particularly strong in
Maryland, where the majority of Catholics lived. Maryland Catholics had
to endure discriminatory laws that restricted their freedom of worship.
When American patriots began regarding the British Crown as despotic
and demanding more liberties, such a message resonated with Catholics,
who overwhelmingly supported the Revolution. However, the attempt to
convince Canadian Catholics to join their cause failed.[12]

After the 1783 peace treaty between the United States and Great
Britain, a new structure of the Catholic Church had to be created. John
Carroll insisted that Catholics "must strive to preserve, cultivate, and promote" the new republic "with all their prudence, always behaving as good
subjects faithfully to their political government."[13] He further stated to
parishioners in Philadelphia: "To our country we owe allegiance ... to
the Vicar of Christ [the pope] we owe obedience in things purely spiritual. Happily there is no competition in their respective claims on us."[14]
Nevertheless, many of his fellow countrymen had trouble believing such
patriotism because Catholics continued to depend on Rome for every
important administrative decision. Catholicism was still believed to be
a foreign body in the new republic, a sect that was a puppet controlled
by a "foreign power." Only at Carroll's insistence did the Roman Curia
allow American Catholics to have a bishop in residence with full authority.[15] Carroll, influenced both by European church reform movements
(Cisalpinism, Conciliarism, and Gallicanism, discussed in Chapter 1) as
well as the American Enlightenment's emphasis on self-government and
individual liberties, insisted that the clergy should elect their own bishop.
The pope, however, permitted such an election only once, despite Carroll's
reasoning that an election for all future bishops by the clergy would better
suit the American temperament of a free democracy. In 1788, Carroll was
almost unanimously elected bishop, and only a few months later the first

American diocese, Baltimore, was established. But Carroll rejected the idea that the laity could or should participate in such episcopal elections, in particular because he saw it as connected with "trusteeism."

Democratic sentiment was even stronger among the laity than among the clergy. Since laypersons raised money for new churches, schools, and endowments, they usually oversaw the governance of church property as well. Very similar to the political idea of "no taxation without representation," American Catholics wanted to have a say in the appointment of a pastor if their funds were used for his salary. This practice, called trusteeism, had a long tradition in European Catholicism.[16] In Europe, members of the nobility funded churches and received in return the right to appoint or nominate pastors. In the Republic of Switzerland, lay organizations assumed such rights. In America, however, the ancient privileges were forged with the idea of democracy. A council of laypersons was the superior authority in a parish because it "represented" its constituents. Trustees felt they had a "right" to appoint and nominate personnel.[17] On their side was American law, which recognized churches as religious societies represented by parishioners; the authority of bishops pertained only to the spiritual realm.[18] Because trusteeism mirrored Protestant organization, some Catholics worried that it undermined a crucial element of Catholic belief, namely, hierarchical authority. In fact, many trustees were influenced by Protestant thought because they were married to Protestant spouses. Even an enlightened bishop like John Carroll could not tolerate trusteeism because it ran against Catholic teaching.

American Catholics also quickly adapted a much more tolerant view of their Protestant brethren. They appealed to the recovered tradition of inclusivism, which the Catholic Enlightenment championed. Inclusivism did not compromise the claim that the Catholic Church was the one true church Christ had founded, but it made clear that there was salvation for those outside the church. Carroll made clear that the church had never taught that only her members were saved but rather that those who are in communion with her and thus seek God with a truthful heart and accept Jesus Christ as savior would also reach heaven. Quoting from the French Enlightenment theologian Nicholas Bergier, Carroll insisted that baptized and practicing Protestants were on the way to salvation because they would embrace the Catholic faith if their ignorance could be lifted. Consequently, "these candid and upright persons, from the disposition of their hearts, are children of the Catholic Church."[19]

Another feature that American Catholics adopted, bringing them in line with other more progressive streams of eighteenth-century Catholicism, was the acceptance of the new political reality of the United States. Carroll was by no means a liberal on doctrinal questions, but he saw the necessity for the church to adapt to new circumstances. Against polemical attacks, he unswervingly insisted that Catholicism was compatible with the new civil liberties of the Republic. He and other Catholics were important voices in the debate about religious liberty, which—due to the strong influence of Baptists, James Madison, and Thomas Jefferson—ended with the separation of church and state.[20] Carroll even contradicted the pope, who had spoken about the dangers of a state in which different religions were tolerated. For the American bishop such a statement was "contrary to our experience in America."[21] Carroll's family also thought along these lines. His brother Daniel, a member of the Constitutional Convention and a signer of the US Constitution, and his cousin Charles Carroll, the only Catholic signatory of the Declaration of Independence, both strongly supported the First Amendment.

For the Carrolls, religious freedom was consistent with natural law and human rights. Charles Carroll had studied Enlightenment thinkers during his European education in St. Omer, Rheims, and Paris. He found Montesquieu's ideas about the separation of powers convincing, as it provided a system of checks and balances, federalism, and liberty. At the same time, he disliked Locke, especially because he had denied toleration to Catholics in England. Later, Charles Carroll, together with President John Adams, incorporated Montesquieu's basic ideas, such as the institution of a senate and an electoral college, into American political life. Always an ardent advocate of church-state separation, Charles Carroll protested the attendance of the members of Congress at an Episcopal service after George Washington's first inauguration because it looked like a state endorsement of a specific religion.[22] With men like the Carrolls, the Catholic Enlightenment had arrived in North America and quickly established strong roots.

Confucius, China, and the Jesuits

Despite the conflicts between Enlightenment reformers and the Jesuits, the Enlightenment owed a great deal to this religious order. Enlighteners and Jesuits shared a similarly optimistic view of free will, the power of education, and the love of science. In fact, many of the missionaries established themselves as leading scientists, most famously as astronomers of the Chinese emperor. And without the erudite works of Jesuit missionaries, knowledge of India's religious diversity, as well as of Chinese history and philosophy, would never have reached Europe. The Jesuits collected such information scrupulously and disseminated it widely in order to find supporters for their missions. But their accounts of the highly sophisticated Asian religions unintentionally provided critics of Christianity with ammunition to question the exclusivity and superiority of the Christian faith. Secular Enlighteners began to wonder whether Confucianism possessed a more advanced set of ethical rules than Christianity or whether biblical history could be trusted if Chinese history proved that the world was older than six thousand years, or whether an atheist could be (against Christian prejudice) a good citizen and a moral person.[23]

Some European theologians had been seeking common ground between Protestant and Catholic theology since the sixteenth century. At the core of this trend, which later brought forth ecumenical theology, lay a stance of benevolence toward the other. Instead of reading the documents of another tradition through a lens of distrust, one attempted to see goodwill and sincerity. A similar mindset was at work among Jesuit missionaries in China. Catholicism was often seen as unwilling to acknowledge truth in other religions, and missionaries were charged with trying to superimpose a European form of Christianity on their converts. But Jesuit missionaries, especially in China, engaged in a fruitful bicultural enterprise and early interreligious dialogue. These efforts were untainted by Enlightenment influence but instead grew from the impulses of the Council of Trent, and they demonstrate how the religious zeal of such open-minded Catholic missionaries contributed to the rise of modern values such as respect for diversity and interreligious understanding.

When the first Jesuit missionaries arrived in China in the sixteenth century, they quickly noticed that their plan to baptize the masses would not work. Instead, they realized that if they could convince the intellectual elite they would be able to have a broader impact. This strategy paralleled what the Jesuits attempted to do in Europe, converting Protestant princes and political leaders to Catholicism in order to gain influence over a larger number of people. Thus, the missionaries began identifying themselves not so much as priests but rather as Western sages and masters of enlightenment. They dressed like Confucian scholars, learned the local languages, and gained a reputation for their grasp of the Chinese classics. Christianity was "accommodated" to Chinese circumstances and presented as the ultimate key to Confucian thought. The converted literati consequently saw Christianity not as a replacement for their ancient beliefs but rather as a new dimension of them, so that some historians have spoken of a "Confucian Christianity" brought about by Jesuit missionaries. The biggest theological challenges were that Christ died on a cross and was resurrected, because the brutal execution of a man was regarded as something vulgar, and it was difficult for the literati to grasp how God could want his son to undergo such punishment. Likewise, the egalitarianism the Jesuits preached, especially the equal dignity of man and woman, was troubling for many, as it undermined traditional Confucian patriarchal control.[24] The most important proponent of Jesuit accommodation was Matteo Ricci, who is currently being considered for canonization.[25]

It cannot surprise us that the literati also retained traditional rituals. The most important of these honored the ancestors. Setting food offerings in front of the ancestral tablets was not only an act of gratitude to earlier generations but also a prayer for their protection and material benefits. Some missionaries tried to convince their converts to pray for their ancestors like Catholics in the West did for their deceased relatives in purgatory, but this made Christianity look like Buddhism, which performed services for the souls of relatives and made it seem as if the ancestors were in need of help. Nevertheless, the Jesuits came to believe that acts of "ancestral worship" were not idolatrous but rather were acts of filial piety and respect, performed for the sake of harmony. Likewise, the veneration of Confucius was not seen as idol worship. The Jesuits instead saw him as a teacher of morals, very similar to Socrates in Ancient Greece, whom one could admire just like any great philosopher of the West. Whenever it was clear, however, that local deities were invoked, the missionaries instructed their converts always to transmit their requests to the "Lord of Heaven," the Chinese Catholic name for God, in order to make clear that it was the Christian God, not Chinese deities or ancestors, who heard their prayers. In 1615, the missionaries were even allowed to celebrate the Mass in Chinese—vernacular liturgies were not permitted in Europe until the twentieth century—and in 1656 the Chinese Rites, which officially condoned the veneration of the ancestors and adaptations of the sacraments, were officially approved. A Catholicism that was intellectually flexible enough to fit into Chinese culture was highly regarded even by the Chinese emperors.[26]

Not all Catholic missionaries approved of the Jesuit strategy. Dominicans and Franciscans demanded the papacy put a stop to the experiment. In 1704, Pope Clement XI forbade the Chinese Rites and reiterated his decision in 1715. The Chinese Kangxi emperor was furious. He could not fathom why the pope would do such a thing, because now the missionary efforts had to be discontinued: "This is definitely not the will of your God," he said, "for he leads men to good deeds. I have often heard from you Westerners that the devil leads men astray—this must be it."[27] Christian missionaries were ordered to leave the country, and in 1724, Catholicism was officially outlawed as an "evil sect." Benedict XIV confirmed the proscription of the Chinese accommodations in 1742 and 1744. He was concerned with the purity of Christian worship, which he believed was endangered by the Chinese Confucian rituals. Conversions ceased, but Christianity had now become a family tradition among many. The presence of Christian converts among a family's ancestors became a major motivation to keep the family's faith tradition alive, even despite strong discrimination.[28]

The Jesuits not only used accommodation to make Christianity appear less like a European import but also relied on an ancient way of assessing other religions. Already in the first centuries, the Church Fathers had affirmed that other religions contained "seeds of truth." The Jesuits mined Chinese literature in search of truths common to both religions and to explain how Christianity completed what was already present in Chinese culture. This was called Figurism: the events and doctrines of the New Testament were prefigured and foreshadowed in ancient Chinese texts, mostly the I Ching (Book of Changes). It required that the Jesuits read the texts not as historical but as symbolic. This method suffered, as David Mungello has aptly stated, from "excessive enthusiasm," or simply put, from missionary zeal. Jesuits read into texts what was not there. But by reading Chinese classics through a Christian lens, the founder of Figurism, French Jesuit Joachim Bouvet, nevertheless helped to give Christianity a Chinese face. His main goal was achieved: if one desired to become a Christian one did not have to abandon or reject the past; instead, one could say that Chinese culture had prepared the way for Catholicism. This view diminished the importance of the European framing of theology, as it did not expect the Chinese to become copies of European Catholics. For example, Bouvet regarded the founder of the Middle Kingdom, Fu Xi, as a mythical figure who was identical with the universal lawgiver of ancient nations known as Hermes Trismegistus, or Enoch. He was believed to have given ancient peoples laws, customs, religion, and science. Enoch's laws had survived in a number of civilizations, among which was China, where Confucius retold them in his own way. Thus, China could be presented to Europeans, like ancient Egypt, as a highly developed, moral culture antedating the Gospels. The school of thought that tried to unearth Enoch's laws and connections to other religions was called "Ancient Theology." It relied on St. Paul's letter to the Romans, in which he acknowledged the possibility of salvation for all who follow the "law of their heart" (Rom 2: 14) and had been practiced for many centuries.[29]

Many Catholic theologians aggressively criticized the Jesuits for their Figurism. It appeared to them as if the Jesuits regarded the Chinese traditions to be just as theologically relevant as the Old Testament. Indeed, the Jesuit Louis Le Comte taught that if the Israelites had done meritorious acts by sacrificing in the temple, so had the ancient Chinese. For Noel Alexandre, a Dominican, this went too far. He feared the Jesuits taught that salvation was possible without *explicit* belief in Jesus Christ. Against such accusation Vincente Mascarell argued that no theological argument contradicted the possibility that the ancient Chinese had followed God's primeval revelation from Adam to Noah through his natural law and religion and were thus saved by an *implicit* faith. Perhaps the ancient Chinese enjoyed heaven as much as St. Paul, even if they had not known the explicit content of the Gospel.[30] Figurism ended together with the Chinese Rites in 1744.

It has been suggested that the proscription of the Chinese Rites fit the Enlightenment goal of striving for uniform laws, morals, and even behavior. For most Enlighteners, cultural and ethnic diversity were without value. Another motive for Benedict XIV might have been that since the Council of Trent the church had become an increasingly centralized institution and as such desired, like secular governments, uniform global solutions; a unique "Chinese way" was therefore considered inappropriate. Last, the pope was under pressure to preserve the church from harm. The Jesuits had become the source of strife among missionaries and theologians, and no end was in sight. He felt compelled to end their experiment. Nevertheless, he did not regard the Jesuit approach as incorrect. In fact, he prohibited and censored the book of a Capuchin monk who had called the Jesuit missionary strategies inherently evil. This decision left the door open for the popes of the twentieth century to rehabilitate Chinese accommodation.[31]

One of the greatest propagators of Figurist theology, Father Joseph De Premare, lamented that by ending the biculturalism Jesuits had practiced, Catholicism had lost China: "There is one thing that cannot be denied: at the time when we showed respect for their *jing* [history] and showed them that their ancestors knew and adored the same God we are telling them about, the Christian religion flourished. From this fact I have always concluded that if we had taken the next step, showing them the savior in the same *jing*, more than half of China would now have been Christian."[32] At the end of the eighteenth century, the enlightened Cardinal Stefano Borgia tried to resuscitate the Chinese Rites, allowed formerly proscribed Chinese translations of parts of the Mass, and argued fervently that Chinese missionaries should have permission to celebrate the Mass in Chinese and not in Latin. Moreover, he sought to ordain Chinese bishops who would receive full control over their churches—a proposal that was so radical it would not be implemented for a hundred years.[33]

European Enlighteners such as Voltaire, despite being in love with everything Chinese, rejected Figurism. While the missionaries dwelled in the memories of a pure, ancient China but criticized contemporary Chinese morals and politics, Voltaire saw it the other way around. He and those like him saw Chinese politics—a government without religious affiliation—as a model for Europe. Yet both missionaries and Enlighteners agreed that China posed a challenge to Europe. Both views were historically faulty but only the missionaries' ideas were actually based on a solid knowledge of the primary sources. By "finding" central teachings of the New Testament in ancient Chinese texts, the Figurists posed a radical challenge to European Christianity: the Christian message was foreshadowed in other religions, sometimes almost identically. Therefore, no condescending attitude toward such religions could be justified. It was through the failure of Figurism that a sincere dialogue with other religions and their truth claims later became possible. Almost no eighteenth-century scholar was attracted to Chinese culture for its own sake; the missionaries had their interests, and so did the Enlighteners. However, the understanding of Confucianism proposed by Enlighteners such as Leibniz, Voltaire, and Christian Wolff was much shallower than that of the Jesuits because Enlighteners were only interested in the Chinese ethical and political sphere, not in its metaphysical, cosmological, and historical dimensions.[34] By rejecting the Chinese Rites, but also by neglecting to form and educate a large contingent of native clergy due to the widely attested condescending attitude of many missionaries toward the suitability of Chinese converts for the Catholic priesthood, the Catholic Church lost one of its greatest opportunities for growth in Asia.[35]

The Enlightenment in India

As in China, the first Jesuit missionaries to India sought to blend Catholicism into local culture. Roberto Nobili suggested that priests abandon their traditional cassocks and hairstyles and instead dress like members of the Brahmin caste, who were traditionally priests or scholars. The Jesuits even adopted a Brahmin diet, wore sandalwood paste on their foreheads, avoided contact with other Europeans, and studied the Vedas, India's religious writings. Missionizing in this style was a time-consuming task, as a missionary reported in 1778: "One should always consider that a new missionary ... can bring very little fruit to the Mission before four or five years have elapsed. ... In order to talk to them about their religion, respond to their arguments, understand their books ... a long study of the language, ... their maxims and customs" is necessary.[36] Nevertheless, the strategy of accommodation paid off. A considerable number of Brahmins converted.[37] Nobili's methods were sanctioned by the papacy, and his converts were allowed to continue native customs such as retaining membership in their caste, celebrating the traditional Hindu equinox, and maintaining adolescence rituals and marriage customs. However, in 1704 Rome tightened the screws, fearing that the Jesuits would allow too many old Hindu practices to be continued among the newly baptized. Again, critics warned that the order supported "Hindu superstition" instead of reflecting on the inherent problem: how could one convince an Indian to accept Christianity if this meant abandoning ancient traditions? The Jesuits attempted to demonstrate that the New Testament was the lost Veda that explained all the others. Yet again the Jesuits had found a way of acculturating the Catholic message. But all this came to an end in 1744, when Pope Benedict XIV proscribed, as he had done for China, the accommodations for India. From then on, every Indian Catholic was expected to discard the past of his family and accept the European understanding of Christianity. Missionaries had been freed from using saliva in the *effata* rite of baptism and breathing on the newly baptized, since both actions were considered repulsive by devout Hindus. The pope's lack of sensibility was especially obvious in his remark that if the Indian population still found the use of saliva repellent, then they were not worthy of being received into the church.[38]

One of the most successful missions in India was Goa, which remained a Portuguese colony until 1961. Despite their long presence in India, the Jesuits there never accepted Indian novices. Other Asians and Eurasians were also excluded from entering the Society, with the exception of the Japanese. Other religious orders had similar laws of exclusion. While the Jesuits were apprehensive about the extent to which converts had genuinely grasped the philosophical and theological ideas of Catholicism, in other orders such laws seemed to stem from Spanish-American policies. Since the 1580s, both the Spanish and the Portuguese crowns had tightened their control over their colonies. As the kings appointed bishops and ecclesiastical leaders, the governments considered it crucial to restrict such positions to Europeans, who could be trusted to work to the advantage of the colonial powers. The plan for a native clergy waned under such state pressure. The popes, being busy with other crises in Europe, did not intervene in this scheme until the 1630s, when a new papal office for the missions was erected and the power of both colonial regimes had decreased.[39] Now the popes insisted on the education of native clergy in India and the Americas. It is reported that Pope Innocent XI said in 1680 to a missionary bishop who boasted about the number of baptisms he had performed: "We would rather learn that you have ordained one native priest than that you have baptized 50,000 pagans." Three years later the Holy See publicly stated that skin color could never be an impediment to receiving holy orders.[40] Consequently, a native clergy was established in Portuguese West Africa. A visitor from this time wrote about the African priests, who were for him an exotic sight:

> They are all black but it is only in this respect that they differ from Europeans. ... There are here clergy and canons as black as jet, but so well bred, so authoritative, so learned, such great musicians, so discreet and so accomplished that they are envied by those in our own cathedrals at home.[41]

Because some states did not allow unwelcome papal decrees to be published in their dominions, the papal admonition to end discrimination was not heard everywhere. But most religious orders followed the new directive and many endowed fellowships for students from China and

India to study in Europe.[42] While Goans could now become priests and enter some religious orders, only one monastery was entrusted to native leadership, the Goan Oratory. Pressure from the state was required to finally bring discrimination down. The same government that had originally introduced the color ban now reversed it. Pombal, the enlightened influential Portuguese minister, stated in a royal decree of 1761 that the Christian subjects in the East African and Asian colonies should have the same legal and social status as whites, "since his majesty does not distinguish between his vassals by their color but by their merits." Moreover, the decree made it a criminal offense to call Indians "mestizos, niggers, dogs, bitches," and other derogatory names. Nevertheless, the Goan archdiocese did not implement the decree. Instead, a number of protesters approached Pombal thirteen years later and argued that 10,000 native priests were desperately waiting to be considered for vacant parish positions. They lamented that the Goan archbishop continued to exclusively appoint Europeans to parishes and grant the native clergy only auxiliary functions and indecent pay. Pombal acted immediately, replacing the archbishop and the Goan viceroy. He again made clear that any racial discrimination was illegal. Moreover, all parish positions now had to be given to native clergy; only inland missions could be entrusted to Europeans. Pombal even wanted locals to be preferred for military and governmental posts, and he restricted the admission of Portuguese men and women to Goan monasteries; only by royal permission would a Portuguese be allowed to enter the novitiate in a Goan convent.[43] Queen Maria of Portugal also forbade racial and ethnic discrimination within monasteries. While Goan men and women had been allowed to enter religious orders, many still did not entrust them with any leadership positions, or in the case of female convents even grant them the same clothing. In the nunnery of St. Monica, sisters of European background wore black veils, while Indian sisters had to wear white veils. Queen Maria leveled such differences.[44] Slowly, monasteries controlled by members of the Brahmin caste began to receive members from lower castes.[45] One religious order, the Claustral Carmelites, was founded particularly for Goan needs. This order propagated from its beginning in 1750 a mixture of contemplative and active life and stressed the ideals of Catholic Reform as the Council of Trent had formulated it: preaching to the most abandoned, taking care of the sick and dying, making the faith intelligible, and providing solid education.[46] The new order also broke down the caste division by inviting members of lower castes to join them. This enabled numerous Goans to climb the social ladder by means of an ecclesiastical career and also to help their families achieve a better life. While the new archbishop supported the new order, many locals were critical of the breaking of ancient traditions.[47]

One of the most important Enlightenment influences on Goan religious life, however, was the introduction of ideas about toleration. Goa had been a tolerant place in the sixteenth century, but the Goan Inquisition had turned it into a hostile location for Hindus and members of other Asian religions. Temples had been razed, public Hindu rituals forbidden, and conversions to Hinduism severely punished. The Goa Inquisition prosecuted harshly any cases of public Hindu worship; over three quarters of its cases pertained to this, and only 2 percent to apostasy or heresy. Most instances were marital ceremonies, which could hardly be held in absolute privacy as Portuguese colonial law required. The tolerant rule of the enlightened viceroy Count Alva eased interreligious tensions. He permitted new Hindu temples to be built and Hindu marriages to be celebrated in public. But such toleration lasted for just two years. Only at the end of Pombal's reign, in 1774, were the excessive powers of the Inquisition curtailed, giving Hindus again more rights. Under Queen Maria and her conservative government, Goa returned to the previous state of intolerance, before the 1790s again brought relief.[48]

The most remarkable example of Enlightenment to originate in Goa, however, was the so-called Pinto Revolt of 1787. It was the first planned revolt of an indigenous people against a colonial regime with the intention of ending white, European supremacy. The heads of the conspiracy were Catholic priests in good standing. Josè António Gonçalves had left Goa for Rome in order to receive a doctorate at a Roman university. There, and probably before that at the Goan seminary, he became acquainted with Enlightenment pedagogy and thought. This exceptionally smart man swiftly embarked on a successful career and was soon made general vicar of the Goa diocese. When two bishoprics became vacant in the Goan colony, he traveled to Lisbon to ask the government to appoint him bishop. Another Goan priest, Francisco do Couto, had the same plan and joined him. Both engaged Father Caetano Vitorino da Faria, a Goan who lived permanently in Portugal despite the hatred he felt because of the condescending treatment of Indians by the Portuguese.[49] Yet when Joseph Cariattil, a priest of the Thomas Christians in the Syrian rite, was appointed by the pope Archbishop of Cranganore in 1783, Gonçalves and Couto decided to conspire openly against the regime. Both felt unjustly passed over. After all, their entire life had been focused on becoming bishops. They had both received doctorates from a Roman university for this purpose and had built contacts in Portugal and Italy, but now another native Indian had been chosen. They did not understand that by appointing this local priest, king and pope hoped to heal the schism with the Syro-Chaldean Christians. Couto and Gonçalves now came to believe that neither Rome nor Lisbon, but the Goans themselves, should decide important appointments in Goa. They adhered to a mixture of Gallicanism and Enlightenment nationalism. The conspirators regularly referred in their letters to their education and principles of shared government, and they talked, following Enlightenment jargon, about the "future happiness of all Goans." The death of the Goan Archbishop Cariattil in 1786 triggered the execution of the plan. With a network of agents, many of whom were officers, civil servants, or simple farmers, the rebellion was planned for 1787. Imitating the American Revolution, they sought to drive the Portuguese from the colony and erect a parliamentary democracy. New universities would be established to manifest a new enlightened Indian education.[50] But before their first actions could be set in motion, they were betrayed to the government. Fourteen priests were incarcerated without a legal process until 1802, when they were finally released, while a number of military men were executed for treason.[51] Western historians have hitherto neglected the importance of the Goan revolt: it demonstrates that many Indians no longer viewed Catholicism as a European import and that clergymen perceived a clear compatibility between enlightened political principles and their faith. Moreover, the revolt shows that the resistance to white supremacy in India originated within the church, even if the motives of the conspirators were not always entirely altruistic.

Conclusion

Catholic Enlightenment influence can be identified in all European colonies around the globe, but a particularly strong engagement with Enlightenment thought and life can be detected in the Americas and India. Hitherto, historians have hardly acknowledged the Argentinian, Brazilian, Indian, and Mexican Catholic Enlightenments because they challenge the prevailing Eurocentrist Enlightenment narrative. For far too long the colonies were seen as merely receiving European ideas instead of creatively and dynamically engaging with them. But such engagement was frequently aimed at the genuine compatibility of faith and reason and thus was profoundly Catholic. By taking seriously the roles Catholics played for educational reform, the establishment of scientific discourse, and societal progress in the colonies, one is able to demonstrate the existence of a global Catholic Enlightenment and thus the cosmopolitanism of this branch of religious Enlightenment; moreover, such a view would also help to give non-European Enlightenment figures a well-deserved place in history.

Of course, not everything Catholics did in the eighteenth century was influenced by the Enlightenment, as I tried to explain in the context of the Chinese missions; nevertheless, the ideas that the Jesuit missionaries proposed for the acculturation of Catholic theology to the Chinese population were the first steps toward a serious engagement with Chinese culture at a time in which most European Enlighteners were not only extremely eclectic in their assessment of everything Chinese but mostly ignorant of the native languages. The Jesuit missionary method, however, grew out of the Tridentine zeal for missions. By looking at the Catholic Enlightenment as a prolonging of the Tridentine Reform movement, one can not only connect the developments in China with those in the rest of the Catholic world but also gain a better insight into the reciprocal relationship between missions and papal Rome: knowledge of China traveled West, while European theology was received and transformed in the East. Highlighting such reciprocity helps us see the global interconnectedness of early modernity as a whole and establish the Tridentine contributions to modernity.[52]

In India, Catholic clergymen, motivated by European Enlightenment ideas and the American Revolution, began to openly criticize the exclusion of native clergy from high-ranking administrative functions. Their campaign to end European colonialism in Goa was the first of its kind. It has to be emphasized that the priests involved were no theological mavericks but were genuinely orthodox in their faith, which shows that anti-colonialism and the fight for racial equality could be buttressed by personal faith and ecclesial commitment.

As more research is done on Early Modern Catholicism as a world religion, it becomes increasingly clear that historical accounts overlooking the importance of the global Catholic Enlightenment will miss a key player in global history.

5

Devils, Demons, and the Divine in the Catholic Enlightenment

THE PROTESTANT GERMAN philosopher Immanuel Kant once defined superstition as "the belief in miracles as a duty."[1] When we suspect frequent divine interventions, we overlook natural explanations and become slaves to magical thinking. Enlightenment is, in Kant's words, a "liberation from superstition."[2] Catholicism was seen by many as superstitious. This sentiment was especially common among the Protestant reformers of the sixteenth century; after all, Catholics believed in miracles, they participated in a variety of ostentatious rituals, they had priests who supposedly mediated between the godhead and the people, and they believed in saints. In sum, Catholics believed in things besides the word of God, and that was reason enough to see them as superstitious.

None of these elements, however, is legitimately "superstitious" if one brackets the confessional polemic of the time: and, beginning with the Council of Trent, the Catholic Church itself had worked ceaselessly to counter superstition. Even as early as 1530, a Catholic reformer had warned about widespread prayers in which "superstitious formulas are mixed with holy and pious words."[3] Medieval mendicant orders attempted to establish rational criteria for deciding when divine intervention had occurred. This did not mean that, in the post-Reformation era, miracles were considered impossible but that one became very cautious in declaring an event a miracle. Likewise the veneration of images and saints was subjected, after Trent, to careful revision: questionable images were banned, approved ones promoted. Stricter criteria for the recognition and veneration of relics were introduced, and the faithful were taught that prayer is not magic, not an incantation that bequeathed automatic, machinelike power over natural things but rather a dialogue with God. These changes took time, especially when governments impeded the spread of the reform. In fact, the reforms were not widely implemented until the eighteenth century.

The plan to eradicate superstition targeted remnants of pagan beliefs that could be found throughout Europe and had sometimes been given a Christian veneer. The Roman Inquisition not only pursued heretics but also investigated devotional literature suspected of promoting such superstitions. The censors acted quickly and harshly when magical powers were attributed to prayers: some promised the forgiveness of all sins when recited, but there were also love spells or prayers to secure financial gains or better health. There was nothing wrong, of course, with asking God for these favors, but to suggest the words themselves had incantatory power was superstition.[4] At the time of the Enlightenment, one could find superstitious practices even in Rome: the statue of the Christ child of the Aracoeli church was believed to foretell the future, and sick people requested that it be brought to their bedside. Some among the faithful believed that the color of the statue's face changed according to the outlook of the sick person. If it remained pink she would get better, but if it turned gray she would probably die. Even small reforms, like the illumination of the dark streets of Rome, could not be implemented because, according to local custom, only candles in front of the innumerable images of the Madonna were allowed to give light; public illumination was considered sacrilegious.[5]

These accounts suggest that progress often had to overcome considerable resistance from the population. In fact, because of the increase in pilgrimages, exorcisms, apparitions, and miracles in the last two decades of the eighteenth century, many historians have suggested that this rise in superstition was provoked not only by political instability but also the population's opposition to the hegemony of "reason."[6] Even church reformers within the Roman Curia encountered resistance, even though their reforms were not even motivated by Enlightenment rationalism. For example, in 1748 Cardinal Ganganelli—who would later become Pope Clement XIV—wrote to his friend, the Enlightener and priest Ludovico Muratori: "The hatred of superstitious people is almost unbearable. One cannot convince them since they regard all ideas, which go through their heads, as dogmas."[7] If one regarded all religious ideas and rituals as "dogmas," then of course anybody who attempted to change them was branded a heretic. It did not matter if the reformer had the Council of Trent and the tradition of the church on his side. Blind conservatism spoke: "It was always like this. We have never done anything else," while the Catholic Reformers responded: "Yet Jesus said: In the beginning it was *not* so" (Mt 19:8).

Flying Saints and Marvelous Cures: Miracles in the Age of Reason

Miracles are by definition events that suspend the course of natural laws or contradict them. Reports of miracles were much more common in the Early Modern period than they are today, given advances in scientific knowledge. Even in that context, though, Catholics were often accused of exaggerating the number of miracles that occurred and of disregarding natural science as a possible explanation for allegedly "miraculous" events. While many Catholic believers might indeed have been as credulous as the Protestant Reformers claimed, the Catholic elite, theologians, bishops, and popes were quite critical when it came to miracles. This was not, however, a concession to Enlightenment skepticism but the continuation of the reform process which the Council of Trent had begun.

Until the thirteenth century, sainthood was a local matter. If a deceased person was considered a saint, her grave was venerated and she was invoked to intercede for the faithful. Then the Roman Curia began to centralize the canonization process.[8] The Council of Trent codified this shift. The miracles that were attributed to the saints were reported and analyzed by theological experts, and the decision of whether the person should be accepted into the calendar of saints was deferred to the pope. By the sixteenth century, however, an abundance of sensational stories about the miracles of saints caused the church to become seriously concerned. Many of these stories were no longer reported in order to lead Catholics to Christ but instead to satisfy a public thirst for entertainment. The Protestant Reformers ridiculed these tales, and Catholic theologians realized that they had to introduce stricter standards for both the dissemination of such accounts and for canonization itself. In 1588, Pope Urban VIII declared that for each new saint a short biography had to be published and a proper investigation into his or her life be launched, unearthing every detail from earliest childhood to death. Only if the person's life was without moral stain and full of heroic virtues could she or he move to the next step, namely, the search for a miracle as evidence that the deceased had been a saint. The reform worked. Bishops and priests became cautious and began to take scientific evidence more seriously, but they also began to systematically question witnesses and thus establish critical doubt. Between 1588 and 1623 the number of reported miracles in canonization cases fell dramatically; reports about clusters of miracles virtually disappeared around 1700.[9] In the 1720s, the Spanish Benedictine Benito Feijoo developed a set of criteria to distinguish miraculous from natural cures: 1. The cured illness had to be serious and naturally incurable. 2. It could not have been in remission or decline before the cure. 3. All natural remedies had failed. 4. The cure had to be sudden, total, and perfect. 5. The recovery had to be permanent, without relapse.[10] A rational frame had been established within which alleged divine actions were evaluated, creating an implicit critique of superstition long before the heyday of Enlightenment.

Enlightenment Pope Benedict XIV thought very much like Feijoo. When a Protestant critic approached him one day and listed dozens of fake miracles in order to prove that Catholicism was superstitious, the pontiff replied with ease: "Dear man, not one of the miracles you mentioned was approved by the Holy See." In fact, when he was elected in 1740, he tightened the rules his predecessors had implemented. He stressed especially the importance of credible evidence. Witnesses had to be heard, especially if they disputed the holiness of a person; in the case of healing miracles, medical scientists were called as expert witnesses. Benedict XIV did not exclude miracles from his worldview, but he was convinced that they happened rarely and only for very specific purposes.

Most likely, the pope's personal friend, the physician Giovanni Maria Lancisi, helped him gain a better understanding of modern medicine. Before becoming pope—under his baptismal name Prospero Lambertini—Benedict served for almost twenty years as "devil's advocate." In this role, he was the man responsible for raising objections and finding counter-evidence against men and women promoted as (potential) saints. His rigorous eye let hardly any miracles pass, and thus only a few canonizations were successful; yet he could not always convince popes and cardinals of his opinion. From 1734 to 1738 he published a multi-volume treatise on how to proceed in investigations into the holiness of persons. He made clear that advanced knowledge of medicine was indispensable and that the investigators had to doubt all sources presented to them before making any judgment. Moreover, he believed in the progress of science and thus wondered what would happen if in the future some miracles could be explained by natural causes. Should the canonization of the saint be reversed? Was that even possible? Nevertheless, he also stated clearly that some miracles, such as the resurrection of Christ, could never be explained. No natural law could explain such singular events.

Lambertini argued that the main criteria for sainthood were not miraculous deeds, stigmata, or visions but rather heroic virtues. This meant that a candidate must have demonstrated in his or her life all the virtues of faith, hope, love, justice, fortitude, temperance, and prudence to an extent that transcended the ordinary. If one followed this path, even a miracle that could later be attributed to natural causes would not undermine the validity of the canonization because the person in question had lived a holy life (this way of thinking, pioneered by Lambertini, is still embraced by the Catholic Church). Lambertini was especially critical of men and women who practiced extreme forms of external piety such as flagellation or excessive fasting. When he investigated the case of a fasting nun who claimed never to take any food but to live only on the Eucharist, he asked, to the surprise of his fellow inquisitors, "Dear sister, do you have a daily bowel movement?" When she nodded, Lambertini concluded that this would be impossible with an empty stomach. The nun was exposed as a fraud. This of course does not mean that Lambertini/Pope Benedict XIV was a rationalist. Instead he was a reformer who attempted to free Catholicism from the older worldview that emphasized the senses, the mortification of the flesh, and external devotion because all of these were for him, as for his friend Muratori, mere instruments to achieve the real goal: the virtues and an inner transformation of the heart and soul.[11]

There were also Catholic voices who found so-called miracles repulsive. These Enlightenment reformers thought the church should abandon all beliefs in non-biblical miracles. In England, especially, Catholics were subjected to the prejudice that they belonged to a superstitious religion. Thus, English Catholic Enlighteners tried to demonstrate that their faith was intellectually on par with enlightened Anglicanism by not only denying the pope's jurisdiction beyond Italy's borders but also by denying the existence of miracles. Joseph Berington was appalled that some Catholics still believed in miracles. His critics pointed out that Berington tried too much to please the English Enlighteners and the Anglican clergy, thus forsaking too much of his Catholic heritage. Be that as it may, the question of miracles became a watershed between "new" and "old" Catholics: the "new" Catholic Enlighteners were skeptical of miracles, while "old" Papal Rome celebrated miracles, after a sound investigation, as a welcome symbol of divine approval. It was the latter view that prevailed, while the lecture halls of Catholic Enlighteners remained scarcely visited.[12]

Muratori and the Spirit of Liturgical Renewal

Nobody exemplifies the spirit of Catholic Enlightenment better than Ludovico Muratori, a librarian and priest in Modena who regularly engaged in literary disputes. Among his closest friends was Prospero Lambertini, who in 1740 became Pope Benedict XIV. Muratori was a man in dialogue with contemporary culture, who read everything he could get his hands on—science, history, philosophy, fiction. That so many of his country-men were ignorant about the true content of their faith, could not see the joy of being Catholic and develop a personal relationship with Jesus, troubled him deeply. What made him angry, however, was when these people wasted their time with superstitious diversions instead of fulfill-ing the essential duties of a Christian life. Yet he also realized how hard it was to battle such ignorance, especially if it was buttressed by intran-sigent clergymen. He thought that it was predominantly pride and blind zeal that caused priests to resist the reforms inspired by Trent. By cling-ing to superstitious practices, they gave ammunition to the critics of the church. When an Italian priest tried to show the truth of Catholicism with some miracle stories, Muratori angrily replied, "The truth of the church is not in any need of fables."[13] Superstition was for him as bad as "heresy," he declared in his major work, *On the Moderation of Our Cleverness in Religious Matters* (1714): "The monster of superstition comes into being due to ignorance, and is fed by immoderate zeal. ... Stupid superstition is often to blame for the worst evils, namely that one resists the aboli-tion of deep-rooted abuses that seem to be devout and pious."[14] Why were these abuses so dangerous? The devil, according to Catholic teaching, was unable to create anything meaningful by himself, yet he was a master of imitation. By making demonic rituals appear Catholic, the devil could tear away the faithful from the church. Muratori saw such dangers in exor-cisms against mice and vermin, but also in prayers for the expulsion of demons from bread, milk, wine, and even bathing water.[15]

Since the end of the Council of Trent in 1563, the church had substan-tially reformed its practice of worship. Muratori joined this reform effort a few years before his death with the publication of a little book called *Regulated Devotion* (1747), whose English edition of 1789 was curiously titled *The Science of Rational Devotion*. At the heart of this book lies the distinction between essential and superficial forms of piety. Muratori argues that the main problem for Catholicism is that many faithful cling to superficial practices of piety and neglect the essential ones. It is, however, these superficial practices that most easily lead to superstition and thus away from the faith. By helping Catholics focus on what is central to their faith and by making it intelligible, he attempted to make Catholicism acceptable to more educated individuals. For Muratori, every essential mode of devotion was grounded either in Scripture or in a direct teaching of the church. He made clear that devotional practices theologians or mystics had invented or received through divine messages, such as devotion to the Sacred Heart (which was at this time not yet liturgically approved) might be helpful, but they could sometimes be a hindrance to the faith. The foundation of all true worship was a "reverential and affectionate attachment of the heart to him who is above all."[16] The "chief and principal mode of devotion" was, in his eyes, the Mass. He took pains to explain every element of the Eucharist, demonstrating that it did not contain any magical elements. He emphasized that the faithful "assisted" at Mass, and that they were thus actively involved in this holy mystery, even if they were not "doing" anything apart from saying their prayers. He went so far as to say that at the consecration of bread and wine the attendants "are united with the minister and thus offer up the sacrifice together with him."[17] Although this was official Catholic teaching, it was widely ignored in parish catechesis. Even an educated eighteenth-century Catholic would have been unaware that she was "offering" up the sacrifice of the Mass together with the priest. Only in the twentieth century, with the liturgical reform movement of the 1930s that inspired the Second Vatican Council, was this theological assertion rediscovered. Muratori was two hundred years ahead of his time.

While Muratori did not reject the veneration of the saints or relics, he diagnosed excessive abuses. If the invocation of a saint or the touching of a relic lifted the mind up to contemplate the core mysteries of the faith, that could be useful. But if they were believed to be "powerful" in themselves, like charms, they had become vehicles of superstition. Examples of this included the widespread belief that by wearing certain scapulars or rosaries, or through the veneration of certain images, one would be guaranteed both a holy death and protection against all kinds of evils. Muratori thought this was an abuse of proper Christian practices because material items could never save. The only material objects that carried such power were the sacraments, and even these required the proper inner disposition for any effect. Thus, such devotionals, the Italian priest said, should be seen as sensible aids to prayer, or aids to combat an irreligious imagination, but nothing more.

Muratori especially detested those devotions that benefited the inventor but did not help the believer to conform her or his life to that of Jesus Christ. The English translation of Muratori, published 1789 in Ireland, carefully eliminated this sentence in order to avoid giving Anglicans further ammunition against Catholics.[18] What did Muratori mean by accusing clergy of making money from superstition? A good example is the hermits of Wallersee in Upper Bavaria. In the 1680s they settled close to a famous Benedictine abbey but had trouble sustaining themselves. Thus they began to use popular beliefs about the poor souls in Purgatory for their own profit. The hermits explained to local farmers they knew the fate of their deceased family members in purgatory, and claimed they could also reveal how many prayers or Mass intentions these souls would need to pass on to heaven. But for such information, the hermits charged a handsome fee.[19] Equally troubling for Muratori was when people exaggerated the veneration of Mary, the mother of God. His position on Marian veneration had already brought him trouble a few years earlier. At that time, every Catholic university student was required to take an oath to defend the doctrine of the Immaculate Conception, even to the point of shedding his own blood if necessary. Muratori called this oath a superstition, not out of disrespect for Mary, but because it was against the faith to give one's life in defense of a religious opinion. After all, the Immaculate Conception would not even be declared a dogma until 1854.[20] Also, excessive veneration of Mary sometimes seemed to attach to her aspects of divinity. Others seemed to expect pardon for their sins from her. Widespread was the belief that anybody who had a devotion to her would not go to hell, even if he or she died in a state of mortal sin. Muratori insisted: "Let the Faithful know that such ideas ... can have no place in the just and pure doctrinal instructions of the Roman Catholic Church" because "Jesus Christ is ... the grand foundation of all hopes of Christians ... whose own merits move the mercy of his divine father to grant us, truly penitent, the forgiveness of our sins."[21] By continuously connecting his criticism of abuses and excesses with the intentions of the Council of Trent, Muratori established a clear continuity between the reform attempts of this council and the ideas of the moderate Catholic Enlightenment he was propagating.[22]

A New Theological Discipline:
Liturgical Theology

The Tridentine liturgical renewal that Muratori championed inspired many Catholics who were sympathetic to Enlightenment values such as simplicity and practicality to treat the liturgy of the church as a separate theological discipline. Theologians had never before analyzed prayers with such rigor nor had they devoted themselves to studying liturgical history and developing new rituals. Especially in the German lands, the new discipline of "liturgical theology" began to take shape, often against considerable resistance. Some conservative theologians called Muratori's thoughts "stinking cabbage" that did not deserve to be taken seriously; they said his followers were heterodox because they frequently cited Protestant authors. The reformers, however, had two aims: first, the extirpation of superstitious or excessive baroque piety, and second, to make worship more intelligible to the masses. It had to be shown that "the ugly Catholicism put forth ... by fanatics" was not the true Catholic religion.[23] The *Prayerbook for Enlightened Catholics* (1803), by the German Philip Brunner, exemplifies the goals of this movement. Instead of perpetuating hatred for Jews, for example, the book contained a respectful prayer for their conversion, asking God to remove all obstacles that would keep them from embracing Christ. Another prayer was for non-Catholic Christians—something radically new in a Catholic prayer book. It went like this: "Let us pray for all Christians, who think differently in religious matters, that we can, even if we do not agree with their religious opinions, live together with them a good life in universal brotherhood. ... With all differences in doctrine, people who hold a different belief can also be righteous and virtuous, and how could you, O holy God, punish virtue and righteousness, even if they are connected with error!"[24]

The mechanical way many people said their prayers was identified by the German liturgist Vitus Anton Winter as a major problem. It had made them passive, had dried up their religious imagination and undermined their personal connection to God. In this tradition, prayer became a mechanical order of business but not a religious experience. Therefore, many liturgists suggested that the liturgy should no longer be celebrated in Latin but in the vernacular. If the Mass were said, he argued, in the language of the people it would be much easier to get their attention and to make the mysteries again part of their faith lives. Benedict Werkmeister would not wait for the popes to bring about such a reform; he decided in

1786 to start celebrating a German Mass in the duke's house chapel in
Stuttgart. Yet liturgists often sounded like bad schoolteachers who tried
to remove the last bit of mystery from the liturgy. Worship became a
"school of humans, which makes them aware of their sublime vocation
and ennobles their immortal soul, a school of citizens which pulls them
out of savagery and infuses them with the spirit of the common good,
and a school for everyone, which helps to solve the problems of an infinite progress in morality."[25] Many wondered, consequently, whether they
could take the "lesson" elsewhere, be it at a university, at home, or with
friends.

The flattening of religious rituals was predominantly what caused this
well-intentioned reform to fail. Without having prepared their parishioners, elitist liturgists robbed the faithful of all popular devotions and thus
of all traditional means of consolation and contemplation. They replaced
them with prayers that were sometimes humanistic, most often beautiful
and biblical, but almost always far beyond the intellectual grasp of the
average Catholic. The reform proved sterile because of its own elitism.
The fact that it was spearheaded by the most radical Catholic Enlighteners
also contributed to its failure. Many of the movement's leaders publicly
rejected papal jurisdiction, ridiculed the saints, or argued that Catholics
could divorce. After 1789 these reformers were accordingly associated with
the dangerous Enlightenment that had brought about the terror of the
French Revolution. Even if someone were inspired only by certain moderate Enlightenment goals, he or she could not throw off the stigma of
being part of a destructive movement. Moreover, many reformers were
also connected with Jansenism, which had been denounced by the papacy
as a heresy, and with the Synod of Pistoia (1786), which the Grand Duke of
Tuscany, Leopold, had convened. This meeting of Italian bishops—many
of whom were sympathetic to Jansenism—sought to restore the liturgy
"as an action common to priest and people by bringing back the liturgy
to a greater simplicity of rites" and by celebrating it in the vernacular.
Yet the synod also scorned the papal claim to jurisdiction over bishops.
Consequently, even the synod's moderate liturgical reforms were rejected
by the papacy, not only because the meeting was regarded as unlawful and
partially heretical, but, also, as Pope Pius VI stated in his bull *Auctorem
Fidei* (1794), because these liturgical reforms implied that the current
order of worship was corrupted, or at best insufficient. The Catholic
Church could never concede this, the pope said, because this would shed
doubt on the infallibility of the church and confirm Protestant prejudices

against Catholicism. This argument remained alive until the liturgical renewal of the Second Vatican Council.[26]

Magical Healers: The Main Target of the Spanish and Portuguese Inquisition

Beginning especially in the first half of the eighteenth century, Catholic intellectuals made ample use of modern non-Catholic thought, including Isaac Newton's physics or John Locke's empiricism. The University of Paris, the Sorbonne, was particularly famous for attempting to merge Enlightenment and Catholicism, at least until the 1750s. One of its professors, the exiled Irishman and priest Luke Joseph Hooke, had shocked some French Catholics because he did not believe in the miracles of some of their favorite saints. Defending his position, he explained that no Catholic was obliged to believe in such accounts and that true faith should not seek the miraculous.[27] Portugal's all-powerful minister, the Marquis de Pombal, was also moved by this new philosophy, and in 1774 he passed a law that explained to the public that the laws of nature, which God had established, could not be altered by human sorcerers. Consequently, wizards and magicians were frauds who deserved hefty punishments for deceiving the public. Most churchmen fought against magic not because they believed that magic was real, as conventional wisdom suggests, but precisely because they did not.[28]

In Spain, accusations of witchcraft as a satanic conspiracy had ceased in 1614, not because one regarded witchcraft as a human invention, as in Portugal, but because new legal standards made proving such accusations impossible. Nevertheless, one can find in Spain regular prosecutions of sorcerers until the end of the century. Yet the image of thousands of burning stakes and inhumanely cruel inquisitors is not a reflection of history, but of fiction. Many modern historians have shown that the accused might have preferred to be prosecuted by the Spanish Inquisition rather than by local secular courts, since the Inquisition's procedural guidelines were stricter and their punishments were milder. The practice of the Spanish Inquisitors regarding sorcery, however, was quite similar to that of Portuguese Inquisitors. Men and women who applied magic were seen as frauds, not enemies of the church. For example, in 1787 an impostor was sentenced to receive two hundred lashes for having used love-charms, and in 1807 a woman was similarly punished for selling instructions for magical potions such as this: "After 11 o'clock at night, place on the fire a vessel full of oil; when it boils, throw in a living cat and put on the lid; at the stroke of midnight remove it and inside the skull of the cat will be found a little bone, which renders the person carrying it invisible and enables him to do whatever he pleases; the bone will ask 'What do you want?' but if carried across running water it will lose its virtue."[29]

While the Spanish, Portuguese, and Roman Inquisitions conducted about twenty thousand trials against offenses of magic between the sixteenth and the eighteenth centuries, only a small fraction pertained to witchcraft proper. Most defendants were tried for relatively harmless practices such as the ones just mentioned, and additionally for fortune telling, healing magic, or treasure hunting. In fact, over the course of the entire eighteenth century, the Spanish Inquisition burned only four persons (none of them accused of witchcraft), while the Roman Inquisition ordered the execution of three. The Portuguese Inquisition sentenced about one hundred to death, all of them Jews, showing that anti-Judaism was a much bigger problem than magical superstition. The rest were either acquitted or received minor corporeal punishments or prison terms.

One magical offense that might strike us today as odd was "treasure hunting." We usually think of it as an adventurous endeavor, but not as magic. In early modernity, however, such quests were undertaken with the help of sorcery; for example, ghosts were invoked to divulge the location of hidden treasures and to release this treasure from those who guarded it. During the Age of Reason such practices became, especially among the poor, quite popular. Catholicism was believed to have the most powerful spells to bind the ghosts, so much so that in 1744 a Protestant treasure hunter hired a Catholic who had learned to use exorcisms to torture an evil spirit. Special prayers to St. Christopher, the patron of treasure hunters, were also common. Priests—even higher ranking clergy—were frequently involved in such practices; for example, two cathedral canons from Bamberg in Bavaria were charged with such a transgression in 1776.[30] In 1736 a Capuchin friar named Guido supposedly exorcised the castle of Katzenstein in Austria and forced the ghosts there to surrender thirteen boxes with treasures. However, when the city magistrate desired to see the gold, the treasure had turned into "flies," because the spirits had forbidden the boxes to be opened—or so Father Guido claimed in his defense.[31] The 1779 case of the former priest and then Lutheran Joseph Niedermeyer of southwest Germany, however, demonstrates why the state government was interested in eradicating such activities. He had conned and ultimately ruined dozens of farmers and other credulous people. It is still hotly debated why treasure hunting became so frequent in the eighteenth century, but one reasonable explanation is that the increased interest in private property and the desire to supplement one's own means in a context of poverty was responsible. Yet a farmer's ethical code forbade the desire for riches, because it was believed that one's increase in revenue was a loss for the wider community since the amount of distributable goods was considered limited. Treasure hunting offered the possibility to gain profit from outside the agricultural society and was thus considered morally indifferent. Although the practice was consequently prosecuted, the punishments were mild; church and state both had pity on the poor who sought rescue through this superstition.[32]

In Spain, the highest inquisitorial court even recognized the grave injustices its officials had committed when in 1614 it stopped prosecuting witches as collaborators of the devil, not because the power of all magic was denied but because the inquisitors realized that they could not find evidence beyond reasonable doubt. By making it almost impossible to collect sufficient evidence, the witch crazes, which also existed in Protestant territories and were worst in the border regions between Catholics and Protestants, ceased, and falsely accused victims received monetary compensation. Preachers were instructed to teach their congregations that even if thunderstorms or earthquakes are occasionally sent as punishment for sin, they are primarily caused by nature and certainly not by malicious witches. A healthy skepticism had finally prevailed by the mid-eighteenth century, at least among the intellectual elite. This of course did not mean that superstition was eradicated, but the "deadly effects" of popular religion, as historian Henry Charles Lea called them, were halted.[33]

One crime that the Spanish Inquisition increasingly prosecuted was, however, magical healing. A few examples will give a sense of this phenomenon: in 1760 a Guinean slave named Manuel Galiano, already seventy years old, was charged with being a *curandero*, a healer, in Lima, Peru. He had cured swellings by making a small incision, inserting a cane, and sucking blood and little animals such as snakes or scorpions out of the wounds. Locals believed that he was in a pact with the devil. Questioned, Manuel conceded that he planted the animals first in the cane so that it appeared he would free the sick person from a demon. The trial lasted for three years, during which he was imprisoned. His punishment required a humiliating public act of faith and five years of service in a hospital. Another example is the case of Juana Martinez, age forty, of Mexico, who had sustained herself by healing through the use of certain roots, which she gathered by invoking the Holy Trinity. "She said that her patients ejected, from mouth and nose, insects, flies, etc., which was a sign that they had been bewitched." Interrogated by the Inquisition, she conceded that she privately invoked the devil and that all miracles she had performed were deceptions. Two hundred years earlier she would have died a gruesome death; in the heyday of the Catholic Enlightenment, when the possibility of any pact with the devil was questioned, the Inquisition released her and reprimanded the local priest, who had denounced her: instead of accusing ignorant and superstitious parishioners he should better educate them about the true nature of the Christian faith and the vanity of sorcery.[34]

In Portugal and its overseas colonies, especially Brazil, the Inquisition had been tolerant of magical healers for almost one hundred fifty years, but at the beginning of the eighteenth century it launched an attack on them. This attack had its origins in the 1690 official policy of the Portuguese Inquisition. It stated that while true medicine was the "scientific application of the divine power found in medicine, placed there by God to be used by men," healers were non-scientific charlatans who abused sacred prayers for their rituals. *Curandeiros* were identified as dangers to both scientific progress and to the faith itself because they impeded the eradication of superstition. Between 1715 and 1774, about 60 percent of all cases the Portuguese Inquisition investigated were about magical healing practices. While sorcerers in Catholic Hungary and Protestant Sweden faced a fifty-fifty chance of survival, the Portuguese Inquisition had not sentenced anybody accused of magic to death since 1626. Under the enlightened Grand Inquisitor Nuno da Cunha, whose tenure spanned from 1707 to 1750, the prosecution of healers meant not only protecting the rural population from being cheated out of their money and deceived in ludicrous cures, but also restoring the Catholic faith as Trent had outlined it. Cunha, for the first time, also employed a great number of physicians, all of whom were friends of the Enlightenment and who saw the healers, whom they now prosecuted, as an unwelcome competition for patients. Yet, in 1774, the Portuguese Inquisition gave up: it stated that it had become pointless to charge ignorant men and women with such offenses and to punish them. Their actions were no longer considered criminal but simply silly. Education was a much better way of dealing with the problem, they now believed.[35]

Of Devils, Demons, and Exorcisms

It was the Spanish Benedictine Benito Feijoo who most vehemently attacked vulgar beliefs about the devil. He affirmed the devil's existence as a person and certainly did not want to ridicule the ignorant masses, but he also considered it necessary to make clear the need for a better catechization of the rural population. Being a skeptical Catholic Enlightener, he was certain that practically all cases of possession could be explained naturally. But he conceded the reality of possession in principle, since the Bible and the lives of the saints reported them, and of course because the church had an approved ritual for exorcisms. His criticism was based on a refined reading of Scripture—influenced by Enlightenment thought that questioned miracle accounts and healings—along with an appreciation for the works of Augustine Calmet, his fellow Benedictine, who avoided metaphorical interpretations of the Bible, preferring a literal reading of the text. A pressing question for a critical thinker such as Feijoo was why God allowed many more real cases of possession in the times of the prophets, of Jesus, and of some great saints, compared to the small number in his own time. For him the only reasonable explanation was that these cases helped to highlight the role of Christ or helped to prove the sainthood of a person: "It was extremely important that God should allow unearthly spirits to enter human bodies. It was necessary to repeat the miracle of exorcising them, the characteristic work of the Redeemer, more than other types of miracles. . . . The same argument can be leveled at those opposing the saints whose virtues God wished to demonstrate in this way."[36] In Feijoo's lifetime it was customary to identify a possessed person by, among other means, holding a smoking aromatic plant under the accused's nose. The demons would then come out and show themselves—or as Feijoo stated, the person so tortured would say anything to stop the cruel treatment. Precisely because the devil was a spiritual being, a fallen angel, nothing material like smoke could "force" him to reveal himself, Feijoo explained.

One thing should be clear, however: Feijoo did not abandon belief in the devil, who was considered a necessary part of the Christian belief system, but he did make doctrinal demonology more coherent and intelligible. Besides a better theological understanding, which seemed necessary especially because of many credulous exorcists, Feijoo was also concerned about people who pretended to be possessed. He was certain that many did this only to justify erratic or vengeful behavior. Such a person "enjoys total freedom to commit as many crimes as he feels like. He can kill, can take away honor, steal, burn down villages and cornfields. ... He knows nobody can touch a hair of his head. ... Could there be a more pernicious kind of person in the world?"[37] Just like priests, doctors were also frequently ignorant, disregarding the real causes of illness and instead explaining the symptoms as demonic. As we have seen, Feijoo was a defender of the rights of women and thus it should not surprise us that he spoke out against the common prejudice that women were more susceptible to diabolic influences than men. He saw right through the misogyny of his fellow countrymen; and although he also conceded that women often faked possession, it was only because of their lack of freedom. A woman might pretend to be possessed because it would enable her to escape her patronizing husband and family: she could get out of her house, go on pilgrimages to find healing, or visit exorcists.

The perspective of the Catholic Enlightenment on the devil is nicely summed up by Carl Schwarzel, professor of theology in Innsbruck. Although branded a radical, he never doubted the existence of the devil, and he felt uncomfortable that many priests at the end of the eighteenth century no longer dared to speak about him out of fear of being ridiculed by Enlighteners. He wrote in 1803: "If we subtly explain away the realm of Satan for whose destruction the savior had come to earth, we lose half the Gospel. These Catholics, with their 'elevated' Enlightenment, have sunk into the deepest ignorance—after all, they believe that in order to be called erudite one has to deny the Gospel or be ashamed of it."[38] How had such a change occurred? A few generations earlier, most people still believed strongly in the devil. Then came the Reformed preacher and freethinker Balthasar Bekker, who, in his bestselling book *The World Bewitched* (1691), argued for a radical disenchantment of the world and the abandonment of all belief in miracles, apparitions, and devils.[39] This new view had quickly gained ground in progressive Protestant theology; in the middle of the eighteenth century, it found its most famous advocate in the German Lutheran Johann Salomo Semler. He declared the devil a mythological figure and Jesus's exorcisms misunderstood accounts of merely physical healings. For him there was no devil in the Old or New Testament. Yet, just when rationalist Enlighteners thought they had convinced the elites, a chaplain from a small Austrian village shook central Europe with a series of exorcisms. Thousands desired to see the man who expelled devils and cured the sick; his name was Father Joseph Gassner.

Gassner was a difficult target for the Enlighteners. He both endorsed the Enlightenment critique of witchcraft and argued that demonic possession was not caused by the spells of evil people. Nevertheless, he believed, demons attacked humans and tormented them with incurable diseases. These possessions manifested no supernatural symptoms, such as the ability to talk in different languages without prior knowledge of them, superhuman strength, or knowledge of distant places and events. By conceding to rationalists that the devil would not manifest his powers in supernatural ways, the rationalist attack on the entire spiritual realm could be averted. In Gassner's view, the devil presented himself in diseases that medical doctors were unable to explain or cure. By relying on medical knowledge and expertise, his exorcisms connected science, medicine, and religion. This new understanding of the devil allowed him to immunize the belief in hellish powers against Enlightenment criticism by employing Enlightenment enthusiasm for medicine and science. Gassner had arrived at his practice because he himself had suffered from chronic headaches and as a last resort exorcised himself. Since this cured him, he began using the same method with other patients. In the 1760s he began touring the German lands, where he healed hundreds if not thousands. Enlightenment critics could have dismissed him as yet another superstitious fraud if his followers had all been uneducated people, but they included many educated citizens of the upper-middle class, noble families, and even university professors. The crowds he gathered were large; in Ellwangen and Regensburg alone he attracted some forty thousand spectators.

Catholic Enlighteners such as Ferdinand Sterzinger and Emperor Joseph II of Austria were not pleased with this development. While authors tried to discredit Gassner, local governments attempted to outlaw his public healing ceremonies. The question of why so many people followed this man, however, has never been fully explained. The best explanation has been provided by the eminent historian Erik Midelfort. He demonstrated that Gassner answered the most fundamental and most pressing theological question of his time, the question of why there was evil, in an especially convincing way. When a farmer suffered from fatigue, chronic migraine, or epilepsy, when he could continue his daily work only with the greatest pain or not at all, he of course asked himself: "What is the cause of my sickness?" The farmer could not find a satisfying answer; even the medical specialist could not help. Gassner, however, was able to provide an answer: by explaining that his disease was caused by the devil, he made the farmer's daily miseries "intelligible" and—through exorcism—curable. Gassner was not alone in this business. Franz Anton Mesmer, also a Catholic, tried to heal similar illnesses with magnets. Our verb "to mesmerize" still echoes this strange man and his belief, based on the findings of the Jesuit astronomer Maximilian Hell, that one could heal by using the magnetism in each living being. While Mesmer, who claimed to be entirely scientific, was condemned by a royal commission, Gassner was able to pass the scientific and theological tests several university professors demanded from him.

How did Gassner's exorcisms, which made liberal use of the approved Roman rite of exorcism, look like? The ritual began with a conversation, after which the priest decided whether the disorder was natural, or inwardly or outwardly caused by the devil. If the exorcist was convinced it was the latter—and according to the Ritual he had to exclude *all* natural causes—he urged the patient to obey him to the letter and to *believe* that the devil caused his discomfort. Then Gassner spoke: "If this illness is unnatural, then I command in the name of Jesus that it should show itself at once." This caused the demon to present himself in swellings, headaches, convulsions—all the symptoms got worse. After a while, Gassner applied a second exorcism that eased the pains, and finished with a third, expulsive exorcism.

Under Gassner, exorcism turned into a healing ritual of "unnatural disorders" caused by the devil, but they no longer had a connection to the traditional understanding of illnesses caused by spells or charms. Based on his apparent ability to heal many people suffering from madness or epilepsy—he even claimed to exorcise animals—Gassner insisted on the success of his methods. His critics, on the other hand, claimed that the cures were only temporary easements and relied on the patient's imagination. This debate generated a flood of publications in favor of or against Gassner. After his death, his followers painted him as a master of "spiritual formative powers" and an inspiration for the new movement of Romanticism that defied the hegemony of reason. Especially in the early nineteenth century, exorcisms were again *en vogue*, even among Pietists. The full story of Father Joseph Gassner, however, demonstrates that he cannot simply be characterized as a Counter-Enlightenment figure, as if he were untouched by Enlightenment thought. Even critics of the movement's rationalism like him used Enlightenment thought, or deviated from traditional mindsets, and contributed to the emergence of what we call "modernity." Even today, Gassner is hailed by historians of psychiatry and psychoanalysis for taking an important step toward the "discovery of the unconscious," and the fact that he taught his patients how to control their symptoms still inspires modern day hypno-therapists.[40]

Most Catholic Enlighteners, however, had a different view of the devil and of exorcisms than Gassner. For most, it was clear that the world was created good and that the devil's power had been restricted by Christ. Consequently, the prayers for deliverance from evil in approved liturgical books were mostly superstitious, except, of course, the petition for deliverance from evil in the Our Father. For the Enlighteners, most if not all possessions could be explained naturally. Exorcisms should, these scholars claimed, be reserved for very rare instances. All other prayers for protection from evil or delivery from evil should not be called exorcisms because this caused people to think that the devil was as powerful as God. Such confusion was probably most obvious in the rite of baptism, which contained an "exorcism." Catholic Enlighteners saw in this rite an insult to human dignity and an abuse of religious power; for them one could at best speak metaphorically about a newborn being a "slave of sin," which, however, would not justify an exorcism.[41] Thus, a number of Catholic Enlighteners attempted to revise the ritual books. The Enlightener Bishop Joseph Anton von Gall of Linz in Austria came up with a prayer, which is surprisingly close to the current post-Vatican II version: "May the Seducer not overpower you like our forefathers in paradise. The inherited inclination to evil ... may not be victorious in you ... but the Holy Spirit may reign over you, and his grace may guide your spirit and heart."[42]

Of Witches, Ghosts, and Vampires

While the fear of witchcraft certainly receded in the eighteenth century, it faded slowly. Even in cities such as Nuremberg or Salzburg, which could claim to be at the forefront of the Enlightenment, one could still find oneself charged (no longer prosecuted, though) with witchcraft as late as 1790. The last witch in Poland was executed in 1793, and in 2004 a woman in Krakow had to apologize publicly for suggesting that her neighbor would increase his milk production with magical spells.[43] Still, did the Catholic Enlightenment's critical view of witchcraft really come about through the criticism of radical Enlighteners such as Balthasar Bekker?[44]

Bekker and others were certainly the most radical critics of the witch craze that haunted Protestant and Catholic regions alike, and they were usually charged with being lapsed Christians, atheists, or deists. (Deism, of course, is the belief in a watchmaker God who does not intervene in the world.) Yet long before Bekker, Catholic reformers had tried to put an end to the witch craze. Admittedly, this was no easy task for a Catholic theologian; powerful institutions watched over the orthodoxy of the clergy, and criticism of old practices, such as the prosecution of witches, could be seen as suspicious or even heretical. Thus, critics of the witch craze—which was a phenomenon of early modernity and not of the Middle Ages—had to be careful. Anyone who denied outright the possibility of demons and witches acting in the world was only one step away from denying the existence of the devil and perhaps even God's own interventions in history. Some church officials feared a slippery slope that could lead from one denial to the next.

A theologian, therefore, could not reject the possibility of demons, but he could attempt to develop a philosophical and theological framework that would limit their actions. As miracles were more cautiously investigated after the Reformation, so were reports about magical and demonic activities. Criteria were developed to ensure that no innocent person was convicted. Deaths that were supposedly caused by witchcraft were subjected to a thorough medical investigation, and from the time of the reorganization of the Holy Inquisition in 1587 on, popes demanded that women who claimed to have had intercourse with the devil be examined by a midwife to determine the state of their hymens. If the hymen was intact, it was considered clear evidence that no such intercourse had occurred and that the person had just hallucinated.[45] The German Jesuits Friedrich von Spee and Adam Tanner also employed evidence-driven criticism of witchcraft. Tanner was a learned jurist, and he reminded his academic peers that no innocent person should ever be harmed. With the prosecution of witches, however, this principle was violated, because one could never obtain evidence beyond reasonable doubt that a person was a witch. It was this line of reasoning that succeeded in halting the witch-hunt in Spain, even though the prosecutions continued in central Europe until the end of the eighteenth century. For the priest Muratori, belief in magic was mere imagination, as he treated it in his book *The Force of Human Fantasy*.[46] Relying on the Church Fathers, he explained that already in the ancient church reasonable theologians doubted that demons or the devil could mingle with humans or procreate with them.[47] He relied on the expertise of his physician friends, who found that hysteria and illness, such as depression and extreme anxiety, were responsible for the belief in witches. Such beliefs became "epidemics" if their suggestive power was shared with people who were either ignorant or had endured losses or griev-ances, and thus saw in witchcraft an explanation for their misfortune. It is exactly this explanation that modern historians use, not knowing that a Catholic Enlightener had anticipated their ideas by two hundred years.[48]

For Muratori, modern science had shown that words could not bring about mental or physical changes in a person, thus proving that spells and charms are ineffective. He explicitly excluded from this naturalist explanation the efficacy of the sacraments, which work through signs and words. Muratori's idea relied on the presupposition that the material and spiritual world were separated, as the French philosopher Rene Descartes had declared. Charms only seemed to work because they had sugges-tive power—just like a placebo. Muratori recalled that in France people believed that a man could instantaneously lose his virility as a result of a malicious spell. He reminded his readers that the great skeptic Michel de Montaigne had to promise his help to a friend if such a loss should hap-pen on his friend's wedding night. When he indeed could not perform, Montaigne, who did not believe in any superstition or magic, gave him a necklace and explained it would reverse the spell. The newlywed could now "miraculously" fulfill his marital duties. For the priest Muratori, this incident nicely illustrates that sudden impotence had nothing to do with magic.[49]

A ten-year-long dispute about witchcraft in Italy attracted wide atten-tion throughout Europe. The two rival scholars at the center of the debate, Scipione Maffei and Girolamo Tartarotti, were both proponents of the Catholic Enlightenment but had distinctly different understandings of magic and witchcraft. Tartarotti argued that belief in witchcraft was credulous nonsense and that the confessions of witches were worthless because they had been obtained under torture. Yet he could not bring himself to declare magic impossible because he feared he would also undermine the Christian belief in miracles. In his book *Night Congress of the Witches* (1749), he also left open the possibility that both "erudite" magic or alchemy, as it was practiced by Paracelsus, and the devil and his companions, were real, though at the same time he insisted that ever since Christ's ministry the power of Satan was limited. For Maffei, on the other hand, this was an inconsistent stance. Maffei explained that the successful fight against belief in witchcraft required that the virus be fully eliminated; this entailed the eradication of all superstitions, including the belief in all kinds of magic, erudite or demonic. Maffei, an extraordinarily gifted historian and dramatist, did not unreservedly follow Bekker, and thus rejected a radical naturalism that would exclude all supernatural interactions in the world; otherwise he would have been forced to accuse the Bible of lying about wizards and magicians. Instead, he argued that since the time of Christ, magic was a chimera and the power of Satan was limited; from the moment of the resurrection onward the devil no longer had any control over human bodies.[50] Through the bold book of the German Augustinian monk Jordan Simon, *The Great Fraudulent Nothing*, the arguments of Maffei became well known in central Europe.

Some historians argue that although Maffei was nominally Catholic, his views were actually inspired by the "radical Enlightenment" and thus were materialistic. This opinion leaves out the fact that Catholic Enlighteners such as Simon or Ferdinand Sterzinger—who were in complete harmony with the church and were never censored—fully accepted Maffei's position. Moreover, Maffei was a genuine, lifelong Catholic, and while he was perhaps persuaded by Bekker to express strong criticism of magic, this did not mean that he rejected any supernatural activity in the world or the existence of the devil. Still, Maffei articulated a theological view of evil, the devil, and demons that could withstand the criticism of Enlightenment thought. His strategy also featured a defense of God, a theodicy: if possession and magic were fantasies, it would no longer be necessary to explain why God allowed such evil to roam the earth; if, on the other hand, God allowed the devil or any spirits to continue to work on earth, a more elaborate theodicy would be needed. Some theologians did attempt to offer such explanations. For example, some explained that the existence of evil spirits and ghosts served to prove materialism wrong and gave a foretaste of hell. Even an otherwise very critical priest, the Englishman Alban Butler, thought that ghosts possibly existed; however, the only ones were the ghosts of holy souls because divine providence would never allow the damned to haunt the living.[51]

The Maffei/Tartarotti debate coincided with one of the last executions of a witch on German soil. It attracted international attention because the victim was a seventy-year-old nun of the Norbertine monastery in Unterzell near Würzburg, Maria Renata Singer von Mossau. It was not uncommon to find possessed nuns. The most famous possessions were found in the Ursuline monastery of Loudun in 1632, but throughout early modernity one can find about fifty cases of group possessions in female monasteries, although only a handful ended like the Unterzell case, with outright accusations of witchcraft, and fewer still ended with an execution.[52] Renata Singer came from an old noble family, and at nineteen she was forced by her parents into the cloister, although this practice was opposed to the explicit teaching of the church about the freedom necessary for genuine vocations, whether to religious life or to marriage.[53] When some nuns began hearing ghostly voices in the monastery, they came to believe that the nunnery was haunted, but initially nobody suspected Renata. Then, in 1749, a new nun began to suffer from incurable fainting and headaches, and soon afterward five other nuns complained about similar symptoms. Today one explains this by "imitation neurosis," but in 1749 the sick nuns accused their subprioress of bewitching them. The bishop of Würzburg appointed the theologians Kaspar Barthel, a former student of Pope Benedict XIV, and Michael Wentzel to investigate the case. Both were moderately influenced by Enlightenment theology and quite critical of the popular belief in sorcery. Yet they applied torture, and, in agony, Renata finally confessed that she was a witch. The devil, she said, had first appeared to her in the form of a soldier when she was seven years old. He handed her special ointments for bewitching others. At the age of eleven she officially signed a pact with the devil with her own blood. The devil countersigned the pact with brown spots on the skin of her back. Renata continued to confess: she had intercourse with Satan in her sleep, she blasphemed Eucharistic hosts, she created mice and vermin. All of it was taken at face value by the bishop. The nuns who felt bewitched were exorcised and their demons forced to confess. These "confirmed" Renata's story. Dreams and reality, it seems, were for the nuns no longer distinguishable. Renata was now imprisoned. Barthel, the theological investigator, not only doubted the veracity of the confession but also the veracity of the sisters' accounts. He implored the worldly court, to which he had to hand her over, to pardon Renata; but this was the most he could do. On June 18, 1749, the civil judges announced their verdict: she was to be beheaded and her body burnt. Her head should be put on a spike and presented to the public. Three days later, after having received the sacrament of penance, Renata was executed. Empress Maria Theresa in Vienna was shocked. Pope Benedict XIV was outraged by the stubbornness of the bishop and his unenlightened stance. The pope told the bishop that by killing an elderly nun, he had brought scandal to the church.[54]

The Unterzell case convinced skeptical Catholics that no time could be lost in fighting superstition. The sooner witchcraft prosecution stopped, the more lives could be saved. Germans were embarrassed that their record of witch executions was much higher than that of the (unjustly) infamous Spanish Inquisition. Ferdinand Sterzinger, a priest of the Theatine order and professor of church history in Munich, was one of the most influential Catholic thinkers to criticize the belief in magic. As a member of the Bavarian Academy of Sciences, Sterzinger was in close contact with scientists and *philosophes* throughout Europe, and early in his career he began to doubt the existence of witches. When he was invited in 1766 to give a lecture to the Academy of Sciences—the leading center of learning in the duchy and one of the most prestigious in Europe—in the presence of the Bavarian sovereign, he accepted and titled his lecture *Common Prejudices about Witchcraft*.

> Witchcraft is ... an explicit or secret pact with the devil, with which one subjects oneself to him in order to receive the advantages he has promised. These advantages are supposedly such ridiculous miracles as travelling on broomsticks ... to certain places in order to be lustful with Satan ... causing bad storms, hail or rain ... bewitching cattle, children or anybody else, or sending ... demons into their bodies ... and other nonsensical stuff.[55]

It is important to note that Sterzinger calls the belief in witchcraft a "prejudice." For the Enlighteners, "prejudices" stood for unchecked and credulous beliefs—things the Enlightenment attempted to abolish. At the beginning of his speech, Sterzinger concedes for the moment the "possibility" of witches: if something like witches existed then these men and women would have to have obtained their magical powers from a pact with the devil. Such pacts, however, were merely figments of imagination. This was a bold step for Sterzinger to take, since many theologians had defended the existence of such pacts since the 1420s. Sterzinger wondered how a human could even get in touch with the devil to sign such a pact. Certainly one could not force Satan to appear, but neither could Satan materialize at will since Jesus had put limits on his powers ever since his resurrection. God surely would not allow Satan to act freely in the world since this would contradict the philosophical notion of a good, all-powerful, and benevolent God. The pact was, for Sterzinger, mere "fantasy," along with all the supposed advantages of the bargain, such as flying on a broomstick to the witches' sabbath orgy: these were merely hallucinations brought about by drugs.

The belief in a satanic witch-sect that conspired with Satan against humanity arose in the early fifteenth century and grew, not only because of the Little Ice Age and the consequent crop failures but also because a growing number of people indeed practiced some kind of magic. This was quite understandable. After all, many at the time were convinced that it was malicious sorcery that caused the evils of everyday life such as cattle epidemics, mysterious illnesses, and of course the suspicious behavior of fellow citizens who could be accused of witchcraft. It was therefore necessary to use magic to defend oneself against spells, or to gain an advantage, or to take revenge. The idea, however, that male and female witches practiced intercourse with demons, celebrated a witches' Sabbath, and conspired to bring evil to all humanity was entirely the construct of erudite theologians and jurists.[56]

What Sterzinger did not know was that there were also enemies of witches, the *benandanti*, who were something like Catholic shamans and practiced "good" magic. The *benandanti* were found in Italy, Hungary, Croatia, and Slovenia. They cured the bewitched, identified witches, and counter-attacked with white magic and spells. Depending on the outcome of the conflict between witches and *benandanti*, the harvest was either good or bad. For this battle, the *benandanti*, just like the witches, "left their bodies behind"; a hallucinogenic ointment put them into a trance, and they fought the battle in their dreams.[57]

Vampires inspired human fantasy even more than regular witchcraft accusations, since the accused was dead. One did not need to apply torture; hard evidence was found by simply examining his or her corpse. Vampire accusations also made it unnecessary to blame a person of one's own community for misfortune—one could blame the dead. Thus it makes perfect sense that as witchcraft accusations slowly receded, vampire spottings exponentially increased.[58] The Spanish monk Benito Feijoo sarcastically remarked in 1753 that if the stories about vampires were true, then more resurrections from the dead had happened in central Europe during his lifetime than in the entire world since the death of Christ.[59] Yet vampires had theological relevance. Popular stories described them as the evil living dead in incorruptible bodies, lusting for human blood. Catholic doctrine also believed in incorruptible bodies as clear evidence for the saintliness of a person; vampires were thus the negative image of the saints. Like some medieval saints, the fingernails and hair of vampires continued to grow after their death, their bodies did not decay, and they demonstrated vitality long after their earthly demise. Even the bloodsucking had a parallel in Christianity: Holy Communion, which many early modern Christians had depicted as a material absorption of Christ's flesh.[60] Although the Viennese court decided in 1754 that vampirism was a figment of popular imagination, some Polish bishops still wanted to hunt vampires. Pope Benedict XIV, who also denied the existence of vampirism, fought against episcopal enthusiasm for vampire hunts.[61]

In France, a scholar of enormous erudition and acumen, known throughout Europe for his twenty-three-volume commentary on all books of the Bible, decided in 1746 to publish a book on apparitions, demons, ghosts, and vampires. While most of his exegetical work is (deservedly) forgotten, historians of popular religious beliefs still cite his book on ghosts, which made Augustin Calmet the leading Catholic specialist in the field. It was not that Calmet was ignorant of critical thinking—he was capable of good historical research; often, however, he could not resist his apologetic tendencies and so the conclusions he drew did not really follow from his research. Whenever he had amassed enough material to shed doubt on a biblical story, leading the reader to expect Calmet to issue a critical verdict and label the account a fairy tale, he instead caved and refused to judge the veracity of the account at all. Not so Voltaire, who once stated that he had no better inspiration for his biblical criticism than this shy Benedictine monk.[62]

For Calmet it was inappropriate to simply dismiss accounts of things that fell between the supernatural and the natural, such as ghost or apparition stories, since the Bible mentioned these as well. In his book, he grouped together stories that looked alike and amassed material from different cultures all over Europe. In the end, he concluded that only the biblical accounts could stand up to the historian's scrutiny; only they were fully trustworthy. This, however, did not mean that apparitions were impossible or all modern accounts of them untrustworthy; to give up all belief in the possibility of apparitions would endanger the foundations of faith. Therefore, Calmet suggested:

> In these matters it is therefore necessary to steer a middle course between excessive credulity and extreme incredulity: one must be wise and enlightened moderately, *think soberly* [Romans 12, 3]; one must, according to Saint Paul's advice, test everything, examine everything, bow only before evidence and known truth: *Test all things; hold fast what is good* [1 Thessal 5, 21].[63]

This conclusion, however, was only valid for apparitions, not for vampires. The latter he could only reject as outrageous inventions.

Unfortunately, Calmet's message did not spread fast enough. At the eastern outskirts of the Habsburg lands, reports of vampires skyrocketed. The most famous case claimed the sighting of a dozen bloodsucking monsters. In 1755, in the little village of Hermersdorf near the Silesian-Moravian border, villagers and clergy were convinced that the recently deceased Rosina Polakin must be a vampire because several people had testified to weird nightly attacks. The villagers opened her grave and found her body in good condition even though her funeral had taken place several months earlier. There was even blood in her veins, which was accepted as evidence that she was a vampire. Her family was forced to drag her body out of the grave, behead her, and burn the corpse.

Empress Maria Theresa was appalled. For her, influenced by Jansenist rigorism, superstitious beliefs such as vampirism put Catholicism in a bad light. She therefore began a campaign to purge the faith of such fantasies. Superstitious calendars and exorcisms were banned in 1758, and in 1766 a new law against the persecution of witches was passed. Catholic France and Protestant Prussia had already approved similar decrees generations earlier. The empress's law made clear that ignorance kept the belief in magic and vampires alive. Many could no longer distinguish between imagination and reality; they believed every account about the supernatural. Most important, "the children have been infected from the cradle by these terrible fairytales."[64] The new ruling also set new standards for accusations of sorcery: investigators first had to regard all events as naturally caused, and they had to consult scientists. It was necessary to establish beyond any reasonable doubt the presence of supernatural magic or demon worship before the case could proceed. As a result, accusations became virtually impossible and trials ceased.[65] It is important to note that the law did not state that all magic was fake but only that most accounts were superstitious. The empress left the door slightly ajar because she felt it was heterodox to deny the devil any interaction with the world. The government of the Habsburg lands intervened not only because of the bad image vampire beheadings gave to the state and the church, or to protect potential victims in witch crazes, but also because vulgar superstition was seen as a stumbling block for progress, especially economic reforms. As long as the population believed in such stories, they were unable to live and work up to their true potential, unable to turn the country into a new, flourishing Eden.[66]

Conclusion

The Catholic Enlightenment continued the fight of the Tridentine Reform movement to eradicate superstition and to reinvigorate the church by renewing its liturgical life. This was a movement to emphasize in catechesis the salvific message of Catholicism and to explicitly reject the superstitious, sensational marginalia of religious experience, which attracted popular attention. Catholic Enlighteners successfully campaigned against the prosecution of witches and the belief in vampires, but carefully noted that their engagement did not mean a denial of the supernatural world itself, which would have undermined the Catholic faith. Instead, they attempted to show the compatibility of belief in the supernatural elements and miracles of the Christian faith with modern science and philosophy. Catholic Enlighteners applied a rigorous framework of rational theology to reports about miracles and developed philosophical criteria a miracle had to fulfill to count as such. Some—such as the Austrian exegete Johann Jahn or the German theologian Benedict Werkmeister—pushed this agenda so far that they came close to being rationalists, while others such as Muratori stand out as exemplary in their attempt to balance faith and reason. It was also Muratori who realized the importance of a liturgical renewal and suggested changes in the liturgical books of the church. Some of his followers even translated the Latin rituals of the church into the vernacular, composed new prayers, and thus tried to contribute to this liturgical renewal, which anticipated much of the Second Vatican Council. Nevertheless, unlike many proponents of the Tridentine Reform, Catholic Enlighteners lacked pastoral sensitivity: instead of constantly catechizing and carefully implementing changes of popular beliefs on the parish level, they tended to overwhelm the uneducated population with highly sophisticated homilies, treatises, and harsh attacks on their religious practices. Only the educated elite read their books and supported them; not even among the rural clergy could Catholic Enlighteners find a majority supporting them, because of their often arrogant attitude toward traditional piety.

By considering the achievements and failings of the Catholic Enlightenment battling superstition and popular belief, it becomes obvious that this movement was a prolongation of the Tridentine reform. Moreover, the efforts of Catholic Enlighteners to purge the liturgical books of what they considered superstitious and to emphasize the intelligibility of the faith not only shows how they were integrated into the broader phenomenon of religious Enlightenment but also that they shared the secular Enlightenment's abhorrence of prejudice and superstition. Yet Catholics have often been portrayed as "anti-Enlightenment" because they tried to reconcile faith and reason and rejected a naturalist worldview. Behind such a view stands a teleological view of history that sees religious commitments as deviations from the goal of human progress and therefore as "unenlightened." A serious engagement with the literature of the Catholic Enlightenment would instead unearth an intellectual world that eclectically absorbed new philosophies, scrutinized their presuppositions, praised scientific endeavors, and tried to balance all this with the beliefs in the supernatural truths of Christianity. Such a revisionist approach would also allow for a long overdue re-evaluation of the Catholic Enlightenment's contributions to modernity, in particular to the battle against superstition and the belief in witchcraft.

6

Saints and Sinners

DESPITE GREAT CHALLENGES, Catholicism flourished between 1740 and 1800. Catholic Enlighteners updated and reformed the devotional life of the church, though they sometimes acted without much pastoral sensitivity, especially when they robbed commoners of traditional forms of prayer. More remarkable than these Enlighteners and certainly more influential were the saints this half-century produced. Although none of them were Enlighteners, they embody both traditional concepts of saintliness and the challenges of their century. The saints of the eighteenth century continued the Tridentine Reform, embodied a message that was directed against the secular mainstream Enlightenment, and anticipated ideas that only resurfaced two hundred years later.

Recent studies have shown that in the eighteenth century the church canonized saints from much more varied societal strata than ever before, favoring saints who struggled heroically to live virtuous lives and to perform works of mercy over saints who received mystical visions.[1] Yet one can go even further. While during the seventeenth century Counter-Reformation saints were predominantly those who traveled far in search of heroic deeds, such as the missionary to India St. Francis Xavier, the eighteenth-century canonizations seem to emphasize men and women of holiness who stayed home and demonstrated their sanctity "in a narrow geographic radius, instructing, comforting and healing compatriots and neighbors."[2] This emphasis on local sainthood went hand in hand with a change in religious art.

Some art historians have argued that religious art increasingly lost its importance over the eighteenth century. While this is certainly true for areas in which a "de-Christianization" set in, as in Revolutionary France, this change was not reflected in the rest of the world. Religious art was not abandoned; instead, it was transformed, particularly in the last three decades of the century. Continuing a trend that began during the Renaissance, more and more religious art was found outside churches and monasteries, in city halls and living rooms, and its purpose shifted as well. On the one hand, religious art had to be relatively neutral to fit into the neutral space where it was displayed, but on the other, it had to be a useful tool to lift up the soul of the viewer in prayer. Religious images began inviting more subtle devotion.[3] A marvelous example is Giambattista Tiepolo's (1696–1770) *Rest on the Flight to Egypt,* painted between 1762 and 1770. The Holy Family, consisting of Joseph and the pregnant Mary, occupy not even an eighth of the painting. Both tiny figures are located in the bottom right corner. They rest underneath a gigantic pine tree emerging from a crevasse of rock, their donkey waiting patiently in the back. Beneath their feet is an enormous river without a bridge, majestic mountains in the back, and occupying half the canvas, a blue sky.[4] This new style is associated with the Catholic Enlightenment. It emphasized the natural and circumvented the Baroque exuberance of portraying the supernatural, or as the enlightened Archbishop of Salzburg, Colloredo, stated, "all inappropriate, ambiguous, superstitious, and laughable images, representations and decorations" should be avoided because these "only heat up the imagination" of the faithful. Instead, he and other proponents of Catholic Enlightenment of the eighteenth century aimed at noble simplicity.[5]

Saints Everywhere

In Catholic churches of the eighteenth century, one could find numerous depictions of saints; in fact, images of Mary and other saints probably outnumbered images of Christ and the Trinity. The veneration of the saints had intensified with the Council of Trent's exhortation to give the faithful role models who would help increase their devotion and inspire greater love of God. This made devotion more personal because it motivated Catholics to choose saints of their liking and imitate them in their daily lives. The saints were believed to be with God in heaven, constituting the "church triumphant," in contrast to the "church militant" on earth, which is stained by sin and human frailty. Moreover, they interceded and prayed on one's behalf in heaven and were a reminder that Christian perfection was possible.

Apart from the theological meaning of the saints as role models and intercessors, their feasts had an important social meaning. On many feast days people did not work, so that after the Reformation a "culture of leisure" could develop in the Catholic countries of Europe, which contrasted sharply with the Protestant North. While in Protestant territories only about 15 to 25 days were considered holidays, Catholics had about 80 to 120. The feast day of a saint was usually also a market day, which included public entertainment. Such leisure was especially important for the hard-working rural population. But the holidays also hindered commercial growth. Secular as well as religious Enlighteners argued that reducing the number of holidays would increase agricultural and commercial output. However, one could not increase productivity on a farm by abolishing feast days as farmers had to do the necessary work, such as feeding the cattle or cutting the grass, no matter what. More to the point, saints' day fairs often included drinking, cursing, dancing, and sexual activity outside the bonds of marriage—all of which were detested by Catholic Enlighteners. Therefore, they sought to reduce the number of holidays and imbue the remaining ones with a more profound spiritual message.

This was supposed to generate more social discipline and holiness, but it showed a striking ignorance of rural life. The fairs were the social cement of village society. The "chatting" during religious processions, which the enlightened clergymen hated, was not indifference to religion but a way of maintaining social contacts and conducting business. Also, the alleged "lasciviousness" of rural feasts was a rare source of relaxation and leisure. Instead of gently regulating excessive forms of leisure, the reformers wanted to eliminate a substantial part of rural life. Unfortunately, the arguments of the Enlighteners are much better known than those of their critics, and until today most historians assume that the cult of the saints was bad for the economy and morals. Until recently, hardly any research has been done on the number of saints' festivals, the allegedly excessive forms of celebration, or the charge that such "Baroque" behavior deprived large groups of the population from a real increase in wealth. Even the critics of the holiday reductions are usually passed over by historians. In a number of instances, this is quite understandable. A book arguing against the reduction of holidays, published by the Franciscan Clarentius Pschaider of Salzburg in 1773, survived in only a handful of research libraries. The Archbishop of Salzburg, an ardent supporter of (some) Enlightenment reforms, had successfully destroyed all other circulating copies. Pschaider's insistence that behind the enlightened reforms stood nothing but greed and avarice echoes the criticism of capitalism that nineteenth-century Germans would hear more often not from pulpits but from Karl Marx. A rare exception of an Enlightener who considered holidays to have a somewhat positive effect on public recreation and social life was the father of the Revolutionary Mirabeu, Victor de Mirabeu.[6] Pope Benedict XIV, who had agreed to reduce the number of holidays in Italy, however, was branded by the faithful with the questionable title "papa protestante" or "the Protestant Pope," which indeed summarized the sentiment of the Catholic rural population.[7]

As mentioned above, the Catholic Enlightenment rejected the exuberant devotion of the Baroque and preferred a simpler piety of the heart. It also stressed the essentials of the faith. The veneration of the saints was in its eyes good and commendable, as long as one did not lose sight of Jesus Christ. Yet a number of Catholic Enlighteners thought that many popular practices, in particular Marian devotions, had exactly that effect. While for Alphonsus of Liguori the figure of Mary offered a way to learn how to love Jesus, for others his piety seemed irrational or at least unbiblical. The clearest outline for a recalibration of the veneration of the saints was written by the former Benedictine monk Benedict Werkmeister in his book *To the Immodest Admirers of Mary* (1801). His aim was to convince the "immodest admirers" of Mary and other saints that their actions were either abuses of proper devotional practices, superstition, or exaggerations. Werkmeister was concerned that some ordinary faithful "worshipped" the saints, although the Council of Trent had prescribed that Catholics only worshipped God and "venerated" the saints. Moreover, he reminded Catholics that the council did not require Catholics to venerate the saints but simply stated the usefulness of this practice. Only if the saints were understood properly could church leaders eradicate misunderstandings such as the idea that the saints were somehow "mediators" between the faithful and God. Consequently, Werkmeister was also critical of a veneration of relics: "Enlightened Catholics consider these things as nothing but toys of the masses, and it would be time to open the eyes of the masses about this."[8]

Werkmeister particularly detested the popular practice of invoking the saints' aid for temporal goods such as a good harvest or a cow's safe delivery, and called them "shameful" and "immoral." Yet by ridiculing others, he made his own position look elitist and detached from the needs of the common man—a major problem for most Enlighteners. "Do some people fear God would … not listen if we go to him directly?" Werkmeister asked, not unreasonably. But the question misses a deeper point.[9] While Alphonsus tried gently to teach his flock to come to an appreciation of the love of Christ through Mary and the saints, Werkmeister robbed the faithful of their simple devotional practices instead of slowly reforming them. His position on the veneration of Mary shows that Werkmeister lacked a pastoral sensibility: Marian feasts should be abolished, prayers from approved books and tradition should be erased, and the rosary should be banned as a fantastic invention, he argued. Unlike all saints since the Middle Ages, who held the rosary in high esteem as a form of meditative, biblical prayer, he perceived it as a "brainless mechanism."[10] Praying was, for Werkmeister, always an act of the intellect. There was no room in his mind for the common prayers of the faithful.

The Limits of Government, or Martyrs of the Confessional

One of the most crucial demands of Enlightenment thought and politics, often called "Enlightened despotism," was that because the state was responsible for the welfare of its people it had broad authority over nearly all areas of life. Since religious matters were seen as essential to the people's welfare, states attempted to control as many aspects of religious life as possible. This trend can be observed in practically all early modern states, regardless of confession, from Portugal to Poland, from Naples to the Netherlands. The church, not far removed from the great struggles for supremacy in the Middle Ages, felt as if it were being attacked. It had won those earlier battles, but its moral and political reputation had suffered tremendously during the Avignon papacy and the Western Schism (1377–1415). Since the Reformation, the political influence of the papacy had sunk even more, and was now, in the eighteenth century, at its lowest point ever. What could the church do to defend its rights against the overburdening pressure of the state? After all, the appointment of bishops and priests, the blueprint of dioceses, the life of monasteries and religious orders, the printing and publishing of religious books, the communication of the pope with the faithful—seemingly every aspect of Catholicism was on trial.

Pope Benedict XIII acted in 1728–1729. He tried to install the commemoration day for his medieval predecessor Gregory VII, who had begun elevating papal authority over secular powers, as a worldwide feast day.

The prayer for this event, however, not only stated Gregory's virtues but also mentioned his fight for the primacy of the pope. This was perceived as a direct attack on national pride in France, where the church obeyed the pope in spiritual affairs but was in all other respects governed by the king. Other countries also refused to accept Gregory VII as a saint, seeing him instead as a power-hungry pope and vicious man.

Another example, a few decades later, was the struggle in Austria, northern Italy, and Bavaria over criminal clergymen and nuns. If a monk committed a crime, the prior usually locked him up in a prison cell within his monastery, often without a proper trial. The modern state, however, claimed to have the exclusive right to punish offenders. The state argued that it could not protect the rights of its citizens if an organization such as the church was allowed to run private and secret prisons. Thus, in 1769 and in the years afterward, many states in Central Europe abolished monastic prisons. In the coming decades, more and more ecclesiastical privileges would be abolished.[11]

The most direct attack on Catholic doctrine, however, came when the state attempted to compromise the sacraments. Besides marriage, the sacrament that was most contentious for the state was confession, since some princes claimed that no priest should have the right to refuse to answer his sovereign by invoking the sanctity of the confessional. It was, one could say, an assault on the pride of a ruler. The patron saint of confessors is St. John Nepomuk. This fourteenth-century Bohemian general vicar of the archdiocese of Prague was drowned in the river Moldau for not revealing the sins that the queen, the wife of King Wenceslaus IV, had confessed. Although he was venerated in Bohemia for centuries as a saint, he had not been officially canonized. Now, in the eighteenth century he proved to be the perfect saint to remind the state of its limits. On March 13, 1729, following a thorough investigation, as the rules of the church required, Pope Innocent XIII declared the Bohemian priest a saint. The investigation included a medical investigation (carried out a decade earlier) of the body of the saint, who was buried in the Prague Cathedral. When his coffin was opened, medical doctors verified the identity of the person buried and the likely cause of death (one could see that he had suffered a severe blow to his head as one would expect from the fall from a bridge that the legend reports). Yet something puzzled the investigators. The tongue of the saint had not decomposed. Instead it was dried out and gray and naturally preserved. For future investigations, it was placed in a glass container, and the grave again sealed. A few years later, when it was clear that nothing impeded the saint's canonization, the tomb was reopened. When the doctors took the tongue out of its container, however, it suddenly changed color, from gray to red. In order to make sure that the lighting of the room was not playing tricks, the tongue was placed on a piece of paper. Inspection showed no dyes or other evidence of tampering, and the tongue remained reddish. All surgeons agreed that the sudden change of color could not be explained scientifically. A miracle had occurred that verified the value of the confessional secrecy: the saint had not violated the seal of confession. His tongue had remained silent. The man who was in charge of the whole investigation was none other than the future pope Benedict XIV, Cardinal Prospero Lambertini, who stressed the importance of reliable miracle stories for sainthood.[12] To elevate Nepomuk as the first martyr who died for the confessional was not just a theological message about the importance of the confessional seal but also a political statement that the authority of the state did not extend to the sacraments. The state has no right to pressure priests to give up what Christ demanded must be kept sacred. This principle had not only been under attack by the state but also had been tarnished by immoral priests in Portugal. Nepomuk's canonization led the Holy Inquisition to prosecute clerical violators with the greatest severity.[13]

It took only a few decades until the next martyr died for the exact same reason—put to death on the direct, personal command of a man whom Europe celebrated as enlightened. In 1757 Andreas Faulhaber, a forty-six-year-old priest of the archdiocese of Breslau, became preacher and assistant pastor to his older brother in the city of Glatz. The county of Glatz belonged to Bohemia and thus to the Habsburg territories of the Austrian archduchess and empress Maria Theresa. However, in the third Silesian War, it came under the control of the Prussian philosopher king Frederick II, who had annexed great parts of Silesia in 1740. In the little county castle of Glatz, Austrian troops were interned, yet in September 1757 two prisoners, Josef Rentwig and Johann Veit, escaped. Both were afraid of being punished if they were caught by the Prussians. Prisoners of war were spared if they accepted their internment until a peace treaty was signed; but if they escaped they were to be treated as deserters and subjected to capital punishment. When Rentwig was arrested, he tried to save himself and placed the blame on Andreas Faulhaber. According to Rentwig, he had confessed his plans to escape to the priest but had not been warned about the consequences or been persuaded to stay. He had supposedly asked the priest: "Is it a great sin if I desert and do not keep my oath to a Lutheran king although I am Catholic?" The priest allegedly answered: "Of course this is a great sin, but not too big to be forgiven." Faulhaber was immediately arrested and interrogated. Yet all he could say was ""I cannot confess anything and will not confess anything, and that is because of the sanctity of the sacrament of confession and my priestly dignity." Although soon even military personnel came to the conclusion that Rentwig had lied to save his skin, the investigation continued; meanwhile, Rentwig had a change of heart and confessed to having lied. Initially, the judges refused to accept the recantation of his confession but were forced to when he swore an oath. The judge declared the priest innocent. But this was not the end of the story.

General Heinrich August de la Motte Fouqué took the files with him, and nine days later Rentwig again accused Faulhaber, this time claiming that the priest had said the oath did "not matter much." Faulhaber again refused to speak about anything that had happened in the confessional. He was again found innocent but was advised to take a lawyer and was soon incarcerated. Imprisoned among murderers and thieves, Faulhaber continued to serve as a priest. He shared his food with them, tried to console them, and prayed with them. On December 29 a messenger reached the city with secret orders from the king. A rumor spread that the next day a spy should be hanged. On the morning of December 30 Faulhaber told his fellow inmates of a dream he had had—he was supposed to accompany a prisoner to his execution. A few hours later he found out that he was the prisoner to be executed. The king's decree explicitly forbade Faulhaber to receive last rites—a final arrogant act of deviance according to Catholic beliefs. When he was asked to take off his cassock he refused, declaring defiantly: "The King has not given me my clergyman's cloak, so he cannot take it either." Only when a Catholic officer implored him to take it off did he finally do so. A simple coat over his shoulders and a brass cross in his hands, he climbed the scaffold. His last words were supposedly: "Oh happy day, oh happy hour! Be happy, my heart, for you are a temple of the Holy Spirit!" Then, after the official sentence was read, he was hanged. An official funeral was, as for every traitor, denied. The body remained on the scaffold until the Austrians recaptured the city two years later.

Frederick the Great is often venerated as a king who propagated tolerance, yet he hated Catholics, and in particular the Catholics of Silesia and the surrounding regions; he questioned their loyalty to his crown. Frederick and his generals had long desired to punish the Catholic clergy, whom they despised for their alleged loyalty to the Catholic Habsburgs.

The Faulhaber case was the long-awaited opportunity to threaten the church to rethink its political allegiance. That Faulhaber downplayed the importance of an oath compared with the salvation of one's soul hurt the self-esteem of the Prussian king. Would it not have invited chaos in his army if more priests or even Protestant pastors had followed his example? One cannot but help associate this episode with the conscientious struggle in which Prussian officers found themselves during the Second World War: could they break their oath and assassinate Hitler without committing a grave sin? Could such an act ever be forgiven even if the commander-in-chief was a moral monster? Last, the question remains whether Faulhaber was a real martyr. For him to be recognized as such, one would have to establish that he was killed because of hatred for his Catholic faith. Frederick's inhumane command that deprived Faulhaber of the consolation of a priest and a final opportunity to receive the Eucharist, seems to be sufficient evidence to assume such hatred.[14]

The Holy Spirit Rekindled

Most Catholics of the eighteenth century had only a lukewarm relationship to the Holy Spirit. Of course, the Spirit was present in the arts, even in popular art such the Holy Spirit glass balls that hung over most dinner tables in central Bavaria and symbolized the blessing of the family table. Liturgically, however, only once a year, on the feast of Pentecost, did the church seem to commemorate explicitly the third person of the Trinity. Then the hymn "Come, Creator Spirit" was sung while the priests, dressed in red vestments, celebrated a Mass in honor of the Spirit. Veneration of the Holy Spirit was also observable on certain special occasions, such as at the election Mass for a new pope and the feast days for religious confraternities. Believed to be the power that drives the church, that changes bread and wine into the body and blood of Christ, and that endows the sacraments with supernatural power, the Spirit, of course, was invoked in every prayer. Nevertheless, a personal relationship with the Holy Spirit was not on the devotional horizon. Even theologians had remarkably few things to say about the Spirit. Yet the eighteenth century brought forth a saint who tried to remedy this neglect—and she was a woman.

Crescentia Höss came from humble origins. Her parents were weavers and thus among the poorest residents of the city of Kaufbeuren. Mathias Höss, her father, was a pious man who was formed by the spiritual exercises of St. Ignatius and also by Baroque devotional practices, such as self-flagellation and other forms of mortification of the body, through which one could collect "merits." These merits, many believed, would help in obtaining eternal salvation. Traces of this piety can also be found in the life of Crescentia after she entered the Franciscan convent in Kaufbeuren; the convent accepted her only because the Protestant mayor of the city strongly recommended her, even though she did not bring any dowry to the cloister. Accounts also testify that despite her love for the nuns and for everybody who approached her, she had only contempt for anything worldly, including images of herself. On her deathbed she even implored the nuns to throw her corpse onto the dungheap![15] Convent life, however, was Crescentia's greatest cross. Most nuns initially hated her. When she was a novice her virtues, especially her love and obedience, were so perfect that she was a constant reminder to the other nuns of their negligence and lack of devotion. The prioress and the majority of the convent therefore invented ever more painful "tests" of Crescentia's virtues. Nobody stopped this hazing; instead, the confessors and other Franciscan monks encouraged them as a way to eradicate vice and vanity. For three years they even deprived her of her own cell and a bed, making her sleep on the floor in the corner of a room. The hardest, most physically demanding, dirtiest tasks were always hers, and she was not welcome at the common meal. It comes as no surprise that the physically and emotionally distressed nun often collapsed—yet her superiors saw in this "behavior" mere "viciousness." As punishment she was ordered to play the monastery jester, only to be punished for her inappropriate conduct. Some young nuns tried to convince her that she was not bound to obey such orders, but Crescentia believed that the prioress represented Christ and had to be obeyed, no matter how silly, painful, inhumane, or demeaning her wishes were. Not until ten years later, in 1714, did the situation change under a new prioress. Crescentia now became the spiritual center of the community. Soon she became known as a mystic and visionary, and after the death of the Munich Carmelite mystic Maria Anna Lindmayr, the Kaufbeuren convent successfully established their house as a new center of mysticism. Like Crescentia, Lindmayr had visions that portrayed the Holy Spirit as a young man with curly hair, his head surrounded by seven tongues of fire, as opposed to the traditional depiction of a dove.

When Pope Benedict XIV heard rumors of Crescentia's alleged miracles and visions, he decided to investigate the case. After all, already as a cardinal he had established clear criteria for establishing the authenticity of miracles, visions, and saintly life. A theological commission was formed in 1744 to investigate the nun shortly after her death. Eusebius Amort, the most prominent German Catholic Enlightenment theologian, headed it, along with Giovanni Battista Bassi. Both were extremely skeptical, as they had both been formed by the Catholic Enlightenment. They set out to decide whether Höss had lived the Christian virtues and whether she had possessed any supernatural gifts.[16]

They found that she had experienced visions of the Holy Spirit since her earliest childhood days. The first one seems to date between her third and fourth birthday, when she was alone in the garden of her parents. She held an apple in her hands when the Spirit appeared as a young man and took her to a paradisial garden. At other times Christ appeared to her in the shape of a child. Both kept her company throughout her adolescence. The Spirit came back often and taught her how to pray and how to grow in the virtues. He encouraged her to go to Eucharistic adoration, even during the daily chores in the cloister. When a fellow nun asked her if they could leave their work behind and attend, she replied that they should go "in spirit." "Just like when you pluck a piece of thread, think of Christ when he is tortured and the soldiers pluck his beard ... when you make threads, think that you are creating the true bonds of love in order to attract the heart of Jesus."[17]

It was her way of loving God in all things that ultimately made Crescentia a saint. The only criterion for canonization was that she lived the virtues and her Christian life heroically. The fact that she did not leave any written records of her visions behind proved relatively unproblematic because even the critical investigators judged them, reported by others, as ordinary. However, the theologians found her alleged kidnappings by demons or persecutions by the devil to be the result of hysteria and superstition. Nevertheless, the examiners could only testify that she must have been a profoundly spiritual person, who lived and loved heroically. Even in her last illnesses, she showed superhuman patience in enduring great pain. When, during her last weeks, she was offered a strengthening drink, she refused: "The will of God is sufficient strengthening for me."[18]

The biggest obstacle to her canonization was also her most remarkable insight: her worship of the Holy Spirit. Like most who received private revelations, she was suspected of bypassing the church's tradition and teaching. Catholic officials feared that a direct communication with

God could easily lead mystics to condone immoral behavior or heretical ideas: some false saints had legitimized illicit sexual relations by pointing out that God was working through them so that their actions could not be sinful.[19] While the painting in the Carmelite church in Munich based on Lindmayr's visions depicts the Trinity consisting of Father, Son, and Spirit as three men, pictures of Crescentia's vision showed the Spirit alone. It was simply the portrait of a young man with tongues of fire around his head. This made Pope Benedict XIV wary. After all, the Holy Spirit was according to the creed "breathed by the Father and the Son," and was thus unthinkable without them. He was the loving relationship between the two, who subsists as a person. If one showed him separately, one could easily charge Catholics with worshipping three different Gods. Höss claimed to have seen the Holy Spirit in the form of a young man and Christ in his passion behind bars.[20] When artists disseminated pictures that followed her description, theologians countered that such images had never been used in the church, and indeed Pope Benedict XIV expressed his displeasure in his brief *Sollecitudini Nostrae* of 1745. Nowhere in the Christian tradition was the Holy Spirit worshipped in isolation from the other two persons of the Trinity; such a new iconographic theology was a breach of tradition, he argued. Three years later, when in Altdorf painter Matthäus Günther depicted the Holy Spirit as a man clothed in royal garb with flames around his head, he could do so because he circumvented the papal admonition by also depicting the Father and the Son. In 1928, the Roman Curia decreed once and for all that Catholics cannot tolerate new pictures of the Holy Spirit as a human person.[21]

The approval to begin Crescentia's beatification process in 1775 was not based on any of her visions or on her supernatural encounters, but instead on the sober notion that she had died with the reputation of a saint—a person of heroic virtue. She became a saint despite her mystical visions, not because of them. It is this feature that makes her a good example of a changing religiosity of the eighteenth century, a religiosity that was still rooted in the Baroque but with a new appreciation for virtuous holiness, which other Tridentine reformers such as St. Francis de Sales also espoused. Through Höss, however, the church was reminded of the extent to which it had neglected the worship of the third person of the Trinity, and which would only be resuscitated in the twentieth century.

The "Preferential Option for the Poor"
and Oppressed

A few years after the Revolution, America was shocked at the news that an ordained Congregationalist minister, who had served during the War of Independence, had converted to Catholicism. In the spring of 1783, John Thayer traveled to Rome to dispel the myths about Catholic miracles and other such nonsense. His critical and theological mind was particularly offended by the case of a beggar named Benedict Labre, who had recently died and was being venerated like a saint. Miracle after miracle occurred at his gravesite in Rome, Thayer had heard. So he began collecting evidence, visiting the witnesses of such miraculous cures, and consulting medical doctors about these cases. Instead of proving the miracles wrong, he found the evidence for them overwhelming. Shortly thereafter, he became a Catholic.

Benedict Labre was born to a farming family in Amettes, France, in 1748. He demonstrated precocious intelligence, so his parents sacrificed to send their eldest son to private school. Benedict's uncle, a priest, took him in and trained the twelve-year-old in Latin and religious instruction. By living with him, Benedict learned what was expected from a country priest: saying Mass, visiting the sick and dying, hearing confessions, marrying young couples, and instructing schoolchildren. He also learned about the spiritual writers of the day, including some close to Jansenism. The seventeenth-century writer Père Le Jeune especially impressed him and motivated him to practice extreme mortification. He saw his life as an exercise of penance and expiation to gain heaven and to avoid hell. It became clear to him that the best and most secure way of obtaining his goal was to join a religious community, where he could concentrate on the spiritual battle with regular prayer and admonition. Yet he was not sure which order, because he was impressed by Le Jeune's exhortation not only to do penance but also to give heroically to the poor. He wanted to be like the "chosen soul" St. Vincent de Paul, selected by God for heaven: "The chosen soul, when he finds a poor man in the street, filthy, lacerated, wan, stinking and covered in vermin, brings him into his house, sets him near his fire, washes him and puts him to rights; a worldly soul would find this astounding. Whence is the difference? The chosen soul knows the hidden meaning of poverty."[22]

The acknowledgment of the poor as an important reminder of Christ was also present in the theology of the great theologian-bishop Jacques

Bossuet. In a famous homily of 1659 he even spoke of the "eminent dignity of the poor." Since the world had abandoned the poor, God would take up their defense, and because people scorn them, God will "raise up their dignity." The poor were, for Bossuet, the most genuine citizens of the church, because it is they whom Christ addressed most directly. Because Christ emphasized the poor so much, Bossuet was convinced that only through them and the sacraments did heavenly grace flow on earth. Society is not just called to help them out of pity but to have "great sentiments of respect" for them as they are the "firstborn" of the church.[23]

Benedict Labre was fascinated by what twentieth-century liberation theologians would call a "preferential option for the poor." Yet to see in a beggar the image of the firstborn of the church took a supernatural amount of willpower. The smell and the vermin on them made even the young Labre nauseous. He began to share his food and money with them, and to take care of their sick. He revolted against the commonplace notion that beggars are the outcasts of society. The Enlighteners wanted to lock them all up, force them to work, or punish them violently until they changed their behavior. Philosophers, in general, showed no mercy toward the poor. They certainly wanted to end poverty, but with the most inhuman means. The church, on the other hand, valued the poor in principle; as Bossuet's homily shows, it gave alms and set up institutions for their betterment, but ultimately did not wholeheartedly commit to reform unjust social structures. Benedict, however, wanted to fulfill what the church assented to and what the Franciscan friars, and in modernity in particular the Capuchin Friars, were practicing.[24]

Benedict Labre believed that if he joined a religious order the vow of poverty would make him one of the poor and thus secure his path to salvation. It was only natural that he desired to join the strictest of all Catholic orders, the Carthusians. The monks of St. Bruno of Cologne were known to live like hermits, in complete silence, poverty, and fasting, but also as especially holy men, whom the riches of the church had not corrupted. The prior, however, considered the young man too frail and not yet educated enough to join the order. After a year of intense studies with a rural priest his parents had chosen, without access to any more books on mystical theology, Benedict was finally allowed to enter the monastery as a novice. He left a few weeks later. He had "fallen into misery," so deeply depressed that he could no longer stand life as a monk. Living again with his parents, he continued to chastise his body, as many Baroque saints did, with chains and flagellations, until his parents finally allowed him to join the Trappists. After weeks of painful travel on foot, Labre reached La Trappe only to be refused: the abbot would not receive him, but instead asked him to return in a few years. Perhaps then he would show signs of a real vocation and a better physical stature. Labre was heartbroken but did not give up. At home he declared that he would try again to enter La Trappe and, if refused again, would then seek to enter the monastery of Septfonts. Since the local bishop admonished Labre to follow his parents' wishes, he tried again to join the Carthusians in 1769, and succeeded. Yet, after a few months, he was dismissed.[25] As he was too young to be accepted in La Trappe, in November 1769 he entered the Trappist monastery of Septfonts as a novice. Yet his prayer life again became "paralyzed," and he slipped into a state of despair and desolation, with excessive feelings of sin and guilt. His fellow monks began to question his sanity and in 1770 asked him to leave. He had already left his family several times, and each time he entered a religious order he thought he had followed God's voice. Labre was devastated. Not knowing what to do, he sought spiritual counsel and, as a result, undertook a pilgrimage to Rome.

Pilgrimages reached their peak during the Enlightenment, despite the sharp attacks of the Enlighteners, who thought them a waste of time and money and temptation to debauchery. It is certainly true that many participants sought in a pilgrimage not so much spiritual goods, such as the presence of the sacred in their lives, but worldly ones. By traveling the countryside people got to know the world, had their first sexual encounters, and found amusement at pilgrim fairs or in the big city. Even so, one should not underestimate the importance of pilgrimages for dealing with personal hardships. By traveling to a certain shrine, a pilgrim could, for a short time, perhaps only a few days, distance himself from the pressing needs of daily existence, reflect on his own needs and personal desires in the light of the sacred, and thus gain a new perspective on life.[26]

At the end of the century, however, pilgrims were often mistaken for beggars and therefore arrested and lumped together with suspicious tramps in prisons. This is exactly what happened to Benedict Labre, who found himself among the beggars he had once pitied, and was likewise humiliated and scorned. He had not given up his plan to enter a monastery. In fact, he would try just that in Italy; again in vain. So he remained on pilgrimage, waiting for God to make his plan clear. From 1770 to 1777 he traveled to all the great shrines of Europe, poor like a beggar, preaching the Gospel by his actions and simple but kind words, including exhortations from the Bible, which he always had with him. He once explained to an Italian woman: "To love God you need three hearts in one: a heart of fire for him, a heart of flesh for your neighbor, and a heart of bronze for yourself." When begging, he would only accept the bare minimum to sustain his life: "What we need is very little; all the rest goes to feed the worms."[27] Labre came to Rome for the seventh time in 1777, sleeping in one of its famous landmarks. The city was, as usual, swarming with beggars, so nobody took notice of the man who soon was nicknamed "the beggar of the Colosseum." He had often been treated with disrespect, denounced as a religious fanatic, spat at or pushed aside. Such hazing was constant. Nonetheless, the priests who knew him, as well as hundreds more, venerated him as a saint when he died, still homeless, during Holy Week of 1783. Yet the people of Rome mourned: "The saint is dead! The saint is dead!"[28] Instantaneously, a veneration of his body began: his last garments, rotten and vermin-infested, became relics. He had been canonized by popular acclamation long before his official canonization in 1881. During the reign of terror following the French Revolution, his fellow countrymen looked up to "their" strange saint for protection and intercession.

Not everyone was impressed. Benedict Labre became the laughing-stock of the philosophers. Some even spread the rumor that he had been a Jansenist. A leading German Enlightenment journal published an essay titled "Labre's Stupidity." The author, Peter Adolph Winkopp, a former monk, explained his rejection of Labre in this way: "Revelation and reason command to work, if one can, to live cleanly and not like a pig, to fulfill one's duties towards society and not to become a burden to her. A person who does not fulfill such rudimentary duties cannot be pleasing to God, cannot be called 'venerable,' and even less 'saintly.' "[29] For Winkopp, who had become a radical Catholic Enlightener, Labre was an idle, filthy tramp who belonged either in prison or in a madhouse. It was irresponsible, he claimed, to recommend such a man as a role model. To do so would seduce the faithful to become idle and parasitic on the state. In addition, Winkopp brought forth a philosophical argument. God would use always the simplest means to reveal his truth, and thus would not work miracles if there were other ways. If somebody has a tumor, then he needs a surgeon and not a holy card. Thus, according to Catholic doctrine, miracles are rare and can only be established after a careful scientific and theological investigation. But Labre's gravesite was used by the Romans as a universal "medicine" against blindness, deafness, tumors, stroke, epilepsy, lameness, fistulas, cancer, and more. The sheer number of miraculous healings supported the view that the whole affair was fraudulent. Like most Enlighteners, however, Winkopp felt that he belonged to the educated elite. As all miracles happened in front of simple, uneducated people, not in front of critical, intelligent Enlighteners, how could one believe them? Another journal decried that the church probably buried Labre with all honors "because he was a tramp and a bad citizen."[30] The German Enlightener Christian Salzmann even wrote that in Berlin or Vienna Labre would have been arrested for idleness.[31]

According to secular Enlightenment critics, the church was supporting idleness, lack of hygiene, and superstitious enthusiasm. The pope should have arrested the beggar and put him in a workhouse. A beggar was, in the eyes of the Enlightener, a worthless human being. When Pope Pius VI allowed pilgrims to come to Labre's gravesite, the world understood this as "canonization," although he was not added to the calendar of saints until 1881. Pius's action was a slap in the face to the enlightened elite of Europe, a hurtful reminder that Jesus himself had always elevated the lowly. The pope made clear that the church had, as twentieth-century liberation theology would call it, a "preferential option for the poor."

Benedict Labre is *the* anti-Enlightenment saint. He embodies radical discipleship in the footsteps of Jesus. No other saint since Francis of Assisi was known to have become so poor. Labre, who was found too frail to be a monk and too weak to work with his hands, gathered, despite extreme bodily mortification, the strength to walk several times through Europe while serving his fellow beggars. He was a thorn in the flesh of Enlightenment philosophy: he was either too weak or too asocial to work, they argued. For the church he symbolized the opposite, namely, the medieval appreciation of the beggar as an exemplar of Christ, and the affirmation that there are no useless people.

Gentleness and Practical Wisdom

Despite the fact that Jansenists proposed a number of interesting reforms and emphasized the ideal of a poor church, it also taught a rigorist moralism. According to Jansenists, the elect of God were predestined from eternity and endowed with grace and therefore could act virtuously, while those who were predestined to hell lacked such grace and could never obtain it. This view also influenced many Catholic moral theologians, who argued that in a situation in which a law or obligation is doubtful, one must always follow the letter of the law, unless one could prove the law was wrong. There could never be any reasonable doubt about what to do. Rigorism was a reaction to Jesuit laxity. The Jesuits, however, did not defend lax morals but only argued that, in cases of doubt, one did not have to follow the law if one could give reasonable arguments for one's actions. This teaching was called *probabilism*. The Jansenists successfully portrayed the Jesuits as destroying Christian morality. The result was that probabilism steadily receded and rigorist positions took root. Confessors in the Italian countryside of the eighteenth century were known for their Jansenist sympathies and thus we should not be surprised that they even withheld absolution in the confessional if the penitent only repented out of fear of going to hell. According to sacramental theology, this was called imperfect contrition or attrition, but the Council of Trent had accepted it as minimum requirement for the sacrament of reconciliation. Perfect contrition included sorrow over one's sins because they offended God and the will to improve oneself. For the Jansenists only perfect contrition was a gift from God. Attrition was worthless. Therefore, a person who approached the confessional only with attrition could be refused absolution because such a person was not filled by grace to receive the sacrament. The results were devastating. People who were never fully catechized in their faith were rejected and left with the burden of mortal sins, which they believed would exclude them from eternal life. Sooner or later many of them abandoned the faith, or they despaired. In the eighteenth century one saint stood up to change this: Alphonsus of Liguori. Alphonsus is the official patron saint of moral theologians and was made the first modern doctor of the church, but he remains little read among academic theologians today. This is surprising, because the saint's works are remarkably modern.

Alphonsus was born into a noble family in Naples, and nobody thought he would become a clergyman. Instead, his parents agreed that he should either join the military or become a lawyer. He chose the latter and studied at the University of Naples, where the famous Enlightenment thinker and father of modern philosophy of history, Giambattista Vico, was among his teachers. When Alphonsus lost his first case in 1723, he underwent a spiritual transformation and decided to become a priest. In the first years of his service he learned to know the needs of the rural population and tried to address them, like Paul of the Cross, in "missions." In 1731, he founded a new religious order, the Redemptorists. Its motto was and is: "With him there is plentiful redemption." It means that with and in Christ everybody can be saved. This was the message Alphonsus wanted to bring to a world that was either too busy with physical work to think much about redemption or rejected it because of feelings of unworthiness. In order to reach out to Catholics who had been abandoned by their priests, he also wrote 111 books and pamphlets between 1728 and 1778, many of which remain in print.[32]

The first theme of Alphonsus's theology could be summarized simply: redemption is real. He believed that humans can change and that the sacraments, together with proper catechization, had the power to bring such transformation about. How could a poor soul who had been refused absolution improve her ways if she lacks the power of the sacrament? He argued vehemently against the moral rigorism that left so many abandoned and burdened. A priest should never withhold absolution if the penitent showed signs of remorse, because if he does he only freezes the sinner in her ways and perhaps motivates her to despise the other sacraments as well.[33] It was for those who had been rejected that he wrote many of his spiritual treatises, such as his 1745 Visits to the Blessed Sacrament. This work illustrates well his conviction that everybody can be saved and that—and here he follows his hero, the Catholic reformer St. Francis de Sales—everybody is called to holiness. The latter message had been forgotten in the first third of the eighteenth century. Now, in a time of spiritual renewal, it once again became a central focus of the church, especially in parish missions. If holiness meant the transformation of a sinner into a person who truly loves God, then, Alphonsus thought, one would have to teach how to love God. Unlike other contemporary theologians, Alphonsus was convinced that loving God had to be simple. He recommended the Eucharist as a first step. Just as one visits a friend often, so the believer should visit Christ often through the Eucharist. There he could begin to enter a dialogue with God:

> Prayer is communication with God. In your own simple words tell him your feelings, your desires, your fears and what you wish to receive from him. In return, the Lord speaks to your heart, making you aware of his infinite goodness, his love for you and what you should do to make yourselves pleasing to him.[34]

According to Jansenists, God had chosen only a few for heaven and had predestined the rest for hell. According to Alphonsus, however, every person had received sufficient support (grace) from God to pray, and with prayer even more graces, and thus salvation, were obtainable. His greatest bestseller, *The Glories of Mary* (1750), was translated into about eighty languages and printed in countless editions in hundreds of thousands, if not millions, of copies. The book was controversial because Catholic Enlighteners found that it went beyond the legitimate boundaries for the veneration of Mary. Some found that he introduced a competition between Mary and Jesus as to who really saves humanity, while others charged him with making Mary part of the Trinity. Neither accusation is correct. The book is certainly full of hyperbole for Mary as the "refuge for sinners" or as "co-redeemer," but his goal is to show God's love. Alphonsus knew from many encounters with people in the countryside that if one began preaching about "loving Jesus" most would close their ears and hearts. Jesus was for them too high to reach; he was the Christ and savior, but one could not have a real, personal, intimate relationship with him. The founder of the Redemptorists set out to change that. Through Mary, those who felt abandoned, who did not dare to lift up their hearts to Jesus, could experience God's love and thus arrive in the arms of Jesus Christ. The idea of a personal relationship with Jesus was a theme of the eighteenth century—in Pietism, Methodism, and other awakening movements that spread over Europe and the Americas. Alphonsus, however, did not found a new church but reformed his old one. His remarkable little book of 1768, *The Practice of the Love of Jesus Christ*, is probably the most evangelical book a Catholic theologian had ever written until that point. Like Methodist or Pietist theologians of his time, Alphonsus emphasized the personal encounter with Christ and the inner conversion of the sinner. Like St. Ignatius and other masters of prayer—but much more practical—Alphonsus encouraged his readers to use their imagination to bring Holy Scripture alive. One's emotions and desires are not shut off during prayer, but opened up to God, so that the whole person can be transformed. No one before him had ever taken the time and energy to teach ordinary Catholics such profound truths, and nobody before him had taken emotions so seriously.

Alphonsus of Liguori, the apostle of a gentle, people-oriented theology, died in 1787, not having seen the fruits of his work. His religious order lay in disarray, divided by internal conflict. After his death, the Redemptorists somewhat distorted the heritage of their founder by portraying Alphonsus as a staunch defender of papal claims, and they also forgot much of his message.[35] Alphonsus's gentleness in dealing with sinners in the confessional, where he gave them practical advice without condescension, contrasts with the hard-hearted reforms many Enlighteners proposed, which not only demonstrated their ignorance of the living conditions of the unprivileged but also their elitist indifference to their suffering.

Jansenist Miracles

France also had its enthusiasts but could never equal the number of miraculous shrines and events found in eighteenth-century Spain, Germany, or Poland. One reason was that French Catholicism had, through its early interaction with Protestantism, become more austere, more centered on the essentials, on interior piety and devotion, and much less ostentatious. It was a "classical" Catholicism that differed dramatically from Catholicism in Spain or Italy, where the faithful still preferred public penance, lavish processions, and other forms of Baroque piety. Yet a contemporary remarked that the political situation in France also helped to prevent new enthusiastic pilgrimages to miraculous sites. False miracles were considered sacrilege in France, punished by the secular courts. As a result, France was almost free of such supernatural events.[36] This was almost, but not entirely, because in the midst of the eighteenth century even the otherwise rational French church was shaken by a series of miracles that happened not to good and devout Catholics but to the Jansenists, who the pope had labeled heretics.

The Jansenists, however, considered themselves the only true, faithful Catholics, since in their view the "rest" of the church had abandoned its crucial doctrines on predestination at the Council of Trent. Cornelius Jansen argued that the church had deviated from the teachings of its most important Church Father, St. Augustine. According to Jansen, nobody could fulfill God's commands by his own power; one always needed divine assistance, that is, grace. This grace was given to humans with irresistible force, which meant that one could not refuse it. This seemed to eradicate human freedom. However, for Jansen, one was sufficiently free as long as one was not compelled to do this or that; even if grace itself was irresistible, it did not force a person to perform certain actions and thus left the individual sufficient freedom. Most important, the bishop denied that Christ died "for all" and instead argued that he died only for the elect. While Jansenism emphasized the depravity and wickedness of the human person in the fallen world, the Jesuits viewed the world much more optimistically. They believed that the human person was fallen and inclined to sin but could still achieve good by her own powers. Jansenists attracted followers by their example more than by their doctrine. By living very austere lives, following a rigorist and moralist code, referring to the Bible in the vernacular, they became an impressive protest movement. However, they did not protest just Catholic teaching but also the corruption and decline of Catholic morals. The church should repent, give away its riches, abandon its privileged status, and become again the poor church of the apostles. Such a lifestyle, such simplicity and purity, was attractive, and men such as Blaise Pascal, the great mathematician and philosopher, were staunch defenders of Jansenism. In 1713, Pope Clement XI prohibited Jansenism, and French law soon followed. The Jansenists, however, did not give up. They appealed to courts, ran their own underground journal, and held to their beliefs. In 1731 heaven seemed to have taken their side when miraculous cures occurred at the Paris gravesite of a Jansenist deacon, François de Pâris.[37]

The first miraculous cure happened during the deacon's funeral, when a woman, whose right arm had been paralyzed for twenty-five years, was instantaneously healed when she touched the coffin.[38] Jansenists set out to prove the credibility of the miracle accounts. That the church rejected such miracles in the St. Médard cemetery was therefore considered proof that it had apostatized from true faith.[39] The situation became even more complicated when, from 1731 onward, regular convulsions happened at the gravesite: pilgrims fell to the ground with contorted grimaces, yelling and screaming for hours on end: "Police reports described the sight as 'terrifying,' 'scandalous,' 'diabolical,' 'indecent,' and 'obscene.'"[40] According to the Jansenists, these events were proof that God was working through the deceased deacon to heal the bodies of those afflicted by sin and evil. In December 1731 some four thousand bystanders stared as several hundred were afflicted with convulsions. Tormented by their twitching, these Jansenists claimed that they were imitating Christ's passion as the only remaining true Catholics. The king ordered the cemetery to be closed, but this did not stop the "miracles," which continued to undermine his power. The healed now met in private séances, which often featured violent outbursts followed by police arrests. These activities split the Jansenist movement further and radicalized one wing to become even more subversive toward state and church authorities. Historian Dale van Kley even sees in Jansenism an overlooked root of the French Revolution.[41] Recently, the Jansenist contributions to the discussion of what constitutes virtue and a moral life have been rediscovered. Taking Jansenist thinking about saintliness seriously helps not only to enrich the scope of historical anthropology and intellectual history but also to identify its contributions to modernity, allowing us to understand ourselves better.[42]

Martyrs of the French Revolution

By insisting on toleration for their views, criticizing the crown for its persecution of Protestants, and undermining the divine rights of kings, Jansenists became a source of growing discontent in French politics and society. Many rural clergymen supported some aspects of Jansenist ideology, especially its pastoral ideals, which insisted on fair compensation for priests. When the Estates General were elected to solve France's dire fiscal and social problems in the spring of 1789, many priests, called *curés*, switched from the Second Estate for clergy to the ranks of the Third Estate of the commoners. Thus they not only demonstrated their disappointment in their bishops and prelates, who remained in the Second Estate, but also their support for a substantial reform of the country. But soon the Revolution turned against its former supporters. On October 28, 1789, all religious vows were suspended (permanently on February 13, 1790) and on November 2, 1789, all church property was confiscated for the benefit of the state. On July 12, 1790, the so-called Civil Constitution of the Clergy was passed by the National Assembly against the resistance of its 290 ecclesiastical members. It dissolved the traditional hierarchical church structures and replaced them with elected offices of bishops and pastors. For most clergy, this was an attack on the integrity of the church. The constitution was nevertheless an official law that required clergymen and nuns to accept it. Just as many had abstained from taking a similar oath during the English Reformation more than two hundred years earlier, many now, including 220 clergy members of the assembly, refused to sign it. Yet throughout the country, about 52 percent of the parish clergy accepted it.[43]

Among the most famous "refractory" nuns who rejected the oath were the Carmelites of Compiègne. In 1784, the monastery had elected a new prioress, Mother Theresa of Saint Augustine, or Mother Lidoine, a thirty-four-year-old nun. Interested in the history of her cloister, she found in the archives the report of a nun's dream from 1694. The nun had seen the scourged and suffering Jesus followed by four Carmelite nuns, robed in their habits. Only two nuns resisted "following the lamb."[44] The nun foresaw what would happen a hundred years later, when the

Carmelites of Compiègne would be executed. The prioress foresaw that God had a plan for the monastery that involved self-sacrifice by "following the lamb," the symbol of Christ in apocalyptic literature. Mother Lidoine shared her finding of this dream with her community on Easter 1792.

The Revolutionary government first intruded into the cloister of Compiègne in August 1790. Since religious vows were abolished, all nuns were free to leave, and government officials interviewed each of the eighteen members about their desire to stay. Many invoked their vocation to monastic life "until death." Pressure on the community grew when Pope Pius VI officially condemned the Civil Constitution of the Clergy in 1791, causing a schism in the French church between those who followed the pope and those who swore an oath on the constitution. Catholics who refused the oath were identified as royalists, since King Louis XVI had delayed signing it. The still-existing monasteries were full of men and women who abstained. Consequently, the government decreed all monasteries to be evacuated on August 4, 1792. Violent measures against the church increased. When the Prussian troops finally approached Paris in an attempt to overthrow the Revolutionary government in September 1792, a violent Parisian mob killed hundreds if not thousands of formerly imprisoned Catholics in a most gruesome manner. Stanford historian Dan Edelstein has argued persuasively that it was ideology, not wartime threat, that led to the massacres as well as to the reign of terror. The Revolutionaries believed that their ideology had freed human nature and restored its inherent rights. Critics of the Revolution were branded as "enemies of the human race" and declared pests of mankind. Because such an enemy had "reduced himself to the savage state of nature, by declaring war against all mankind, all mankind must declare war against him: so that every community has a [natural] right, by the rule of self-defense, to inflict" capital punishment upon him.[45] Arrests and executions became arbitrary.

Despite lacking a proper home, the nuns maintained their religious vocations. They rented small apartments and met for prayer. They were forbidden to wear their precious habit, but they were too poor to buy new clothes. Clothed in "unfashionable, second-hand-civilian clothes," the nuns renewed daily their promise to "follow the lamb."[46] In 1794, this phase of their lives came to an end. On June 22, all the nuns (except the three who were absent) were arrested and deported to Paris. There they were charged with "crimes" against the Revolution as well as religious fanaticism, because they adhered to the pope and rejected the constitutional church the Revolution had erected. The accusation bill was signed on July 16, the feast of Our Lady of Mount Carmel, the patron of their religious order. The little devotionals found in the nuns' possession; a picture of King Louis XVI, who was venerated by many as a martyr; and especially prints of the sacred heart of Jesus were associated with the Counter-Revolution and thus treasonous. None of the nuns was intimidated by their interrogators; instead, they all prayed together, and eyewitnesses confirm their joyous anticipation of the things to come. On July 17, the sixteen nuns were transported to their place of execution. On the way, they sang the psalms from their breviary. "Such a salutation of the guillotine was unprecedented. A visceral revulsion could usually be detected when the condemned arrived at the hideous, repugnant site with its loathsome smell. An unbearable stench emerged from a plank-covered pit of putrefying blood at the head of the scaffold."[47] Once they arrived, the singing did not stop. The nuns sang a hymn to the Holy Spirit while they one by one walked up to the guillotine to be beheaded.

The Carmelite nuns of Compiègne died because they did not accept the new, government-sponsored church. They never participated in any political revolt but only desired to live their vocation as cloistered nuns, in silence and solitude. The new totalitarian regime did not permit it. Soon after their execution they were invoked as saints but were not beatified until 1906. Hundreds of other religious men and women were killed for similar reasons.[48]

Conclusion

If one looks at the lives of the canonized saints of the eighteenth century, one cannot detect in them any meaningful engagement with Enlightenment. Nevertheless, they embody religious views that twenty-first century observers would describe as "modern." Their common characteristic was their excellence in what the Catholic Church calls heroic virtues. In the realm of saintliness, it is the lived virtues, not miracles or supernatural marginalia such as bilocation or levitation, that qualify one as a saint. This made the saints role models for the idea of the Catholic Reform that God calls everyone to a state of holiness. This universal call to holiness did not discriminate according to social status, wealth, gender, or race. Therefore, the lives of the saints contrast sharply with the lives of many Enlightenment *philosophes*, who did often not excel in the virtues of prudence, justice, temperance, and courage. Especially in regard to courage, the saints stand out as remarkable examples: as the powers of the state increased and claimed more and more rights over the church, the church commended saints such as St. John Nepomuk or Andreas Faulhaber as role models of courageous resistance. Jansenism is meanwhile acknowledged as an important influence on the French Revolution because it activated religious resistance against royal despotism, but research on the influence of eighteenth-century Catholic spirituality on the formation of modern individualism and individual resistance is still lacking.[49]

The contributions of the saints to eighteenth-century intellectual life are hardly adequately appreciated by historians and theologians: the challenge that the visions of Lindmayr and Höss posed to the theological establishment of their time are known only to a handful of specialists. With their brave reminder that Catholicism had marginalized the Holy Spirit they anticipated the twenty-first century, in which the dialogue between Catholics and Pentecostal churches began to flourish.[50]

A similarly overlooked contribution of the saints is their practical anthropology: both St. Alphonsus of Liguori and St. Benedict Labre put the human person at the center of their concern and called for gentleness and care for the most abandoned. At a time in which secular Enlighteners argued for workhouses, sought rigorist punishments for beggars, justified slavery, and overemphasized the rights of the state, the Catholic Church commended their desire to elevate the poor and abandoned above all others—a stance that is similar to the concerns of twenty-first century liberation theology.[51]

Traditionally, the canonized martyrs have been of great interest to historians, theologians, and artists, but the numerous executions of oath-taking clergy, killed in many cases out of hatred of their faith commitment, have largely been overlooked. Since the hatred of faith is crucial for martyrdom, the theological question of how to treat these victims, either as collaborators and schismatics or as martyrs, remains. This question becomes even more complicated if one adds to the number of Catholic victims the executed Catholic Enlighteners, such as Bishop Adrien Lamourette, who were certainly killed in defiance of their faith. This conundrum also suggests that discussions of early modern and modern martyrdom could profit from studying the French context.[52]

All this is testimony that the lives of eighteenth-century Catholic saints deserve an adequate place in the cultural history of the century, but these saints should also be taken seriously as challengers to their societies. The intellectual history of modern Catholicism is a caricature without the contributions of the saints of the eighteenth century. We must understand them, without romanticizing them, in order to gain a complete picture of Catholic struggles with the Enlightenment world and modernity as a whole.[53]

7

Slaves, Servants, and Savages

SLAVERY IN CATHOLIC COUNTRIES

THE AGE OF Exploration led directly to the Age of Empire. Colonization of the Americas, Africa, and Asia accelerated in the eighteenth century. In the Catholic world, Spain controlled South and Central America, many smaller islands in the Pacific and Atlantic, and some African colonial areas; Portugal reigned over Brazil, and Goa in India; France had large territories in North America, as well as Senegal, Mauritius, the Seychelles, and areas of India. However, with colonialism came a great moral evil, namely, slavery. Colonial governments saw forced labor of either the native population or imported slaves as the key to profitability.[1] While many abhorred the living conditions of slaves, only a few demanded the abolition of slavery, and most enjoyed the products of slave work, such as sugar or chocolate. To give the horror a numerical dimension: Between 1750 and 1825, France imported about 960,000 slaves into its colonies; Spain 215,000; Portugal 1.9 million. Historians estimate that 11 million Africans were enslaved between 1519 and 1867.[2]

While in the sixteenth century Dominican friars such as Bartolomeo de las Casas voiced concern about the enslavement of the Indians, the enslavement of Africans was condoned. One reason was that Africans were usually identified as idolaters or infidels, who had lost the proper purpose of religion—to elevate the human mind toward God. Even for radical materialist Enlightener Diderot, a critic of slavery, Africans were intellectually "limited to present life, with no inkling of a future state."[3] Moreover, by the reasoning of theologians, Africans and Asians could be enslaved because they had lost their freedom when they resisted in a "just war" that the West had waged against them. This idea was key to almost universal enslavement because, of course, most nations resisted European attempts at mission or colonization. Christian theologians argued that Christians could possess, buy, and sell slaves who were legally in a state of slavery—for example, because they were prisoners of war—but that Christian slaves should not be possessed by infidels. Baptism did not free slaves from bondage.[4] Even a Catholic champion of human rights such as the Enlightener Nicola Spedalieri did not deviate from the standard view that slavery was permissible if it was the consequence of a just war. If one has the right to kill another person in combat during a just war, then one also has the right to enslave him. This was infinitely less cruel, he argued.[5]

A slave is defined by historians as a person who is legally the property of someone else and bound to absolute obedience. Slaves have no control over their personal fate, their family life, the conditions of their work, or a right to own property. Most Catholic philosophers and theologians of early modernity viewed slaves as persons, some as inferior persons, but rarely as animals or things. While some rulers conceded more rights to slaves than others, one characteristic of slavery that did not change over time was that a human being was considered the property of someone else. Therefore, some historians have argued that colonial slavery evolved out of the forced indentured labor of whites in Europe. Following this train of thought, the many Catholic Irishmen deported for petty crimes to British colonies would qualify as white slaves.[6] In the eighteenth century such deportations, especially to Barbados, occurred on a grand scale, particularly after the Jacobite uprisings of 1715 and 1745.[7] A similar group were galley slaves, often captives taken in wars or smaller military encounters.

Enlightenment and Slavery

How did the major Enlightenment thinkers view slavery? Most Enlighteners, such as John Locke, disliked slavery, yet almost all of them condoned it in one way or another. Even Montesquieu, who in the *Spirit of the Laws* (1748) ridiculed the rationalization of slavery, was not an abolitionist. Only a few "radical Enlighteners," as historian Jonathan Israel calls them, argued for the immediate abolition of slavery. Yet, how could slavery grow in a climate in which it was regarded with, at least, moral distaste? Those who argued for the abolition of slavery, as well as those who insisted on its economic necessity, relied on arguments about the moral and intellectual inferiority of Africans. Pro-slavery thinkers attempted to show that Africans were utterly different, possibly not even human. Humanity had, so they claimed, many different origins (*polygenism*), but most branches on the tree of humanity were intellectually and morally inferior compared to white Europeans. *Monogenism*, supported by the abolitionists, argued against such a view and insisted on the unity of the human race. In 1744, Pierre Maupertuis suggested abandoning talk of "races" for "varieties" of humans, and expressed his scientific belief in the relatedness of all people. George-Louis Buffon argued in his *Natural History* (1749) that humanity had a single origin. *Monogenism* coincided with the traditional biblical account. Nevertheless, most monogenists continued to view Africans as degenerate or inferior, as cursed descendants of Noah's son Ham. According to them, the hot climate of Africa had corrupted them morally and intellectually.[8]

The abolitionist Catholic clergyman Pierre Joseph André Roubaud reported in his *General History of Asia, Africa and America* (1771) that black Africans would change skin color if they lived in different climatic conditions. Roubaud's account gained crucial exposure when Diderot referred to it in his edition of the Abbé Raynal's *History of the Indians* of 1780, which became the basis for the first coherent program of the French anti-slavery movement. He debunked the scientific nonsense of polygenism that Enlighteners such as David Hume and Voltaire had embraced, and along with it the myth of a genetic degeneration of Africans.[9] Both Diderot and Roubaud thus rejected a growing scientific view that regarded Africans as a subhuman race. Yet in the nineteenth century, the polygenist scheme returned and gave white colonialism a pseudo-scientific footing.[10] It is striking that monogenists, who often unintentionally defended the biblical unity of the human race, provided with their scientific explanation of human variations the arguments for calling Africans inferior and degenerate, while polygenists argued outright for a multitude of human species and a scientifically "proven" degeneration of non-whites.[11]

In the intellectual climate of the eighteenth century, talk about the equality of all humans regardless of skin color was heard only at the margins. Few even thought slavery was a pressing issue because Europeans believed they were bringing fortune and happiness, morality and culture to inferior races. Protestant missionary Pierre Poivre formulated this vision thus: "Our simple religion ... will return them [the slaves] beyond what they have lost. Its consoling truths will enable them to bear patiently the harshness of their fate. .... Despite the horrors of slavery, they will be able to be happy by retaining that precious freedom of the soul that only vice can take away."[12] It was only societal outsiders who advocated abolition—predominantly Quakers, themselves evangelical dissenters from the Church of England.

The most prominent Catholic voice in favor of equal rights for blacks was the priest and later bishop Henri Grégoire. His vision of a just society in which humans had equal rights did not rest on materialism. On the contrary, he criticized freethinkers for their defense of the slave trade and of a hierarchy of races in which whites were indisputably at the top. He was convinced that the equality of mankind was grounded in the creation and redemption of all humans by God, regardless of color. He rejected as rubbish racial classifications and anthropological findings that attempted to show the inferiority of enslaved people.[13] As a member of the National Assembly convened after the French Revolution, he fought tirelessly in favor of granting equal rights to blacks in the French colonies. He could see no justification in the exploitation of slaves for France's economic profit. He finally succeeded with a 1794 bill that established equal constitutional rights for Africans in the French colonies and officially abolished slavery.

It was Grégoire who accepted Toussaint Louverture's offer to help stabilize the Haitian Revolution by bringing order to its ecclesiastical system. Beginning in 1795, Grégoire, as a bishop of the constitutional church shunned by the papacy, gathered volunteer priests to go to Haiti to rebuild the country and church. Grégoire established dioceses and appointed bishops without papal approval, acts that certainly made his schism with the Church of Rome deeper, but these actions should be seen in the context of the time. He was a bold fighter for the emancipation of blacks, even after Napoleon reinstated slavery in 1802. By rebuilding Haiti's church he tried to prevent the country from sliding into paganism or de-Christianization—a trend he perceived in his own country. He can be credited as one of the ideological fathers of anti-racism, seen especially in his 1808 book *On the Cultural Achievements of Negroes*. In its conclusion he addresses Europeans directly:

During the last three centuries, tigers and panthers were less terrible to Africa, than you. For three centuries, Europe, which calls herself Christian and civilized, tortures without pity, and without remorse, the people of Africa and America, whom she calls savage and barbarian. To procure indigo, sugar and coffee, she has

introduced amongst them drunkenness, desolation, and a forget-
fulness of all the sentiments of nature. Africa is not even allowed
to breathe when the powers of Europe are combined to tear her to
pieces. Yes, I repeat it, there is not a vice, not a species of wickedness, of which Europe is not guilty towards negroes, of which
she has not shown them the example. Avenging God! Suspend thy
thunder, exhaust thy compassion, in giving her time and courage
to repair, if possible, these horrors and atrocities.... There is nothing useful but what is just: there is no law of nature which makes
one individual dependent on another: and all these laws, which reason disavows, have no force. Every person brings with him into the
world his title to freedom. Social conventions have circumscribed
its use, but its limits ought to be the same for all the members of a
community, whatever be their origin, color or religion.[14]

The Popes and Slavery

While the popes resisted the enslavement of North and South American
Indians, they condoned slavery as an institution. The often-repeated
claims that Christianity humanized the institution of slavery because
it regarded slaves as persons has been falsified—ancient Roman thinkers, such as Seneca, had brought about this innovation. The popes were,
however, influenced by the new ideas of natural law and unimpressed by
voices that attempted to demonstrate that the Africans were the cursed
descendants of Ham, and thus "natural" slaves. These long-standing theories prescribed legal obligations without recourse to the Bible and were
espoused especially by the Dominicans of Salamanca in Spain. One of
them, Francisco de Vitoria, argued that some people could be natural
slaves if they lacked reason. In order to enslave a nation or tribe, this lack
of reason had to be proven, although, according to Vitoria such a case
could not be made for Indians of the Americas. For Bartolomeo de las
Casas, slavery was not inhuman as such, but legal as long as the slaves
were captives from a just war or purchased in a proper transaction. But
every war against infidels was justified, theologians taught, especially
against Africa, a formerly Christian and now "infidel" continent.

The popes denounced the enslavement of the Indians in the Portuguese
territories many times after 1454. As early as 1537, they also embraced the

idea that there was no natural law basis for the enslavement of Indians. Between the most outspoken attack on South American slavery by Pope Urban VIII in 1639 and the next major public announcement, a hundred years passed. In this time the international slave trade grew dramatically. Benedict XIV did not denounce slavery universally in 1741—just in the Portuguese territories, mainly to protect the Jesuit missions. His papal brief recounted the many efforts, financial and otherwise, to bring the Catholic faith to faraway regions of the world. Therefore, he found it appalling that Catholic colonial powers degraded Indians to slaves and thus wrecked the missionaries' efforts to Christianize them. He regarded the colonists' "inhuman behavior" as the primary cause of the Indian aversion to Catholicism. Yet the pope's main objective was not to improve the conditions of the Indians but to convert them to Catholicism. In his view, their eternal salvation was at stake, and this was incomparably more important than their temporal flourishing. Only if the Indians were free could one successfully missionize in the Portuguese colonies. Everybody who deprived Indians of their liberty or preached that such conduct was permitted was excommunicated.[15] Despite its very limited context, the pope's document can be regarded as a first step toward granting slaves more freedom or even full liberty because it called generic slaveholding "inhumane"; this was also the understanding of abolitionist Father Rocha in 1758. Only in 1831 was slavery officially abolished in the Papal States, and the international slave trade was not publicly denounced until 1839, both times by Pope Gregory XVI.[16]

If the popes had no problem with slavery as such, did they own slaves? Although we know little to nothing about the private slaves of the papal household, archival material exists on the slaves of the Papal States. As state property, these were predominantly galley slaves, who were forced to row the ships of the fleet. Some were volunteers who had been bribed to enlist, some were criminals whose galley sentence was considered equal to the death penalty, and others were captives from wars. The last group comprised the largest number of slaves. While some minor differences among these three groups existed, historians have argued that all three should be subsumed under the category of slaves. The papal fleet had its heyday in the sixteenth century but continued to work into the nineteenth century. In 1611, about 1,300 men rowed on the ships, of whom about 300 were slaves. In 1720, the number of slaves had dropped slightly to 257, and in 1812, 86 slaves were still held. The slaves were sometimes directly captured in combat—for example, after battles with Muslim pirates or the

Turkish fleet—or bought in the markets of Livorno in Tuscany, or Malta. Papal slaves were also sold—for example in 1758, when Pope Benedict XIV allowed the sale of 165 Turkish slaves but allocated the revenue to the Gonfalone Confraternity for the redemption of Christian slaves from North Africa. Slaves could also be exchanged, especially for enslaved Christians in Algeria or Tunisia; between 1550 and 1800 about one million Europeans and Americans fell victim to raids of Muslim pirates from the North African coast. The conflict between the Papal States, supported by the Knights of Malta, and pirates resulted in a flourishing slave market in the Mediterranean that only ended around 1800.[17] The slaves of the papal fleet were legally protected from excessive and unjust treatment and could appeal to the papal court, which they often did. In some Italian territories, such as Livorno, ruled by the Catholic Medici family until 1737, a slave could sue someone in a court of law, found a confraternity, engage in small trades, own other slaves, and buy back his freedom.[18]

Most remarkably, non-Christian papal galley slaves were allowed to elect their own religious ministers, Jews and Muslims alike, and could practice their faith on board the ships and in the slave houses on shore in relative freedom. In some Catholic cities outside the Papal States, even mosques were tolerated, for example, in Genoa or Malta.

However, papal slaves also regularly encountered missionaries, who attended to the needs of Catholic slaves. If a galley slave desired to convert, he could do so after receiving permission from the ship's captain, but he often encountered other impediments. The popes were not happy about such conversions, especially not those of Muslim galley slaves who escaped to the holy city to receive catechetical instruction. The popes feared that publicity about conversions could reach the North African coast, where they would be used to enforce stricter anti-Christian laws or coercive conversions of Catholics to Islam. Thus in May 1780, Pope Pius VI ordered the infliction of eighty lashes on a Tunisian slave named Ali who desired to convert. Since he still desired baptism after this punishment, he was accepted into the church, but he was not freed. While the conversion of public slaves was a political nuisance, the conversion of private slaves was often exploited for publicity, because it could allow the owner to appear in a light of piety and integrity—after all, the slave had converted in his household. These private slaves had much better chances of receiving their freedom after becoming Christians.[19]

The popes supported the efforts of Catholic religious orders to free Christians from slavery under Muslim regimes. They feared for their souls, should they convert to Islam. The most efficient rescue missions were headed by the Trinitarians and Mercedarians; both orders had been founded specifically for the redemption of Christian captives. In the Papal States, the Confraternity of the Gonfalone had long had the privilege of collecting alms for this purpose, until Benedict XIV extended it to the Trinitarians. Approximately eighty thousand slaves were freed by the Trinitarians between 1500 and 1800. Such liberations were not easy, and often the friars relied on mediators. In North Africa, the Trinitarians ran hospitals and missions; therefore, they were well informed about the slave trade and were permitted to attend to the needs of Christian slaves. In other areas, Capuchin missionaries were middlemen for such operations.[20]

Jesuits, Maltese Knights, and a Rebel-King

Jesuits have an ambivalent record on slavery. While the members of the order were certainly at the forefront of missionary efforts in all parts of the world, calling for more humane treatment of slaves, they did not participate in the abolitionist movement. However, they undertook great efforts to shelter the Indians of South America from enslavement, enlisting 100,000 of them in so-called reductions, or self-sufficient farming communities. Every adult Indian had to work two to three days a week for the community. From the products of this work, all common expenses were paid. The houses belonged to the community; private property was allowed but restricted to small items. These Indians were never regarded as slaves; on the contrary, the reductions were a means to keep them independent of the colonial power, Portugal. The Jesuits were officially in charge of these virtually autonomous settlements and successfully proscribed foreigners and European settlers from entering the territories. Moreover, Indians in the reductions could not be forced to work for Spanish *encomenderos*[21] and were protected from slave hunters.[22]

Historian Frank Tannenbaum has argued that slavery in Iberian Catholic regimes was softer and more humane than in Protestant countries, yet this amounts to only a few features, such as the Catholic insistence on the rights of slaves to marry or to receive baptism. Harsh punishments and poor working conditions existed everywhere. In their economic projects, which were undertaken to fund their schools, colleges, and parishes, the Jesuits were no different from other colonial powers.

They forced Indians to work for them and they also held black slaves. In Chile, the Jesuits owned more slaves than all private landowners combined. In Brazil, they owned thousands of slaves. The Jesuit college of Luanda alone had 350 in 1759.[23] Similar numbers apply in Mexico. Only two major differences distinguish Jesuit slave owning from that of other colonials. While in the second half of the century many private landowners began to employ free workers, Jesuits held on to their slaves and even increased their numbers, especially in Brazil, until the order was expelled in 1767. Historian Arnold Bauer has shown that this was not an economically wise decision because much of the Brazilian slaves' work was seasonal, for example, in vineyards; however, it provided the slave families with food and shelter while freelance workers often had to endure harsher living conditions. The Jesuits, Bauer argues, seem to have taken better care of their slaves than some farmers of their employees. Compared to secular slaveholders, Jesuits allowed slaves some autonomy, including the ability to elect elders who acted as liaisons between priests and slaves. There were no slave revolts in Jesuit-controlled areas, and the rate of escapees was much lower than from private owners. Like their founder St. Ignatius of Loyola, the Jesuits also paid extreme attention to holy obedience and taught this obedience to their slaves. A slave revolt would therefore have been a revolt against God that deserved God's chastisement.[24] Jesuits mostly kept slaves and their families together and recognized the natural right of slaves to marry. None of this, of course, made slavery a benevolent institution. Jesuits were fully complicit in this contemptible enterprise. They merely seem to have practiced it with a bit less brutality than others.

Data from North America support these findings. As early as 1638, Jesuits ministered to indentured Catholic servants in Maryland, and sometimes even bought their contracts so that imprisoned workers could practice their faith freely. In 1729, the Jesuits in Maryland had slaves bequeathed to them. Evangelization and not economic interest seems to have been the initial motive for their first active acquisition of slaves. They bought individuals who desired Catholic baptism away from Protestant slaveholders, who barred them from receiving the sacrament. In 1749, the Jesuit George Hunter exclaimed that slave masters should recognize their baptized slaves as equal members of the body of Christ. Jesuits also allowed their slaves, who increasingly worked on their plantations, to marry and to worship with them. Often enough Jesuits even joined their slaves in domestic or agricultural manual labor, and in order to set an example in society they dressed their slaves better than others.

Yet the Jesuits did not question the institution of slavery as such, see-ing it as a necessity.[25] The early Maryland Jesuits understood themselves as fully English, and owning property, including slaves, was essential to this understanding. Following natural law theory, the Jesuit Peter Atwood articulated this right, which was under attack: "All Christians enjoyed not only the free use of their religion, but an equal share, in all their Rights, Places, and Privileges . . . both Clergy and Laity of all persua-sion, and consequently of the Roman Catholics among the rest."[26] Four decades later, attempts to strip the Jesuits of their property resurfaced when they were charged with inciting a slave rebellion, especially because the Jesuits preached to large mixed crowds, not separating whites from blacks. Protestants were successful in passing a law in 1756 that doubled the property tax for Jesuits. Slaveholding and landowning became cru-cial in the struggle for Catholic civil liberties in Maryland in order for people to prove their status as English Catholics, and the Jesuits fiercely defended this right. At the end of the eighteenth century, the Jesuit planta-tions appeared to be extremely rich, comprising thousands of acres, but they were in fact unprofitable. "The spiritual concern," states historian Thomas Murphy, "to treat the slaves as equal in dignity to all other bap-tized Catholics restrained the Jesuits, in conscience, from material exploi-tation of them."[27] While private slaveholders abandoned old and sick slaves, the Jesuits held on to them, providing medical assistance. This, however, rendered their farm production unprofitable. Even when prices for tobacco collapsed, the Jesuits (and later ex-Jesuits) still cultivated large tobacco plantations to provide work for their slaves, even though their farm could not produce enough manure to fertilize the plants. Almost everything the slaves produced was consumed by them, the Jesuits in their ministries, and the students in the Jesuit-run college of Georgetown.[28]

The Jesuits in Maryland backed the institution of slavery until well into the nineteenth century. Brother Joseph Mobberly was a staunch pro-slavery advocate. Mobberly believed that Jesuits should abandon the practice of slaveholding, but that the institution of slavery should continue. The Maryland Jesuits, archival evidence suggests, could not appreciate aboli-tionism because they saw it as a liberal Protestant movement. Moreover, racist ideologies were widespread among them, so Mobberly was probably not alone in his belief that the black skin of a slave was a sign of both his ancestral sins and his future moral failures. To sum it up, most American Jesuits did not seem to have much hope for moral and spiritual progress among their African slaves, and saw instead in slavery a divinely founded institution that had its faults only because of individual, personal failures. Yet another reason to resist abolitionism was the Jesuit stance toward Enlightenment ideals. Although Bishop John Carroll and other Jesuits recognized that American religious liberty derived from Enlightenment ideals, they rejected the idea that reason and nature alone were sufficient for building up a society—especially when these contradicted Scripture. Enlighteners such as Diderot called slavery irrational, but the Bible portrayed it as part of the hierarchical order. Enlighteners seemed to preach liberty for everyone, including slaves, which was contrary to the Bible. Humanity was not entirely free, Mobberly observed: "No sooner was man created than he was commanded to obey."[29] It was the colonial trend toward egalitarianism, supported by many Protestant churches, that the Jesuits and former Jesuits in Maryland fought, relying on a traditional hierarchical view of society, paired now with racism. Mobberly wanted the Jesuits to fit into the newly emerging American culture and thus argued for slave-free Jesuit plantations, but he also did not want to give up traditional Catholic views or sell out to the ideas of Protestant theologians. Thus, he defended slavery as an institution.

The Knights of Malta were a religious order founded during the time of the Crusades. Beginning in the sixteenth century they were sovereign over the little islands of Malta and Gozo in the Mediterranean. Especially in the eighteenth century the Maltese knights harassed the pirates of Barbary in order to impede their slave trade—not for humanitarian reasons but to make profits from seizing the ships and selling the inmates into slavery. In fact, the greatest revenues from slave sales were gained in the years 1773, 1783, and 1790. The slaves on the island of Malta were allowed to have an official representative, the *cadi*. If the slaves were badly treated, Muslim governments often retaliated against Christians in their dominions, and vice versa. Most of the slaves in Malta were galley slaves, who had to remain in slave houses, so-called *bagnos*, at night, yet until the middle of the century, exceptions were often granted. Many also worked on the fortifications of the island, some in private households, and some even as doctors in the famous hospitals of the order. Furthermore, slaves had to be recognizable in public. A special haircut was obligatory—a clean-shaven head, except for a small pigtail. In 1758, a con man had the hair of a free boy cut this way and sold him to a priest. Then the seller sought refuge in a church, demanding asylum. Meanwhile, the priest realized that he had bought a free Christian person, who by law could not be reduced to slavery. He tried to recover his money, but the seller was in religious asylum and thus untouchable by law. The Grand Master of the Knights denied the priest any damages. The fact that a free Christian could not be reduced to slavery did not mean that the knights did not also own Christian slaves. However, these slaves had to have been enslaved previously, so that the knights became "rightful" title owners. Unlike in Jesuit territories, the slaves of Malta attempted several times to rebel and overthrow the oppressive government—yet all these insurrections failed. After an attempted uprising in 1749, dozens of slaves were barbarously punished or executed. Just like the corsairs, the knights also blackmailed the relatives of their captives to obtain money to ransom important captives from Muslim territories. Slaves were exported from the island to Tuscany, the Papal States, France, Sicily, and other markets.[30]

One eighteenth-century Catholic sovereign distinguished himself by his attempt to grant equal rights to all of his people and to free all his slaves: Theodore von Neuhoff, elected king of Corsica. Despite his short reign (1736–1743), during which he defended the autonomy of the island against the Republic of Genoa, one of the greatest slave-trading states in the Mediterranean, he instituted freedom of conscience for all Christians and Jews, and abolished slavery. Neuhoff was equally formed by Enlightenment philosophy and a strong Catholic faith. The slaves that Neuhoff freed were not all Christians; many were Muslims or Jews, and he made no attempt to evangelize them nor did he expect them to receive baptism. They could remain in Corsica, build mosques and temples, worship, and live as free persons among equals. Until Theodore's reign, Corsica's coat of arms showed a Moor with a blindfold; but with his reforms that reinvigorated freedom for the Corsicans and abolished slavery, the blindfold became a bandana and remains the proud symbol of the island until this very day.[31]

Slavery in Portuguese Brazil

Brazil had been a Portuguese colony since the sixteenth century. Like most colonial powers, Portugal tried to consolidate its power over and economic exploitation of its overseas territories. Slave labor was a key element of the Brazilian economy, especially in mining. Slaves were imported from African colonies, where they were captured and sold by their local chiefs. Many newly apprehended Africans believed the Europeans cannibalized them. Stories that Europeans ate slave flesh or manufactured goods from

them were widespread.[32] After a demeaning physical exam and a successful bargaining over the price—a Portuguese slave was valued in the 1720s
and 1730s at about six or seven ounces of gold—he or she was branded
with an iron on the shoulder or chest, and brought to a warehouse to wait
departure for the colonies. A considerable percentage died aboard the
slave ships.[33]

Carmelites, Jesuits, and Benedictines were the biggest slave owners in Brazil. Between 1746 and 1749, many slaves ran away from the
Benedictine monastery in Olinda because of the extreme cruelty of one
of the monks.[34] Others showed genuine interest in the well-being of their
slaves and reminded slave owners who dumped sick and dying slaves into
the woods—and thus avoided paying for their medical bills—of their
responsibilities. Bishop Manuel Alvares da Costa of Pernambuco tried in
vain to convince King John V to issue a decree that slave owners who
abandoned their sick slaves would lose all property rights to them—even
if the slaves recovered.

The bishops of Brazil were aware that slaves imported from Africa
could only slowly be incorporated into society and considered them therefore in great need of spiritual assistance. In 1707, the Archbishop of Bahia
instructed his priests that arrivals from Mina and Angola would first have
to learn the language and receive some catechetical instruction before
being baptized. Owners of "infidel" slaves should work hard to convert
them. He stressed especially the right of baptized slaves to marry, because
the church considered marriage a universal human right, and it helped to
prevent cohabitation or concubinage:

> In conformity with divine and human law, the slave men and
> women may marry other captive or free persons, and their masters
> may not deny them matrimony, nor the practice of it at a conve-
> nient time and place, nor ... treat them worse, or sell them to other
> faraway places where one of them ... cannot follow; and acting in
> a contrary fashion they commit mortal sin, and take upon their
> own consciences the guilt of their slaves, and thus ... fall into and
> remain in a state of damnation.

Slave owners were admonished not to deny their Catholic slaves participation in the religious rites of holy days, which were, like every Sunday, to be
kept free from work. The archbishop was also aware of the horrible treatment many slaves suffered at the hands of brutal owners, who even denied

them appropriate food, water, and shelter: "To banish such an evil abuse against God and mankind, we exhort and ask all our subjects, recalling the wounds of Christ ... that from now on they grant their slaves the needed support."[35] It is also important to note that the Brazilian Catholic bishops, as well as the Spanish-speaking bishops of the Americas, always insisted on the equality of slaves and masters regarding salvation. Despite racial separation in many religious confraternities, on many plantations owners and slaves worshipped together on Sundays. Missionaries also often encouraged the freeing of slaves.[36] Yet the institution of slavery was defended as late as 1794 (and even beyond), when the Archbishop of Bahia informed the district government of a renegade Italian Capuchin monk who preached abolitionist views, which "if propagated and adopted, would disturb the consciences of this city's inhabitants and bring future results disastrous to the perseveration and welfare of this colony."[37]

The Lisbon-born priest and lawyer Ribeiro Rocha, who lived most of his life in Bahia, Brazil, is a notable outlier among the Catholic Enlighteners of Portugal. In 1758 he published a book titled *The Ethiopian Ransomed, Indentured, Sustained, Corrected, Educated and Liberated*, which was a prophetic call for the end of slavery. At the time of its publication, the Marquis de Pombal was Portugal's secretary of state. Pombal's thinking was influenced by Enlightenment ideas, and in 1755 he restored freedom to all enslaved Indians, but not to African slaves. A royal decree of 1761 freed slaves brought to Portugal, abolished slavery in the state of Portugal itself, and banned the slave trade to its colonies, but it did not end slavery in the colonies themselves. Only in 1775 was another royal charter promulgated, which took up Rocha's important idea that also the children of slaves were by natural law free.[38] Still, this decree did not free Brazilian slaves because according to Pombal's *Law of Good Reason* of 1769, economic usefulness was sufficient reason to uphold slavery in the colonies. The ideas of the Catholic Enlightener Rocha were far more radical than those of the pragmatic Enlightener Pombal. Officially, slavery was not abolished in Brazil until 1888.

Rocha called into question the legitimacy of slavery altogether. In his view, slavery was always an act of piracy or theft. Thus it was necessary to restore slaves' freedom and to compensate them for what they had suffered. Nevertheless, probably in order to evade censorship—Pombal still relied for most of his economic endeavors in Brazil on black slave laborers—Rocha added a legal concession regarding the problem of slavery. Outside "righteous titles"—such as captives in a just war or sentenced criminals—slavery was illegitimate. Among the titles he rejected most vehemently was the notion that every child born of a slave mother was a slave. Instead, Rocha proclaimed the womb "free" and that every child was born into liberty. By stating the possibility of legitimate slave ownership with "righteous titles" and by proposing a process of liberation, he did enough to have his book pass censorship; a radical pledge for the immediate end of slavery would almost certainly have not gained the permission to be printed, since Pombal still relied for most of his economic endeavors in Brazil on black slave laborers.

The priest's main argument, however, questioned the foundations of the colony's most important economic institution. Human dignity, Rocha insisted, required equal treatment of all people and an end to human trafficking. He implored the pope and the Portuguese king to pass a law that would liberate every baptized Christian from the yoke of slavery—which meant for Brazil the end of slavery itself. His pragmatic solution was to restore the freedom of African slaves and to pay them for damages they had suffered. Slaves should no longer be the property of others, but paid workers who take a pledge to provide services for a fair wage. In exchange for this compensation the freed person would pledge his service for room and board for up to twenty years, after which he would have to be paid a regular fair wage or would be free to seek employment elsewhere. Historian Hugo Fragoso points out that the "rescue under pledge" system that Rocha suggested was a revolution in thinking about slavery because it meant the beginning of a "a process of liberation." Much of Rocha's argumentation about the dignity and freedom of all humans rested on Catholic moral theology. His book treated slavery as the theft of human freedom. Following this idea, he came to the conclusion that a contemporaneous moral theologian suggested for other cases of theft: restitution of the stolen goods and fair compensation for the loss.[39]

Contrary to this view, a number of Catholic theologians defended the slave trade. In 1788, the Spanish Jesuit Don Raymondo Hormaza published his *Scriptural Researches on the Licitness of the Slave Trade, Shewing Its Conformity with the Principles of Natural and Revealed Religion* (1788). In Britain the pamphlet stirred anger among the abolitionists and they publicly denounced it as a work of "Jesuitical sophistry."[40] Hormaza conceded that many had been enslaved in unjust circumstances and that many abuses existed, but he insisted that these criticisms did not touch on the question of whether slavery in itself was immoral and illicit. For him, neither tradition alone nor philosophical arguments could decide the question, but only sacred Scripture. In Genesis 16—the story about Abraham's slave mistress Hagar—Hormaza saw a clear vindication of slavery. When Hagar wants to flee with her offspring Ishmael, an angel of the Lord orders her to submit to Sara and return to Abraham's tent. Hormaza commented:

> This solemn sentence ... declared her to be her master's indisput-
> able property, and the original bargain or contract, by which he had
> acquired that property, to be just and lawful in nature: that is, that
> the slave trade, even when attended with circumstances not alto-
> gether conformable to the feelings of humanity, is essentially con-
> sistent with the sacred and inalienable rights of justice, and has the
> positive sanction of God in its support.[41]

Because the Bible permitted slavery, no malpractice could ever make it illicit. Moreover, he stated, the abolitionists' use of the Golden Rule (Mt 7: 12)—namely, that whatever one wishes that others do to oneself, one should also do to them—to buttress their claims would not prove that slavery was immoral. Instead, it demonstrated that the rule was not appli-cable to social circumstances, and consequently all social order, because otherwise every subordination and obedience itself would be questioned.[42]

Slave Brotherhoods—A Place for African Spirituality

Despite the fact that slaves were regarded equal in terms of salvation, some religious confraternities were racially segregated. The Brotherhood of Carmo of Ouro Prêto in Brazil, for example, accepted only those of "clean blood, good life and customs."[43] Such brotherhoods had been founded in medieval Europe and served after the Council of Trent to ignite new reli-gious fervor among the laity, but they also provided a network of social help and support that resembles modern unions and health insurance. In Mexico, confraternities for Indians existed from the 1620s, which helped to give farmers much-needed mortgages or other assistance with their finances.[44]

The brotherhoods in Brazil's gold mining region, Minas Gerais, served these purposes too, but were also the primary place to develop a Catholic devotional life, since most priests had abandoned the slaves for the sake of gold mining.[45] Most religious brotherhoods (*irmandades*) that sponsored churches and chapels did not discriminate. If one was Catholic and could afford the annual membership fee, one could usually become a member. In Brazil there were many such brotherhoods, which not only provided for the spiritual progress and earthly needs of members but also for a proper funeral celebration. When the former slave Francisco Gomes died in 1741, he had acquired so much wealth that a magnificent funeral was held. His body was dressed in a Franciscan habit and carried through the city by the members of the three confraternities to which he belonged.[46] In regions where mixed marriages or concubinages were common, as in Minas Gerais, mixed brotherhoods were common; in areas where mixed marriages were rare, a stricter racial divide can be detected. There were white brotherhoods for the European colonists and black brotherhoods for African slaves and those of mixed origin. Brotherhoods also provided religious instruction for the newly baptized and a place for them to engage in devotions.

In Portugal, the leaders of a brotherhood often elected their own king and royal court. Brazilian brotherhoods followed this example. The members of the brotherhood would march several times a year through the city streets, "dressed in regal splendor and collecting charitable contributions."[47] King and queen always appeared under a huge, lavishly decorated parasol, accompanied by bodyguards. Often slave owners enhanced the pomp of the parades by lending jewelry or costumes. For one of Brazil's most famous brotherhoods, the *Brotherhood of the Rosary*, the annual celebration consisted of "religious ceremonies and the *congado* (or *reinado*), which involved a reconstruction of the battle between the black and white monarchies and various dances. . . . Throughout the duration of the festival, the emperor exercised real power over his 'subjects,' even going so far as to free the village prisoners, which really scandalized the imperial officials."[48] King and queen received a throne, crown, and miter, giving audiences and expecting reverent bows, even from whites. In 1763 such processions were prohibited in the capital of Rio because government officials feared chaos, disorder, and pagan rituals: some of the brotherhood dancers had put chicken blood on their faces and ate special cakes for good fortune. For them, mingling such elements of African native belief with Christianity was unproblematic, but for the colonial government and the Inquisition it was not.[49]

Although the brotherhoods were not seedbeds of anti-slavery protest, they certainly served as places in which slaves could find some

self-determination because they allowed for a greater experience of freedom and social recognition. After all, the members could publicly "protest"
against their owners through religious rituals without being punished.
They sang African songs; played the drums, marimbas, rasps, and other
percussion instruments; and dressed in native clothes. "All of this was
legal in the church-sanctioned context and only needed prior authoriza-
tion from the local authorities."[50]

Why Slaves Became Catholic

During the eighteenth century the rulers of the Congo increasingly sold
their own subjects—most of them baptized Christians—into slavery to the
French, Portuguese, and British, as well as to Danish colonies. However,
the Christianization of the Congo was not so much the work of priests, as
in other areas of Africa, but of lay missionaries.[51]

The faith that was practiced by the Congolese was as everywhere in
Africa mixed with native elements. Some historians go so far as to say
that most African Christians practiced a syncretism that was condoned
by the church because it lacked any better solution to the problem of catechesis. Even a catechism approved by the Inquisition in Spain in 1658
for the West African mission of Allada identified God with "Vodu" and
Jesus Christ with "Lisa." Lisa was in the Allada cosmology a white man
linked to a black goddess named Mawu. Of course, the priests tried to
suppress nocturnal dances, fortune telling, and healing activities that
were connected with witchcraft and superstition, but anything that
seemed not to be in harsh contradiction to Christian values was tolerated. This approach dated back to early medieval times and persisted well
into the early modern period. Despite such associations with native religions, one cannot assume that Africans who were sold into slavery and
thereafter baptized were badly instructed in their faith. In fact, a number
of documents testify to their solid knowledge of Christian faith. This
instruction, however, was not brought about by missionary priests but
by African laypeople who spoke the many languages and dialects the
Europeans had difficulty comprehending. The clergy performed only the
rite of baptism and the other sacraments. The lay missionaries ensured
that the Catholic message was "naturalized" or adapted to the context
of their listeners. Jesuits and catechists met each ship that arrived in
an African or American port to offer baptism or last rites, while slave

catechists provided catechetical instruction. The Allada catechism was also used in Brazil, and thus African Christianity provided the context for South American religious instruction. This helps us understand why so many slaves converted to Christianity. They were not converted after "hasty instruction in a complex and foreign religion in a language they could barely understand, but rather they were told how best to make a syncretic blend of their own tradition and what was essential to being a good Christian."[52]

Seventeenth-century slaves from St. Christopher Island in the Antilles were known to have escaped from their British masters, despite better living conditions, to the French West Indies. In the French colony they did not gain liberty, but were treated as human beings and allowed to receive the sacraments about which they had been instructed by priests and lay missionaries. In the absence of priests, the Catholic slaves among the British continued to marry secretly in the presence of witnesses, and met on Sundays to say their prayers before a crucifix. This shows how profoundly Catholicism had been accepted by many slaves. One slave family is even known to have rejected a white Frenchman leading them in prayer because they recognized him as a Protestant.[53]

The Jesuit missionaries in Haiti trained baptized slaves to convince their newly arrived countrymen to accept Christianity. A flourishing lay apostolate among slaves was the consequence. The order that had also founded the first confraternity for slaves on the islands faced strong opposition from the government when it allowed free and captive blacks to conduct unsupervised prayer meetings in their churches. The government feared that such events without priests but "only" with lay missionaries could get out of control and also criticized the possibility of slaves holding church offices such as choir leaders, beadles, and church wardens as early as 1761. Most disturbing were the lay missionaries who went to their fellow captives in the suburbs and preached the good news. The government feared that "in addition to the fact that the truths and dogmas of our religion could be altered in the mouth of this kind of missionary, the good order and the public security was necessarily harmed."[54] Another successful missionary strategy was the separation of blacks from whites, a practice invented by the Jesuits. We should not attribute this entirely to racism, though that certainly played a role, but also to the fact that slaves had pastoral needs that a regular working parish could not fulfill. Moreover, "black" parishes could gain autonomous leadership and demonstrate to the public their equality and the qualifications of their leaders.

Slaves and freed blacks could gain ecclesiastical offices that were highly regarded in society—something that would never have happened in a regular parish. After the expulsion of the Jesuits in 1763, the Capuchins took over the pastoral care of the islands but kept the idea of a chaplain for blacks in force. In 1777 a Capuchin friar, Michel de Vesoul, was even expelled from Cap Français for preaching against the institution of slavery and encouraging a slave revolt. In fact, Capuchins and Dominicans were deported because they were linked to the abolitionist movement. Their preaching had taught the slaves about the equality of humans. While Catholicism per se did not challenge the institution of slavery, courageous missionaries used their authority to contest the colonial system and to empower the captives. When the production and exportation of goods from the French colonies reached its culmination, the missionaries were banned and their ideas deleted from public memory. In such a dire situation many slaves abandoned Catholicism and returned to their African rites and religions.[55]

Yet another reason for slaves to accept Catholicism was that African and Catholic cosmologies seemed to share common ground. For example, a candidate for baptism could see in both religions a God who directly intervenes in the world, hears prayers, has instituted a priesthood, and approves of certain rites. Catholic saints looked a lot like powerful African spirits who could intercede on behalf of individuals and thus help them to endure the fate of slavery. Baptism also had social advantages. Priests often gave little presents to catechumens and climbing up the social ladder was infinitely easier for a baptized slave. Most important, however, baptism put slaves and their owners on the same spiritual footing. A seventeenth-century Jesuit wrote: "One cannot tell the joy and the consolation that these slaves [attend] the same mass as their master, being treated with equality, and in the same manner by the priest whom they go to confess, to not be distinguished from him at communion . . . and finally to see that the religion does not make any distinction of their persons with those who make masters of their liberty and persons."[56]

Last, entering the Catholic Church also meant entering a new family. Newly arrived slaves from Africa were separated from their families and social groups, with whom they had "built dwellings, tended cattle, harvested crops, engaged in trade, cooked, raised children, and protected the community in war."[57] They suffered social death and the erasure of their personal identities. They had become "nobodies." Only because slaves were able to rebuild patterns of kinship that were similar to their extended families in Africa could they bear the hardships of slavery. A family gave a person social standing, normality, and stability. In Catholicism, "god-families" provided just such a structure. In general, slaveholders rejected being godparents to their own slaves due to a conflict of interest, but they often acted as such for the slaves of others. For white Catholics in most areas of the world, it was a well-regarded service and act of mercy and compassion. Wealthy patrons could provide what formerly a tribal chief or a priest achieved for his kin. A slave with prestigious godparents could improve his reputation and had a much better chance of becoming liberated. However, male African slaves were three times less likely to be manumitted than African women; four times less likely than Brazilian-born males; and seven times less likely than Brazilian-born females. Females were twice as likely to be freed or manumitted because they could have sexual relations with their masters. After this group, it was domestic servants who were more likely to be freed, since they had been selected to be part of a white household.[58] Former slaves who had climbed the social ladder, such as the Brazilian woman Chica da Silva, also acted as godparents and thus provided protection for the newly baptized. The godchildren often formed a network and created a new kinship that replaced lost tribal connections. Their godparents were now their "elders," whose wisdom was appreciated and who helped them form a new group identity. That the priests in New Orleans accepted Africans as godparents shows that they were regarded as religiously equal to whites. In the 1730s only 1 percent of Africans or people of African descent served as godparents for slaves; by the 1760s it was over 20 percent, and by 1775 89 percent. This is the best evidence for a sustained religious life, although some historians think that one could explain the numbers also by an increasing withdrawal of whites from godparenting because it had become socially unacceptable.[59]

These accounts should not lead us to expect that slaves everywhere embraced Catholicism. Where priests were perceived to be self-interested and not supportive of the slaves, baptisms were less common. Slaves on Bourbon/Réunion resisted baptism by missionaries on a large scale because they suspected that in the afterlife their existence as slaves would continue. When in 1775 a priest tried to baptize a dying slave, he turned away and said: "After death, everything is finished, at least for us Negroes."[60]

Catholic African and Indian Slaves in New Orleans and New France

Although originally a French colony, New Orleans had been handed over to Spain in 1763 and remained Spanish until the early nineteenth century. This change of national control also had effects on the slave community there. When the Spanish Capuchins took over the missions, the friars were shocked by the state of their fellow religious. The French Capuchins of New Orleans had not lived up to the order's standards of poverty but had instead owned slaves, silverware, and porcelain, and had used snuff even during choir. Eighteen slaves lived in their household in 1772, one of whom was the mistress of the prior. Some of the other female slaves regularly left the monks' cloister and met their lovers in the city—something the French Capuchins had obviously tolerated. The church's condoning of racial mixing reinforced the fluidity of interracial relations in the city. Conflict between French and Spanish Capuchins became more substantial in the 1770s when the Spanish demanded adherence to the Spanish slave code. This prohibited miscegenation but also regularized slave marriages and their catechesis. When a runaway slave of the Capuchin household was sentenced for the murder of three other slaves in 1784 without proper trial, Bishop Cirilo and his confreres threatened the governor with appeal to the Spanish crown. Their protest did not prevail, so they refused to accompany the sentenced to the scaffold but instead protested with loud voices from the gallery of their church across the execution place. When in 1791 a slave girl was interred unlawfully in a garden instead of the sacred grounds of the cemetery, it was again a Capuchin, Joaquin de Portillo, who publicly criticized the Louisiana governor for the inhumane treatment of the devout slave family. A year later he even ordered slaves he saw working on Sunday on a plantation to stop and honor the holy day. After the transfer of Louisiana to the United States in 1803, any public influence of Catholic clergy, which had profited from the slaves, ended.[61]

The Ursulines of New Orleans were among the major slaveholders of the city. During the French reign, following the French Code Noir of 1685, marriages between slaves were forbidden. Under Spanish law these were again possible; matrimony was required if two adult slaves wanted to have sexual relations. Yet many only had common law marriages because the clergy charged fees no slave or poor person could afford to pay. Hence the Ursulines sponsored the marriages of slaves themselves and stood out in their unwavering support for slaves' right to get married. The nuns even tried to arrange marriages of couples who had fallen in love but were owned by different masters. The nuns, who were certainly not influenced by any Enlightenment thought, educated the girls of New Orleans regardless of their racial or social background—enslaved girls, wives of traders, and upper-class daughters of Louisiana's high society.[62]

Not only Africans but also indigenous people were enslaved and imported to the colonies. A good example is New France, the western Great Lakes region, and the upper Mississippi Valley, where French colonists could participate in the ancient slave trade Indian tribes had established long before.[63] Indian slave women and children performed domestic and agricultural duties. While sometimes subordination could become kinship, enslaved women were without rights in the hands of their masters, who were often sexual predators or rapists. Some of these sexual relations, however, were consensual. The priests, who baptized the offspring of mixed relations, mentioned the father of the child in the official church records if the mother identified him. Often it was the slave owner himself, but slave women were also "offered" to voyagers as a sign of "sexual hospitality." Records exist that testify to priests' efforts to shield women from coercive intercourse, as some Illinois Jesuits did when asked for help by a number of women. One missionary, for example, encouraged a slave girl to devote herself to Christ alone to escape a marriage with a violent fur trader.[64]

Some historians have charged the church with being too stingy in offering shelter to abused female slaves or escaped slaves in general. They overlook, however, that such behavior would not only have been highly inappropriate in the eyes of early modern Europeans, who would have suspected the priest of having sexual relations with a young slave girl, but also legally complicated. While the church certainly had the right to grant asylum, such cases became rarer in the eighteenth century as states tried to reduce the privileges of the church. Thus it was no longer possible for a criminal safely to seek asylum in a church or monastery—often the state authorities arrested such persons by force, even on holy ground. Eighteenth-century Jesuits, in particular, had to be careful not to get involved in such cases as they were already targeted for political activity in almost all Catholic states and were associated with sedition and even regicide. Legally, a slave *never* had the right to seek asylum and leave his master unless he or she had been treated with extreme violence. Then the slave could stay until the owner had promised to mend his ways and no longer mistreat him.[65]

Since only a few male slaves were held in New France, most sexual relationships with slaves involved male French settlers and female Indian slaves. It was possible for an Indian slave girl to gain control of some areas of her life, including her own body, as some enslaved women who had consensual relationships with Frenchmen achieved full legal recognition of their children. Catholic rituals helped to embed slaves in a set of social relationships with the French colonial powers. The 1685 ordinance that prescribed baptism for every new slave in the Caribbean did not apply to New France. Instead, slave owners wanted their slaves to become part of their church on an individual basis. The extended family of the owner participated in godparenthood for the newly baptized slaves. This spiritual bond not only incorporated the slaves into the body of Christ, the church, but also brought them closer to their owners, though they remained, of course, subordinate. The most obvious sign of such incorporation was the new Christian names that the slaves received with baptism—names such as Jean-Baptiste, Pierre, or Madeleine.

Even at the end of the eighteenth century most French priests seem not to have had a problem with slavery, in part because the Indian slaves constituted a large contingent of converts. In some areas they accounted for a third of all baptisms. Yet the priests had been admonished by their bishops to baptize them only after careful instruction and probation. To ensure that the slave who was undergoing instruction understood the meaning of her new faith before she committed, the priest explained: "One is obliged to explain all the mysteries of our religion to an adult before baptizing her, that is to say that she is required to believe ... the unity of God in three persons, the mystery of our redemption, that there is an eternal after-life to reward our good works, or similarly to punish our wickedness."[66] Instruction could be omitted for slaves in mortal danger or for children.

Historian Susan Sleeper-Smith was able to show that Catholicism also played an important role in enhancing female autonomy of Indian women married to French fur traders. This led her to reject the notion that the church subordinated them to their husbands. Indian women served as godmothers to Indian slaves, and their daughters imitated them and thus created a network that stretched across time and space, including many different families. Often such a network connected several fur-trading families and racially mixed families. Sometimes such marriages were done "after the custom of the country," which meant that the individuals were not married in the presence of a priest but rather in an indigenous ritual that the Jesuit missionaries grudgingly condoned. Female converts in mixed marriages often allowed Jesuit priests to gain influence over the fur-trading males, whom they frequently despised as worthless drunkards. Already in the seventeenth century, the French government had deplored the influence of Indian wives on their French husbands. While Paris saw the adoption of native lifestyles as degeneration, the Jesuits hoped that it could bring about religious conversion.[67] The wives of fur traders could become the center of a domestic evangelization and were often trained by Jesuits as catechists. Moreover, these women emerged as cultural mediators between the world of the Indians and that of the Western settlers. When talking to members of their own tribes, the female proselytes could now challenge the religion of their tribal leaders with their knowledge of Western theology, giving them a new, elevated social status that had been unthinkable before. In the absence of Catholic priests, especially after the Seven Years' War, Catholic Indian women, most from slave backgrounds, assumed the roles of lay missionaries and shaped what Sleeper-Smith has called "frontier Catholicism." They conditionally baptized children and adults or arranged marriages that were afterward sanctioned by visiting priests.[68]

Conclusion

The Catholic Church has an ambiguous record on slavery. While the church helped to spread the Gospel, and with it the idea of a fundamental equality of all people with regard to salvation, it did not often question racist theories of the eighteenth century. It attempted to shield the South American Indians from Spanish enslavement but did not condemn the slave trade from Africa. Yet if one compares the church with other institutions of the eighteenth century or even nations and states, and its bold preachers of human dignity with anti-clerical French or English Enlighteners, its record is quite remarkable. Many missionaries worked to ease the burden of slaves, and a number of Catholics, such as Henri Grégoire, supported the abolition of slavery, while most Enlighteners were content with a moral disapproval of slavery but passive when it came to actual help.

Conclusion

THE DEATH OF CATHOLIC ENLIGHTENMENT
AND THE BEGINNING OF A PAPAL CATHOLICISM

TO A CASUAL observer, the Eucharistic procession that wove through the streets of Paris on May 4, 1789, was indistinguishable from the thousands of similar processions that had occurred on these same streets over the centuries. Who would have guessed that this very convoy of the deputies of the Estates-General, marching behind the Blessed Sacrament carried by the Archbishop of Paris, marked the beginning of the end of the old world of Catholicism? Within twenty-four hours, the Estates-General officially opened and the French Revolution began.

King Louis XVI had called the Estates together to address the country's dire financial situation, and in a desperate bid for popularity he doubled the number of deputies for the third estate (which represented the common people). But the king's move only created an unstoppable messianic enthusiasm among the farmers and citizens: the popular consensus was that France had to change. In planning these changes, the church was a target for drastic reform from the very beginning of the official deliberations. After all, many saw an opportunity to fill the state's empty coffers, by taxing the church and suppressing the monasteries, which would also liberate the (allegedly) unhappy monks and nuns from their despotic superiors. Some of these proposals overlapped with the objectives of France's parish priests, who despite their zeal were notoriously underpaid and had no say in administrative decisions. Discontent among the clergy grew exponentially because most bishops chose to ignore the complaints of their priests. It should not have surprised contemporaries that many priests embraced the radically democratic vision of Edmond Richer (see

Chapter 1), who had argued that the jurisdiction of a diocese should rest not with the bishop but with the entire clergy. Thus, some among the clergy, inspired by political unrest, insisted that the hour had come to bring about a change within the church, which their superiors were either unwilling or unable to effect. One pastor wrote: "We priests have rights. Such a favorable opportunity to enforce them has not occurred, perhaps for twelve centuries. ... Let us take it ... so that our successors will not be able to reproach us for having neglected their cause and our own."[1] Despite such sentiments, most clergymen resisted the pressure to join the estate of commoners and were hesitant to openly oppose the aristocracy and the bishops. A few, however—including Henri Grégoire, the great fighter for the abolition of slavery—broke up the unity of the first estate and joined the third. By June 17 the third estate declared itself the National Assembly and on June 27 Louis XVI ordered the first two estates to join the third. The Revolution was now unstoppable.

The events of the next few months, up to June 1790, have often been described by church historians as an attack on Catholicism by anti-clerical Enlighteners or atheists. Yet the majority of the reformers responsible for the new laws pertaining to the life of the church were sincere Catholics. The abolition of feudal duties and tithes on August 4, 1789, was certainly an attack on church property, but such legislation also promised fair compensation for the clergy. The disowning of church property and the abolition of monastic vows were also seen as reforms of an idle monasticism, as unfair as this accusation was. These changes especially hurt the poor; when church hospitals, orphanages, schools, and other institutions run by religious orders closed, the poor lost their most reliable advocates. While the bourgeoisie were quick to circulate complaints about the "uselessness" of nuns and monks, the poor—who were at the receiving end of monastic charity—had no voice and could not express their support for the orders. This part of the story is almost always overlooked.

The French church was now a vehicle, quasi-independent from Rome, for the patriotic-democratic renewal of society. The National Assembly took full control of church affairs in order to align the religious sphere with reigning political ideals. On November 27, 1790, the Assembly passed the famous Civil Constitution of the Clergy, which stated that bishops and priests would henceforth be elected by the citizens of a district, including Jews and Protestants. Every clergyman was obliged to swear an oath of loyalty to this constitution if he desired to remain in his post. Because King Louis XVI had publicly endorsed the new law, many hoped that the pope would also condone it, but such expectations were shattered when Pius VI denounced it in 1791. Priests who did not subscribe to the new order either left the country, were deported, or were arrested, and the French church drifted into schism. It was divided between those Catholics who rejected the assault on church tradition and those who wanted to reform the church in accordance with the demands of the progressive political government. The latter increasingly interpreted the Revolution as the voice of God, and the Civil Constitution of the Clergy as a document equal in stature with the Bible, all brought about by divine providence. Those Catholics who had scorned the Civil Constitution of the Clergy were seen as potential traitors to the new system and of the codified natural rights of humanity. The Prussian-Austrian Army, which approached Paris in September 1792, however, seemed to endanger the survival of the Revolution; many feared that its victory would reverse the achievements of the previous three years. As a consequence, thousands of men and women who were suspected of supporting the enemy's cause were massacred, among them many priests, nuns, and bishops.[2]

The new state church, called the Constitutional Church, initially attracted the majority of the French clergy and also idealists from other European countries, including German Catholic Enlighteners. Due to strong resistance from churchgoers, however, many government officials quickly realized that Catholicism could not be the force for progressive renewal that they had hoped and abandoned it for a new sentimental and philanthropic deism. This transition became obvious during the so-called de-Christianization phase of the Revolution, which began in October 1793 with the changing of the traditional Christian calendar. Many former priests were among the most consistent advocates of the de-Christianization movement; they were convinced that even the terror of mass executions could bring about a reinvigorated society centered on values of optimism and progress. About twenty thousand priests welcomed de-Christianization, many gave up their priestly vocations and married, although several thousand were reconciled with the church a decade later. The Constitutional Church was increasingly marginalized and oppressed, and in its place the cult of the Supreme Being was introduced. Non-Revolutionary Catholics were labeled "enemies of the human race" and sent to the guillotine, a fate that terrified critics of the Revolution.[3] The new religion did not attract popular support because, unlike Christianity, it did not offer hope for a profound moral and spiritual transformation, as the French apologist François-René Chateaubriand aptly observed.

More than any other region, the western coastal area called the Vendée suffered from the effects of de-Christianization; here political reforms did not ease poverty, and the devout population protected their priests. What began as protest escalated into open rebellion, so much so that Maximilien Robespierre, the president of the National Convention and a proponent of the new cult of the Supreme Being, declared in response: "We must crush the internal enemies of the Republic or perish along with it; in this situation the first maxim of your policy must be that we lead the people by reason and the enemies of the people by terror. . . . This terror is nothing but prompt, severe, and inflexible justice."[4] His understanding of "justice" required that the rebels' armies—which consisted primarily of impoverished farmers, who wore images of the sacred heart of Jesus—had to be "exterminated," together with their wives and children. From the village Le Luc it was reported: "A woman suffering from the pains of childbirth was hidden in a hovel near the village; soldiers found her, cut out her tongue, split her belly, and took out the child on the point of their bayonets. A quarter mile away, you could hear the howls of this unfortunate woman, who was at the point of death when help arrived."[5] By 1797, about 115,000 had died under the "just rule" of the French government, or as other historians call it, the "first modern genocide."[6]

In the past, church historians were inclined to describe clergy such as the Abbé Grégoire, Claude Fauchet, and Adrien Lamourette as spineless collaborators with an intrinsically evil Revolution and as dissenters from the faith. Certainly, they were affiliated with a congregation the pope had labeled "schismatic and heretical," but their membership in the Constitutional Church does not justify their rejection as traitors. In fact, they struggled sincerely to balance their commitment to the French Revolution with their faith, often not very successfully and often not very boldly, but we should be careful in branding them as opportunistic heretics before we have thoroughly looked at their lives.

If one undertakes such an investigation, men such as Adrien Lamourette emerge as sincere seekers who tried to avoid the extremes of religious rigorism and materialist philosophy and believed that a renewed Catholic theology was a sound middle position. In a number of books he wrote before the Revolution, Lamourette outlined how Catholicism had to reinvent itself. Such an endeavor, he argued, could only be successful if theology better integrated the emotions. Lamourette was convinced that if sentiment was taken seriously as a source of belief, then faith could take root and renew the French church. Moreover, Lamourette also held that it was Catholicism that best answered humanity's search for the absolute, or as he called it, the infinite. Consumerism (or luxury) was for him the "inarticulate and confused search for the infinite"; only by overcoming such a search for *false* infinite goods (such as money and fame) could humans become capable of benevolence, solidarity, and happiness. Thus, his theological vision had very concrete effects on his view of social ethics and community life, and from this insight he also argued for a poor church and supported the dispossession laws of 1791. He was convinced that by forfeiting its property, the church would be restored to the purity of the first centuries and attract virtuous men to the priesthood. Such drastic measures seemed necessary to him because the majority of the pre-Revolutionary clergy sought only financial and not spiritual benefits. Jesus was, in the vision of Lamourette, the divine messenger of equality and fraternity. The Old Regime Church was, to him, worthless since it had betrayed the Gospel by impeding societal equality. By so alienating the faithful, who were critical of the Revolution, and by alienating many priests, who had faithfully worked as pastors before 1789, Lamourette could not count on many supporters. As a bishop of the Constitutional Church, Lamourette implemented radical changes to the worship in his diocese by moving the celebrating priest closer to the congregation and by ordering the use of a French translation of the Roman Missal. Many times he appealed to the "enlightened Christians" of France to support his goals, but never with much success. As a public figure and member of the Legislative Assembly he desperately fought for the compatibility of Christianity and Revolution, coining not only the term "Christian democracy" but also the "kiss of peace" between faith and the modern world; yet, a critic of the Jacobins, he was executed in January 1794.[7]

Lamourette's student Henri Grégoire believed that the Revolution had been guided by the hand of God because he was convinced that democracy would bring about morally better human beings. Moreover, in the Civil Constitution of the Clergy he saw a liberation from papal despotism. It was his belief in Catholic Christianity that also motivated him to work for the emancipation of Jews and African slaves and to stand up courageously when the de-Christianization of France was becoming violent. On November 7, 1793, when the National Convention demanded from him and other priests an abjuration of their faith—or as they called it, "unenlightened" superstition—he reminded the parliamentarians that religion was beyond their purview and that while his position was elected, his mission came from Jesus Christ. Grégoire's theology was shaped by

Gallicanism, which saw the French church as being independent from Rome and reduced the role of the pope to being a spiritual leader without authority, and a Jansensim that no longer focused on grace but rather on the patriotic renewal of France. Jansenist theology in the 1770s and 1780s, after the defeat of its main enemy, the Jesuits, was mostly interested in purging the church from Baroque forms of piety, reforming the tithing system, and advocating the importance of Scripture. Consequently, it lost its theological edge and became a branch of political activism that was more open to Enlightenment impulses. Historian Dale Van Kley has therefore spoken of a "jansenized Gallicanism," by which he means that elements of Jansenist thought were integrated into the Gallican framework, whose most important tenet of faith was independence from papal "despotism." From such antipathy toward papal monarchy to a rejection of the French dynasty was only a small step. Yet it was the aversion to despotism that was also the theological root of Grégoire's political theology: the Revolution had brought about equality, liberty, and fraternity, which were illusory ideals under the Old Regime. Grégoire especially considered equality a core virtue of Christian belief. Between 1790 and 1801 he was the main figure of the (schismatic) French Constitutional Church and did not shy away from becoming the object of hatred during the persecution of the Constitutional Church in the late 1790s. His ability to remain a major political player during these times saved his life. Despite these remarkable features, Grégoire never spoke out against the persecution of Catholics who refused to take the oath on the Civil Constitution of the Clergy or other crimes of the Revolution. In 1831, the Archbishop of Paris refused the dying Grégoire the last rites because he still upheld the oath of 1791. His most lasting theological idea, namely, the celebration of the liturgy in the vernacular and no longer in Latin, only became reality in the twentieth century.[8]

Claude Fauchet is yet another constitutional bishop who demonstrated that support for the democratic ideals of the Revolution did not require apostasy. He believed instead that France was torn between the cultural force of traditional (and despotic) religion and authority, on the one side, and materialist Enlightenment philosophy, on the other. As a sincere Catholic he tried to overcome this dichotomy and establish a third way. He denounced the irreligion of his compatriots and insisted that Christianity was the true fount of liberty, but he also conceded that religion did not have much to say about how to organize society or politics. The latter belonged solely in the realm of reason, and thus to Enlightenment politics; therefore, religion and Enlightenment could work together. Based on his theological insights, Fauchet also argued for the systematic redistribution of wealth and land because he believed, like Rousseau, that everybody should own enough to fulfill his needs and that nobody should have too much. In a 1792 pastoral letter to his diocese he not only equated Christianity with the religion of holy liberty but also emphasized the importance of the Revolution for the development of the faith: "The more the pure light of reason is propagated in the human mind, the more evident will be the great principles of religion. The more the taste for republican virtues and universal fraternity win hearts, the more will the need for evangelical Catholicism make itself felt in all souls."[9] Fauchet, like Grégoire and Lamourette, did not talk openly about transforming the church but rather of "restoring" it, and thus he tried to put to rest the fears of the faithful that they were abandoning traditional Catholic beliefs. Among Fauchet's driving ideas was the revitalization of the apostolic character of the church, cleansing it from its hierarchical overgrowth. The bishops should not act like monarchs but be elected servants of the faithful, he thought. Fauchet's God was heavily adapted to the needs of the Revolutionary regime, and thus it should not surprise us that he saw Jesus mainly as a political activist and social revolutionary, who had been crucified by aristocrats. Despite being ostracized, Fauchet defended the centrality and superiority of Christian beliefs and their necessity for the survival of France. Like Grégoire he defended clerical celibacy, but was not successful in escaping the rage of the Jacobins. In October 1793 he was executed.[10]

Until well after the September Massacres of 1792 began, in which violent mobs killed thousands of incarcerated opponents of the Revolution, enlightened Catholics unapologetically defended the achievements of the Enlightenment. Two remarkable examples are the homilies that Franz Berg and Gregor Zirkel gave during Holy Week in 1793. The Prince Bishop of Würzburg commanded that they speak on the question "What do religion and prudence ask of the higher and enlightened states in these critical times?" More outspoken than almost anyone else, Berg asked whether the Enlightenment had caused the French disregard for religion and a decline in morality. He vehemently denied such an accusation. He even compared the charges against the Enlightenment with the claims and lies brought against Jesus Christ by the Romans.[11] Berg argued that the Enlightenment secured civil rights and maintained the importance of morality. It was the exclusion of Enlightenment and thus of egalitarianism that fostered unrest, with devastating effects on religion and morals. Nevertheless, he identified one important problem within the Enlightenment that some-times led to violence and irreligion, namely, its overemphasis on sensual-ity and on human passions.[12] Most important for Berg, however, was that the Enlightenment did not increase the conflict between faith and reason because it sought an improvement and enrichment of reason with new knowledge and a cleansing of errors and prejudices.

> This inner perfection is a demand of our reasonable nature and the first duty we are obliged to fulfill. No sacred and reverent truth, which humanity cherishes and which sustains the welfare of civil society, virtue and religion, can suffer from such [Enlightenment], because it is only ... truth. The more we exercise our thinking mind the more the whole realm of truth gains.[13]

Faith cannot collide with enlightened reason, as reason knows—and here Berg followed the Protestant philosopher Immanuel Kant—its lim-itations.[14] If the French Revolution brought about brutality, it was only because of a lack of critical thinking—a neglect of Enlightenment, not because it had embraced it. Most innovative, however, was Berg's claim that not the Enlightenment but rather the Counter-Enlightenment led to civil unrest and revolution, since it petrified societal tensions and prejudices.[15] Instead of seeing the future of Catholicism in the embrace of the Counter-Enlightenment, Berg saw grave dangers. Such a move would only increase blind but unintelligent faith as well as disregard for genuine Christian virtues. Anti-Enlighteners, also called obscurantists, were—Berg insisted—not in need of refined virtue because they preached only one virtue, namely, obedience to the authorities.[16]

Such praise for the Enlightenment and understanding of the French situation became unthinkable just a few months later, when the Paris government imposed a heavy death toll on the country in an attempt to eradicate any resistance to the new regime. It is not necessary to describe the great bloodbaths of the French Revolution; the important point here is that this upheaval roiled the Catholic Church worldwide, but especially the papacy. With the support of hitherto tolerated—or sometimes even supported—enlightened Catholics, the "oldest daughter of the Church," as France had proudly called herself, had been torn by the most severe schism since the Reformation. Former Catholic priests organized the decapitation of nuns and monks or were responsible for the genocidal kill-ing of the inhabitants of the Vendée. Churches were destroyed, sacred art ransacked, monasteries razed, and every attempt was made to erase Christianity from the memory of France. Since all this was done in the name of progress and Enlightenment, the conclusion was drawn that *all* Enlightenment, egalitarianism, and democratization were dangerous, and that Gallicanism and Richerism were responsible for the fall of the French church. The executions of countless martyrs seemed to confirm Pope Pius VI in his firm stance against the Revolution and the Constitutional Church, which he regarded as schismatic and heretical.

As a result, Catholic reformers throughout Europe came under suspicion of being a "fifth column" within the church. A strong Counter-Enlightenment movement, backed by church leaders, began to see liberal individualism as the original sin of the French Revolution. Supporters of this movement were convinced that the uprooting of religion led the Revolution into the moral abyss of the Great Terror. In response, Catholics embraced a Romantic theology that downplayed the importance of individualism and reason and instead focused on intuition, emotion, and community. Likewise, state governments became worried as the Revolutionary ethos spread. While European governments came together to try to defeat the French Revolutionary armies, the pope's power dwindled. He fell prisoner to French soldiers and was deported into exile. At the moment of Pius's death in 1799, it seemed that the Revolution had won and that the end of traditional Catholicism was near.

The church, at the brink of death, was reinvigorated (albeit unintentionally) by a most unlikely person: former Revolutionary general Napoleon Bonaparte. Napoleon realized that the de-Christianization of France had led to a moral vacuum, and therefore he agreed to grant the church an important role in his new empire. With the Concordat of 1801 the First Consul and future emperor crushed the ancient tradition of Gallicanism by granting the pope absolute freedom in the appointment of bishops, allowing him to raze the structure of the Gallican Constitutional Church. Ernest Renan, himself a lapsed Catholic, aptly summarized: "Napoleon's Concordat taught the pope that he really had the rights that [the pope] had never doubted he had, in particular of suppressing an entire church with a stroke of the pen and then reconstituting it on an entirely new basis."[17] This was an enormous boost for the self-confidence of Pope Pius VII, who initially succumbed to Napoleon's bullying and crowned him emperor in 1804 but resisted the tyrant in 1806 when the French sovereign demanded the pope's unconditional support against his enemies. Personally offended, Napoleon ordered the capture and imprisonment of

Pius VII. He was not freed until the end of the French Empire in 1814. Napoleon thought the pope's confinement would crush the reputation of the Bishop of Rome, but the opposite was the case. More than anyone else in Europe, Pius VII had resisted a despot—had risked his land, his liberty, and possibly his life—and had lost almost all in order to keep the papacy from becoming the trump card of French nationalism. Catholics throughout the world now looked to him, whom they venerated like a living martyr, as the new moral leader of the church. Ultramontanism—the mindset that looked to the pope for guidance on all matters—grew rapidly and spread through newly founded religious orders and lay organizations. It was at the time a politically necessary and shrewd way of reorganizing a church in a state of chaos. In the post-Revolutionary era, the church suddenly found itself an outsider. It could not abandon its hierarchy for a democratic structure and embrace liberal individualism without sacrificing its identity, so it reasserted itself through Ultramontanism in order to defend both its independence from the state and the religious liberty of the faithful. Within this Ultramontanist church, however, Enlighteners or freethinking Catholics had no space; they were seen as deserters and untrustworthy believers.

The eminent position the papacy gained is all the more understandable if one considers that nobody expected much from Europe's bishops. The reason was quite simple: when Napoleon's armies overran Europe, they destroyed the old alliance of church and state. New governments were installed and church privileges curtailed. Bishops lost their power, their diocesan infrastructure, and their institutional backing, leaving them increasingly unable to lead. In German-speaking lands, for example, the bishops had been rebelling against a strong papacy since the 1760s and had attempted to become quasi-independent just like bishops in the Gallican church. Yet the peace treaty of Luneville (1801), between the Holy Roman Empire and Napoleon, confirmed the demise of the German church: to compensate the secular German rulers for the loss of their territories on the western bank of the Rhine to France, the secular rulers were given permission to seize and absorb church property. As a result, the next year German prince-bishops lost their sovereign territories and soon even the monasteries were dissolved. The pope's strongest critics, the supporters of Febronianism, were in effect silenced by the pope's biggest enemy, Napoleon. The bishops spinelessly accepted their fate because they feared losing their state pensions, and as a result, the German church lost its leadership. Even church universities were taken over by the state—eighteen alone in Germany—such that the old church was robbed of its entire institutional apparatus. Under these conditions, one could only look to Rome for guidance because, despite even the imprisonment of the pope himself, papal authority remained intact. The teaching authority of the bishops was lost because of their moral failure, while the authority of the popes grew until, in 1869, the "ordinary magisterium" was no longer understood as the teaching authority of all bishops but of the pope alone.[18]

The papacy learned an important lesson from the French Revolution and applied it more successfully than any other organization of its time—namely, that real power rested with the "voice of the people." The post-Revolutionary popes began to appeal to the masses to an extent that had not been seen before, and the masses confirmed the papacy as the lonely lighthouse in a world darkened by modern liberalism, which sharply rejected any influence of the church over the life of the state. While the Catholic Enlighteners (the few who still existed after 1800) worked without a Catholic infrastructure—though they continued to enjoy some cultural prestige—Ultramontanists began to build networks, found societies and clubs, and disseminate their message in newspapers and journals that targeted each segment of society, from the common man, to the bourgeois, to the academic. The failure of the Catholic Enlightenment to become a popular movement sealed its fate. It could not win against the well-organized machinery of Ultramontanism, but it also failed to conduct an honest self-assessment to identify its mistakes and make the necessary adjustments. Earlier generations made pilgrimages to Rome to visit the historic churches, but now they came to "see the pope"; the popes had successfully made themselves the centerpiece of Catholicism, a phenomenon that would continue through the twentieth century.[19]

Ultramontanism gave the church a unifying and coherent interpretation of Catholicism, making it a powerful tool to fight the attacks yet to come, but it had the tendency to turn theology into ideology in order to secure societal influence and to silence dissenters. Catholics who still believed that modern liberalism had value, who believed that the church should be in dialogue with modern thought, were branded heretics. This led to deep distrust between the two camps, which is well illustrated by the divisions in the Spanish church after 1800. While Ultramontanist Catholics argued for purging the church of the "moral perversity" of the Enlightenment and supported a theocratic absolutism, Catholic Enlighteners championed a liberal state government. The two sides were irreconcilable, and the ongoing fights not only damaged the reputation of the church but left it open to critics' attacks on religion as inevitably divisive. Moreover, the ideological element of Ultramontanist theology also tended to marginalize or inhibit the mystical dimension of Catholicism, which was perceived as "dangerous" individualism. Thus, the chance to center doctrine on the mystical encounter with Christ was missed. Then, at the beginning of the twentieth century, when modernizing theologians attempted to ground Catholic teaching in human consciousness and history, the modernist crisis erupted. Certainly many "modernists" were undermining the content and self-understanding of the faith, but others merely rearticulated the tradition in new, non-scholastic terminology. Nevertheless, the Ultramontanist apparatus crushed the modernist movement with full force, without differentiation or nuance. The deleterious consequences of this reaction were numerous; for example, until the 1940s historical criticism in biblical studies could cost a theologian his job. The church was not perceived as the "mystical body of Christ" but rather as an institution entrusted to the hierarchy of bishops. Only under the pontificates of Popes Pius XI and Pius XII did a new Reform Catholicism take root, adopting many insights from the early nineteenth-century Tübingen school (which was in itself deeply influenced by the Catholic Enlightenment) and laying the foundations for a new dialogue with modern thought that led to the Second Vatican Council in 1962.

Nevertheless, as a continuous intellectual movement, the Catholic Enlightenment could not survive Napoleon. Certainly a few isolated individuals maintained the engagement with modern thought, but the overall agenda of nineteenth-century Catholicism was no longer a dialogue with modernity. Instead of continuing the Enlightenment tradition, Catholics tried to find in the chaos of the post-Revolutionary period a new space in society and also new areas of engagement. New female religious orders offered an alternative to the traditional gender roles society had developed, and they flourished, as did powerful lay organizations and Catholic political parties. Romanticism allowed for a rediscovery of the community aspects of Catholicism, and neo-scholastic theology continued—unintentionally—the worst aspects of rationalist Enlightenment theology in its endeavor to prove the existence of God. Overall, however, Catholicism withdrew into an intellectual ghetto. The Catholic Enlightenment project, which had reached out to members of other denominations and religions, seemed forgotten and discredited, even though the questions of church/state relations, gender roles and expectations, the intelligibility of faith, the relationship to other churches and religions, and the issue of human rights were not adequately solved. Only in the 1960s did the Second Vatican Council confirm the Catholic Enlightenment's view that the church should engage with the world, enter into dialogue with other churches and religions, increase the importance of the office of bishops, renew its liturgy and its teaching mentality, accept religious freedom as a universal value, and defend human rights. Even if the Catholic Enlightenment did not have a universal impact on the church, many of its ideas were unknowingly rediscovered in the twentieth century.

The engagement of Catholicism with the Enlightenment was diverse in its methods and in its results. While many Catholic Enlighteners wanted to use modern thought to make Catholic theology intellectually attractive and intelligible, some sought to restructure the entire belief system. At its best, the Catholic Enlightenment was the resuscitation of the Tridentine Reform by modern means; at its worst, it amounted to the subjugation of theology to the state—unsurprisingly, with heretical tendencies. The tendency of Catholic Enlighteners to work with the state against the papacy helps one to understand the papacy's resistance toward state interventions in the nineteenth century and its increasing distrust of the Enlightenment, especially after the French Revolution. However one views the church's effort at contending with modern thought in the era of Enlightenment, many sincere Catholic thinkers believed in the complementarity of modernity and Catholic theology, in the possibility of updating theological argumentation, and in the possibility that modern science and modern thought can improve the faith life of the church. The Catholic Enlightenment illustrates where the dialogue of the church with modern thought was most fruitful, and where it failed, and can thus serve as a lesson and potential guide for twenty-first century theology in its continuing dialogue with modernity.

Acknowledgments

A journey is a person in itself; no two are alike. And all
plans, safeguards, policing, and coercion are fruitless. We
find that after years of struggle that we do not take a trip;
a trip takes us.

JOHN STEINBECK

THIS JOURNEY THROUGH the world of Enlightenment Catholicism has been a strange, sometimes terrifying, but ultimately, an incredibly enriching experience. Like any true adventure, it was not planned. The initial theme of the book was a study of German Enlightenment Catholicism, but strong winds took hold of my sails and I suddenly found myself in the midst of a global voyage. I owe this experience to the generosity of the Earhart Foundation, whose grant enabled me to boldly rethink my original research plans and to finish this project in a timely manner. Yet what is a journey without companions? I am grateful to many friends, colleagues, and students who offered support or advice in writing this book, especially Alison Britton, Richard J. Barry, Shaun Blanchard, Jeffrey Burson, Patrick Carey, Anthony Clark, Theo Caldera, Brad S. Gregory, Grant Kaplan, Catherine Kavanagh, D. Stephen Long, Mark Noll, Laura Matthew, Paul Monson, Kellen Plaxco, A. G. Roeber, and many, many others. It is needless to say that all mistakes in this book are my own and cannot be attributed to my mentors and friends. My academic home, Marquette University, has provided me with a precious sabbatical and research support, and the superb Raynor Library has done a magnificent job with obtaining even my most obscure library requests.

The questions driving the book derived from a fellowship at the Notre Dame Institute for Advanced Study, where I was challenged to articulate my research in the context of "big questions," and also from a fellowship at the Princeton Institute for Advanced Study. Without the mentorship of Vittorio Hösle and Donald Stelluto at Notre Dame and Jonathan Israel in Princeton, and the support of Darrin McMahon and David Sorkin, I might not have followed up on these questions.

Last but not least, I thank my wife Angela, my soul mate and the compass of my life, and our five wonderful children, who always seemed to interrupt my writing exactly when I needed a break. Overtaking my research vessel like pirates, they keep steering me toward the most important and greatest adventures in life.

Notes

INTRODUCTION

1. Ulrich L. Lehner, "A Fourth Francis," *First Things Web-Exclusive*, February 2, 2015, http://www.firstthings.com/web-exclusives/2015/02/a-fourth-francis.

2. Peter Gay, *The Enlightenment: The Rise of Modern Paganism* (New York: W. W. Norton, 1966), 207–8.

3. Charles C. Noel, "In the House of Reform: The Bourbon-Court of Eighteenth-Century Spain," in *Enlightened Reform in Southern Europe*, edited by Gabriel Paquette (Aldershot: Ashgate, 2009), 145–65, at 149.

4. Nigel Aston, *Christianity and Revolutionary Europe, c. 1750–1830* (Cambridge: Cambridge University Press, 2002); Robert Bireley, *The Refashioning of Catholicism, 1450–1700: A Reassessment of the Counter Reformation* (Washington, DC: Catholic University of America Press, 1999); R. Po-chia Hsia, *The World of Catholic Renewal, 1540–1770* (Cambridge: Cambridge University Press, 1998).

5. Jean Delumeau, *Catholicism between Luther and Voltaire: A New View of the Counter-Reformation* (London: Westminster Press, 1977).

6. Andy Alexis-Baker, "Spinoza's Political Theology: Theocracy, Democracy and Monism," *Journal of Church and State* 54 (2011): 426–44; Dan Edelstein, *The Terror of Natural Right: Republicanism, the Cult of Nature, and the French Revolution* (Chicago: University of Chicago Press, 2009).

7. Marcus Hellyer, *Catholic Physics. Jesuit Natural Philosophy in Early Modern Germany* (Notre Dame, IN: University of Notre Dame Press, 2005), 178.

8. Ulrich L. Lehner, *Enlightened Monks* (Oxford: Oxford University Press, 2011).

9. Ulrich L. Lehner, *Monastic Prisons and Torture Chambers* (Eugene, OR: Cascade, 2013).

10. *Lumen Gentium*, ch. 17.

11. *Gaudium et Spes,* ch. 44.

12. Ulrich L. Lehner, "Johann Nikolaus von Hontheim and His Febronius: A Bishop and His Censored Ecclesiology," *Church History and Religious Culture* 88 (2008): 93–121.

CHAPTER 1

1. Jonathan I. Israel, *Radical Enlightenment: Philosophy and the Making of Modernity, 1650–1750* (Oxford: Oxford University Press, 2001).

2. R. R. Palmer, *Catholics and Unbelievers in Eighteenth-Century France,* 2nd ed. (Princeton, NJ: Princeton University Press, 1970), 20.

3. Thomas White, *Devotion and Reason: Wherein Modern Devotion for the Dead Is Brought to Solid Principles and Made Rational* (Paris: 1661), 66.

4. Gabriel Glickmann, *The English Catholic Community, 1688–1745* (Woodbridge, UK: Boydell Press, 2009), 237.

5. Francis Young, *English Catholics and the Supernatural, 1553–1829* (Aldershot: Ashgate, 2013), 74.

6. Gerhard Sterck, *Démonstration de la foi catholique, ou réfutation de la sceptique Profession de foi, du prétendu Vicaire Savoyard, précédé d'un Discours préliminaire à M.J.J. Rousseau, ex-citoyen de Genève, par un curé flamand,* 2 vols. (Kortrijk: 1765).

7. Claude François Houtteville, *La religion chrétienne prouvée par les faits,* 3 vols. (Paris: 1740); Jeffrey Burson, *The Rise and Fall of Theological Enlightenment: Jean-Martin de Prades and Ideological Polarization in Eighteenth-Century France* (Notre Dame, IN: University of Notre Dame Press, 2010); William Lane Craig, "The Problem of Miracles: A Historical and Philosophical Perspective," in *Gospel Perspectives,* vol. 6, edited by David Wenham and Craig Blomberg (Sheffield, UK: JSOT Press, 1986), 9–40; William Lane Craig, *The Historical Argument for the Resurrection of Jesus during the Deist Controversy* (Lewiston, NY: Edwin Mellen Press, 1985).

8. Paul Shore, *Jesuits and the Politics of Religious Pluralism in Eighteenth-Century Transylvania: Culture, Politics and Religion, 1693–1773* (Aldershot: Ashgate, 2007), 5.

9. Johann Nepomuk Bartholotti, *Streitschrift wider die verschiedenen Gattungen des Aberglaubens* (1779), translated by A. Kreil (Vienna: 1783).

10. The Concordat between France and the Holy See of 1516 already contained similar provisions. See Joseph Bergin, *The Politics of Religion in Early Modern France* (New Haven, CT: Yale University Press, 2014), 1–43; Joseph Bergin, *Church, Society, and Religious Change in France, 1580–1730* (New Haven, CT: Yale University Press, 2009), passim; R. J. Knecht, "The Concordat of 1516: A Reassessment," *University of Birmingham Historical Journal* 9 (1963): 16–32.

11. Robert R. Palmer, *The Age of the Democratic Revolution. II: The Struggle* (Princeton, NJ: Princeton University Press, 1970), 316.

12. Francis Oakley, *The Conciliarist Tradition: Constitutionalism in the Catholic Church, 1300–1870* (Oxford: Oxford University Press, 2003), 158.

13. Jean Ehrard, *L'idée de nature en France dans la première moitié du XVIIIe siècle* (Paris: S.E.V.P.E.N., 1963).

14. Burson, *The Rise and Fall of Theological Enlightenment.*

15. Donald R. Hopkins, *The World's Greatest Killer: Smallpox in History* (Chicago: Chicago University Press, 2002); Yves-Marie Bercé and Jean-Claude Otteni, "Pratique de la vaccination antivariolique dans les provinces de l'État pontifical au 19e s.: remarques sur le supposé interdit vaccinal de Léon XII," *Revue d'Historie Ecclesiastique* 103 (2008): 448–66.

16. Palmer, *Catholics,* 40.

17. Palmer, *Catholics,* 41.

18. Burson, *The Rise and Fall of Theological Enlightenment*; Mark Curran, *Atheism, Religion and Enlightenment in Pre-Revolutionary Europe* (London: Boydell Press, 2012).

19. Palmer, *Catholics,* 85.

20. Palmer, *Catholics,* 96–102.

21. Jeffrey Burson, "Nicolas-Sylvestre Bergier," in *Enlightenment and Catholicism in Europe* (Notre Dame, IN: University of Notre Dame Press, 2014), 65–90; Jeffrey Burson, "The Catholic Enlightenment in France," in *Companion to the Catholic Enlightenment in Europe,* edited by Ulrich L. Lehner and Michael Printy (Leiden: Brill, 2010), 63–125.

22. Palmer, *Catholics,* 70.

23. Michael J. Buckley, *At the Origins of Modern Atheism* (New Haven, CT: Yale University Press, 1987).

24. Joseph Valentin Eybel, *Introductio in Jus Ecclesiasticum Catholicorum,* vol. 1 (Vienna: 1778), § 1; § 5–9.

25. Ebel, *Introductio,* vol. 2, § 87–88; Fritsch, *Religiöse Toleranz,* 353.

26. Matthias Fritsch, *Religiöse Toleranz im Zeitalter der Aufklärung* (Hamburg: Meiner, 2004), 356–57.

27. Walter Dürig, "Anton Frenzels Breslauer theologische Preisschrift (1817) über die Unauflöslichkeit der Ehe," in *Ius et salus animarum. Festschrift B. Panzram,* edited by Ulrich Mosiek and Hartmut Zapp (Freiburg: Rombach, 1972), 439–51; Ignaz Fahrner, *Geschichte der Ehescheidung im kanonischen Recht* (Freiburg: Herder, 1903).

28. *August Ludwig Schlözer's Stats-Anzeigen* 3, no. 9–12 (Göttingen: 1783), 109–15.

29. Staatsarchiv Münster: A 278 II–Stift Neuenheerse Nr. 74, Bd. 9.

30. Karl Joseph Michaeler, *Unumstößliche Gültigkeit der heimlichen Priesterehe bis zur Aufhebung des Cölibats,* 3 vols. (Frankfurt: 1785–1787); Paul Picard, *Zölibatsdiskussion im katholischen Deutschland der Aufklärungszeit* (Düsseldorf: Patmos-Verlag, 1975).

31. Augustin Schelle, *Über den Cölibat der Geistlichen und die Bevölkerung der katholischen Staaten: aus Gründen der politischen Rechenkunst* (Salzburg: 1784).

32. Nicholas Bergier, *Ein Amulett für Coelibatsfeinde* (Vienna: 1783), 12.

33. Benedikt Stattler, *Wahre und allein hinreichende Reformationsart des katholischen Priesterstandes* (Ulm: 1791), 93.

34. Georg May, *Das Versöhnungswerk des päpstlichen Legaten Giovanni B. Caprara. Die Rekonziliation der Geistlichen und Ordensangehörigen 1801–1808* (Berlin: Duncker & Humblot, 2012); see also Claire Cage, *Unnatural Frenchmen: The Politics of Priestly Celibacy and Marriage, 1720–1815* (Charlottesville, VA: University of Virginia Press, 2015).

35. Marius Reiser, *Bibelkritik und Auslegung der Heiligen Schrift* (Tübingen: Mohr Siebeck, 2007), 185–329; Marius Reiser, "Catholic Exegesis," in *Oxford Handbook of Early Modern Theology*, edited by Ulrich L. Lehner, A. G. Roeber, and Richard Muller (Oxford: Oxford University Press, forthcoming).

36. *Catalogus Scriptorum Ordinis Minorum St. Francisci Cappucinorum, 1747–1852* (Rome: 1852), 37; Emmanuel de Lanmodez, "Société royale des études orientales et Académie clémentine établies chez les capucins de Saint-Honoré à Paris (1765-1768)," *Bulletin de la Société de l'histoire de Paris et de l'Ile-de-France* 19 (1892): 98–115.

37. Ulrich L. Lehner, "Against the Consensus of the Fathers? The Conundrums of Catholic Biblical Scholarship in the Eighteenth Century," *Pro Ecclesia* 12 (2013): 189–221.

38. Ulrich L. Lehner, "The Bible among Catholic Enlighteners," in Ulrich L. Lehner, *On the Road to Vatican II: German Catholic Enlighteners and Reform of the Church* (Minneapolis, MN: Fortress Press, 2016).

39. David B. Davis, *The Problem of Slavery in the Age of Revolution, 1770–1823* (Ithaca, NY: Cornell University Press, 1975), 530–31.

40. Ulrich L. Lehner, "Catholic Theology and Enlightenment," *Oxford Handbook of Catholic Theology*, edited by Lewis Ayres (Oxford: Oxford University Press, forthcoming); Johannes Altenberend, *Leander van Ess (1772–1847): Bibelübersetzer und Bibelverbreiter zwischen katholischer Aufklärung und evangelikaler Erweckungsbewegung* (Paderborn: Bonifatius, 2001).

41. Samuel J. Miller, *Portugal and Rome, c. 1748–1830: An Aspect of the Catholic Enlightenment* (Rome: Gregorian University, 1978), 1–27.

42. Miller, *Portugal*, 259–65.

43. Michael Arneth, *Das Ringen um Geist und Form der Priesterbildung im Säkularklerus des siebzehnten Jahrhunderts* (Würzburg: Echter Verlag, 1970).

44. António José Saraiva, *The Marrano Factory: The Portuguese Inquistion and Its New Christians 1536–1765* (Leiden: Brill, 2001), 225–26.

45. Evergton Sales Souza, "The Catholic Enlightenment in Portugal," in *Companion to the Catholic Enlightenment in Europe*, edited by Ulrich L. Lehner and Michael Printy (Leiden: Brill, 2010), 393.

46. Miller, *Portugal*, 172.

47. Miller, *Portugal*, 169–72, 269.

48. Gabriel Paquette, *Enlightenment, Governance and Reform in Spain and Its Empire, 1759–1808* (New York: Palgrave Macmillan, 2008).

49. Stanley J. Stein and Barbara H. Stein, *Apogee of Empire Spain and New Spain in the Age of Charles III, 1759–1789* (Baltimore, MD: Johns Hopkins University Press, 2003).

50. Andrea J. Smidt, "Luces Por La Fe: The Cause of Catholic Enlightenment in 18th-Century Spain," in *Companion to the Catholic Enlightenment*, edited by Ulrich L. Lehner and Michael Printy (Leiden: Brill, 2010), 403–52, at 408.

51. William Callahan, *Church, Politics, and Society in Spain, 1750–1874* (Cambridge, MA: Harvard University Press, 1984), 1–109; Joel Morales Cruz, *The Mexican Reformation* (Eugene, OR: Pickwick), 77–118.

52. Pamela Voelker, *Alone before God: The Religious Origins of Modernity in Mexico* (Durham, NC: Duke University Press, 2002), 25.

53. Francisco Sanchez-Blanco, "Benito Feijoo," in *Enlightenment and Catholicism in Europe*, edited by Ulrich L. Lehner and Jeffrey Burson (Notre Dame, IN: University of Notre Dame Press, 2014), 311–27.

54. Callahan, *Church*, 34.

55. Pablo Olavide, *Triumph des Evangeliums. Memoiren eines von den Verirrungen der heutigen Philosophie zurückgekommenen Weltmenschen*, translated by J. des Echelles, vol. 1 (Regensburg: 1848), xx; Joseph Weiss, *Die deutsche Kolonie an der Sierra Morena und ihr Gründer Johann Kaspar von Thürrigel, ein bayerischer Abenteurer des 18. Jahrhunderts* (Cologne: 1907); Jonathan Israel, *Democratic Enlightenment: Philosophy, Revolution, and Human Rights, 1750–1790* (Oxford: Oxford University Press, 2011), 374–95.

56. Olavide, *Triumph*, vol. 2, 237.

57. Pablo Olavide, *Triumph des Evangeliums. Memoiren eines von den Verirrungen der heutigen Philosophie zurückgekommenen Weltmenschen*, translated by J. des Echelles, vol. 4 (Regensburg: 1848), 322–79. The character of faith and secularism as options are analyzed by Charles Taylor, *A Secular Age* (Cambridge, MA: Belknap Press, 2007).

58. Christopher P. Albi, "Derecho Indians vs. Bourbon Reforms," in *Enlightened Reform in Southern Europe*, edited by Gabriel B. Paquette (Farnham: Ashgate, 2009), 253–70; Juan Marichal, "From Pistoia to Cadiz: A Generation's Itinerary," in *The Ibero-American Enlightenment*, edited by A. Owen Aldrigde (Urbana: University of Illinois Press, 1971), 97–110, at 104.

59. Paola Vismara, "Ludovico Muratori," in *Catholicism and Enlightenment in Europe*, edited by Ulrich L. Lehner and Jeffrey Burson (Notre Dame, IN: University of Notre Dame Press, 2014), 251–70.

60. Vincenzo Ferrone, *The Intellectual Roots of the Italian Enlightenment: Newtonian Science, Religion, Politics in the Early Eighteenth Century* (Atlantic Highlands, NJ: Humanities Press, 1995), 137.

61. Henry C. Clark, *Compass of Society: Commerce and Absolutism in Old-Regime France* (Lanham, MD: Lexington Books, 2007), 177.

62. Larry Walter Lupo, *The Abbe Galiani in Paris, 1759–1769* (PhD diss., University of Georgia, 1971), 107.

63. Lupo, *The Abbe*, 108.

64. Ferrone, *The Intellectual Roots*.

65. Isaiah Berlin, *Three Critics of the Enlightenment: Vico, Hamann, Herder*, 2nd ed., edited by Henry Hardy (Princeton, NJ: Princeton University Press, 2013), 62.

66. Vittorio Hoesle, "Einleitung: Vico und die Idee der Kulturwissenschaft," introduction to Giovanni Battista Vico, *Prinzipien einer neuen Wissenschaft*, vol. 1 (Hamburg: Meiner, 1990), xxxi–cclxxx.

CHAPTER 2

1. Gisela Schlüter, *Die Französische Toleranzdebatte im Zeitalter der Aufklärung* (Tübingen: Niemeyer, 1992); Matthias J. Fritsch, *Religiöse Toleranz im Zeitalter der Aufklärung: naturrechtliche Begründung—konfessionelle Differenzen* (Hamburg: Meiner, 2004), 37–59.

2. Rainer Forst, *Toleration in Conflict. Past and Present* (Cambridge: Cambridge University Press, 2013).

3. Charles A. Bolton, *Church Reform in 18th-Century Italy* (The Hague: Nijhoff, 1969), 123.

4. Ulrich L. Lehner, *Beda Mayr—Vertheidigung der katholischen Religion* (Leiden: Brill, 2009), 211.

5. Forst, *Toleration*, 96–265; Sven Grosse, *Das Christentum an der Schwelle der Neuzeit* (Kamen: Spenner, 2010), 55–84; on Kenny, see William Battersby, *A History of All the Abbeys, Convents, Churches … Particularly of the Hermits of St. Augustine in Ireland* (Dublin: 1856), 111; Ludovico Muratori, *The Science of Rational Devotion*. Translated by Alexander Kenny (Dublin: 1789), preface. Catholic Enlighteners also used the term "dissident brethren," e.g., see Karl Schwarzl, *Praelectiones Theologiae Polemicae* (Vienna: 1783). To my knowledge there is no history of the term "separated brethren."

6. Benjamin Kaplan, *Divided by Faith: Religious Conflict and the Practice of Toleration in Early Modern Europe* (Cambridge, MA: Belknap Press, 2007), 8.

7. Dale K. Van Kley, *The Religious Origins of the French Revolution from Calvin to the Civil Constitution, 1560–1791* (New Haven, CT: Yale University Press, 1996).

8. Dominik Burkard and Tanja Thanner, eds., *Der Jansenismus—eine "katholische Häresie"?: das Ringen um Gnade, Rechtfertigung und die Autorität Augustins in der frühen Neuzeit* (Münster: Aschendorff, 2014); Nigel Abercrombie, *The Origins of Jansenism* (Oxford: Clarendon Press, 1936).

9. Bernhard Groethuysen, *The Bourgeois; Catholicism vs. Capitalism in Eighteenth-Century France* (New York: Holt, Rinehart and Winston, 1968);

William Doyle, *Jansenism* (Houndmills: Macmillan, 2000); Daniella Kostroun, *Feminism, Absolutism, and Jansenism: Louis XIV and the Port-Royal Nuns* (Cambridge: Cambridge University Press: 2011).

10. John McManners, *Church and Society in Eighteenth-Century France* (Oxford: Oxford University Press, 1998), vol. 2, 426.

11. Van Kley, *Religious Origins*, 75–135.

12. S. J. Barnett, *The Enlightenment and Religion: The Myths of Modernity* (Manchester: Manchester University Press, 2003), 152.

13. Daniel Mornet, *Les origines intellectuelles de la Révolution française, 1715–1787* (Paris: A. Colin, 1933).

14. Van Kley, *Religious Origins*, 372.

15. Georg Schmidt, *Wandel durch Vernunft: Deutsche Geschichte im 18. Jahrhundert* (Munich: C. H. Beck, 2009).

16. Fritsch, *Religiöse Toleranz*, 236–47.

17. Hans Wicki, "Bernhard Ludwig Göldlin (1723–1785)," in *Festschrift Oskar Vasella* (Freiburg: 1964), 456–500.

18. Thomas Aquin Jost, *Bildnisse der Freyheit und Inquisition wider die Freygeister* (Freising: 1779), 26.

19. The reforms, however, did not accept Jewish culture and intended an assimiliation of Jewry in the image of Joseph II's enlightened ideals. See Derek Beales, *Joseph II: Against the World* (Cambridge: Cambridge University Press, 2009), 196–213.

20. Josef Karniel, *Die Toleranzpolitik Kaiser Josephs II* (Gerlingen: Bleicher, 1986).

21. Ernst Wangermann, *Die Waffen der Publizität: zum Funktionswandel der politischen Literatur unter Joseph II* (Vienna: Verlag für Geschichte und Politik, 2004); Charles O'Brien, *Ideas of Religious Toleration at the Time of Joseph II* (Philadelphia: APS, 1969); Reinhold Wolny, *Die josephinische Toleranz* (Munich: Lerche, 1973).

22. Beales, *Joseph II: Against the World*, 176; Wolny, *Die josephinische Toleranz*, 40–42.

23. O'Brien, *Ideas of Religious Toleration*, 21–22; Wolny, *Die josephinische Toleranz*, 44–45.

24. Wangermann, *Die Waffen der Publizität*, 15; Beales, *Joseph II*, vol. 2, 168–83.

25. Wolny, *Die josephinische Toleranz*, 75–76.

26. Pietro Tamburini, *De tolerantia ecclesiastica et civili* (Ticini: 1783); Francesco Ruffini, *Religious Liberty* (New York: Putnam, 1912), 466–73; Beales, *Joseph II*, 214–38.

27. Harm Klueting, *Der Josephinismus* (Darmstadt: WBG, 1995), 289–94, at 293; Zdenek V. David, Realism, *Tolerance and Liberalism in the Czech National Awakening: Legacies of the Bohemian Reformation* (Baltimore, MD: Johns Hopkins University Press, 2010), 58; 68–69.

28. David, *Realism*, 58–75; Caspar Royko, *Geschichte der grossen allgemeinen Kirchenversammlung zu Kostniz* (Prague: 1785), 214; Otto Steinbach von

Kranichstein, "Versuch einer Geschichte der alten und neuern Toleranz im Königreich Böhmen und Markgrafenthum Mähren," in *Abhandlungen der Böhmischen Gesellschaft der Wissenschaften zu Prag auf das Jahr 1785, Zweite Abteilung* (Prague: 1785), 200–233.

29. Peter Adolph Winkopp, *Geschichte der böhmischen Deisten nebst freimüthigen Bemerkungen über die Grundsätze der Duldung der Deisten* (Leipzig: 1785), 56.

30. Winkopp, *Geschichte der böhmischen Deisten*, 85, 88.

31. Tristan Coignard, *L'apologie du débat public: réseaux journalistiques et pouvoirs dans l'Allemagne des lumières* (Pessac: Presses Universitaires de Bordeaux, 2009), 169–76.

32. Richard Butterwick, *The Polish Revolution and the Catholic Church, 1788–1792* (Oxford: Oxford University Press, 2012), 251.

33. Butterwick, *The Polish Revolution*, 308.

34. Butterwick, *The Polish Revolution*, 309; Richard Butterwick, "Catholic and Enlightenment in Poland-Lithuania," in *Brill's Companion to the Catholic Enlightenment*, edited by Ulrich L. Lehner and Michael Printy (Leiden: Brill, 2010), 297–357.

35. Hans-Wolfgang Bergerhausen, *Friedensrecht und Toleranz: zur Politik des preussischen Staates gegenüber der katholischen Kirche in Schlesien 1740–1806* (Berlin: Duncker & Humblot, 1999); Max Lehmann, *Preussen und die katholischen Kirche seit 1640*, vol. 2 (Leipzig: 1881), 91.

36. Hubert Wolf, ed., *Verbotene Bücher: zur Geschichte des Index im 18. und 19. Jahrhundert. Römische Inquisition und Indexkongregation*, 11 (Paderborn: Schöningh, 2008).

37. Cecil Roth, *Ritual Murder Libel and the Jew: The Report of Cardinal Lorenzo Ganganelli* (London: Woburn Press, 1934).

38. Ronnie Po-chia Hsia, *Trent 1475: Stories of a Ritual Murder Trial* (New Haven, CT: Yale University Press, 1992).

39. Marina Caffiero, *Forced Baptisms: Histories of Jews, Christians, and Converts in Papal Rome* (Berkeley: University of California Press, 2012), 7.

40. Caffiero, *Forced Baptisms*, 79.

41. Caffiero, *Forced Baptisms*, 78–100.

42. Caffiero, *Forced Baptisms*, 130.

43. Owen Chadwick, *The Popes and European Revolution* (Oxford: Clarendon Press, 1981), 20.

44. Benjamin J. Kaplan, *Divided by Faith: Religious Conflict and the Practice of Toleration in Early Modern Europe* (Cambridge, MA: Belknap Press, 2007).

45. David Kertzer, *The Kidnapping of Edgardo Mortara* (New York: Random House, 1997).

46. François-René Chateaubriand, *Génie du christianisme* (1802) (Flammarion: Paris, 1966). Appears under the title *Genius of Christianity* in many English translations.

CHAPTER 3

1. Joseph Bergin, *Church, Society and Religious Change in France, 1580–1730* (New Haven, CT: Yale University Press, 2009).

2. Theresa Ann Smith, *The Emerging Female Citizen: Gender and Enlightenment in Spain* (Berkeley: University of California Press, 2006), 24–34; Benito Feijoo, *An Essay on Woman, or Physiological and Historical Defense of the Fair Sex* (London: 1778).

3. Monica Bolufer Peruga, "Neither Male nor Female: Rational Equality in the Early Spanish Enlightenment," in *Women, Gender and Enlightenment*, edited by Sarah Knott and Barbara Taylor (Houndsmills: Palgrave Macmillan, 2005), 389–409.

4. Elizabeth Franklin Lewis, *Women Writers in the Spanish Enlightenment: The Pursuit of Happiness* (Aldershot: Ashgate, 2004), 23–60.

5. Margaret R. Hunt, *Women in Eighteenth-Century History* (London: Longman, 2010), 218.

6. Lewis, *Women Writers*, 45.

7. Paula Findlen, "Science as a Career in Enlightenment Italy: The Strategies of Laura Bassi," *Isis* 84 (1993): 441–69.

8. Beate Ceranski, *"Und sie fürchtet sich vor niemanden." Die Physikern Laura Bassi (1711–1778)* (Frankfurt: Campus, 1996), 92–94; Luciano Guerci, *La discussione sulla donna nel Settecento* (Turin: Tirrenia, 1987).

9. Massimo Mazzotti, *The World of Maria Gaetana Agnesi, Mathematician of God* (Baltimore, MD: Johns Hopkins University Press, 2007).

10. Mazzotti, *The World of Maria Gaetana*, 145.

11. Frans Ciappara, "Perceptions of Marriage in Late-Eighteenth-Century Malta," *Continuity and Change* 16 (2001): 379–98, at 381; Frans Ciappara, *Marriage in Malta in the Late Eighteenth Century, 1750–1800* (Qormi, Malta: Associated News, 1988).

12. Patricia Seed, *To Love, Honor and Obey in Colonial Mexico: Conflicts over Marriage Choice, 1574–1821* (Stanford, CA: Stanford University Press, 1988), 234.

13. Anne Jacobson Schutte, *By Force and Fear: Taking and Breaking Monastic Vows in Early Modern Europe* (Ithaca, NY: Cornell University Press, 2011).

14. Seed, *To Love, Honor*, 133; 227–43.

15. Seed, *To Love, Honor*, 109.

16. Jean-Louis Flandrin, *Sex in the Western World: The Development of Attitudes and Behavior*. Translated by Sue Collins (Chur, Switzerland: Harwood Academic Publishers, 1991), 53

17. Hunt, *Women*, 91.

18. Peter Hersche, *Musse und Verschwendung: europäische Gesellschaft und Kultur im Barockzeitalter* (Freiburg: Herder, 2006), vol. 2, 742.

19. Hunt, *Women*, 96.

20. Hunt, *Women*, 112.
21. Hersche, *Musse*, vol. 2, 744; John Thomas Noonan, *Contraception: A History of Its Treatment by the Catholic Theologians and Canonists* (Cambridge, MA: Belknap Press, 1965); Leslie Tuttle, *Conceiving the Old Regime: Pronatalism and the Politics of Reproduction in Early Modern France* (Oxford: Oxford University Press, 2010), 3–17.
22. Ciappara, "Perceptions," 385.
23. Alphonsus of Liguori, *Homo Apostolicus* (Regensburg: 1854), vol. 2 part 18, ch. 2, nr. 50.
24. *Conceiving the Old Regime*, 18; Hunt, *Women*, 98.
25. Nadia Maria Filippini, "Die 'erste' Geburt. Einen neue Vorstellung vom Foetus und vom Mutterleib (Italien, 18. Jahrhundert)," in *Geschichte des Ungeborenen. Zur Erfahrungs-und Wissenschaftsgeschichte der Schwangerschaft*, edited by Barbara Duden et al. (Göttingen: Vandenhoeck & Ruprecht, 2002), 99–128; Stefano Cecchin, *L'Immacolata Concezione: breve storia del dogma* (Città del Vaticano: Pontificia Academia Mariana Internationalis, 2003).
26. Franz X. Mezler, *Ueber den Einfluss der Heilkunst auf die praktische Theologie. Ein Beitrag zur Pastoralmedizin* (Ulm: 1794), vol. 2, 253.
27. Ciappara, "Perceptions," 389.
28. Prospere Eve, "Forms of Resistance in Bourbon, 1750–1789," in *The Abolitions of Slavery: From Léger Félicité Sonthonax to Victor Schoelcher, 1793, 1794, 1848*, edited by Marcel Dorigny (Paris: UNESCO and Berghahn, 2003),17–39, at 29.
29. Hersche, *Musse*, vol. 1, 215.
30. Hunt, *Women*, 141.
31. Tuttle, *Conceiving the Old Regime*, 135.
32. Tuttle, *Conceiving the Old Regime*, 135.
33. Hunt, *Women*, 144; for the broader history of "maternalism," see Seth Koven and Sonya Michel, *Mothers of a New World: Maternalist Politics and the Origins of Welfare States* (New York: Routledge, 1993).
34. Rebecca Kukla, *Mass Hysteria: Medicine, Culture and Mothers' Bodies* (Lanham, MD: Rowman & Littlefield, 2005), 31.
35. Jose Pardo-Tomas and Alvar Martinez-Vidal, "The Ignorance of Midwives: The Role of Catholic Clergymen in Spanish Enlightenment Debates on Birth Care," in *Medicine and Religion in Enlightenment Europe*, edited by Ole Peter Grell and Andrew Cunningham (Aldershot: Ashgate, 2007), 49–62, at 55.
36. Tomas and Vidal, "The Ignorance," 59.
37. Jan de Vries, *The Industrious Revolution: Consumer Behavior and the Household Economy, 1650 to the Present* (Cambridge: Cambridge University Press, 2008), 208.
38. De Vries, *Industrious Revolution*, 102–3; Eva Tanner Bannett, *The Domestic Revolution: Enlightenment Feminisms and the Novel* (Baltimore, MD: Johns Hopkins University Press, 2000), 140–43.

39. Keith Thomas, *The Ends of Life: Roads to Fulfillment in Early Modern England* (Oxford: Oxford University Press, 2009), 23.

40. Marion W. Gray, *Productive Men, Reproductive Women: The Agrarian Household and the Emergence of Separate Spheres during the German Enlightenment* (New York: Berghahn Books, 2000), 139.

41. Gray, *Productive Men*, 89–120.

42. Helen Fronius, *Women and Literature in the Goethe Era, 1770–1820: Determined Dilettantes* (Oxford: Clarendon Press, 2007), 16; cf. Anne-Charlotte Trepp, *Sanfte Männlichkeit und selbständige Weiblichkeit. Frauen und Männer im Hamburger Bürgertum zwischen 1770 und 1840* (Göttingen: Vandenhoeck & Rupprecht, 1996).

43. Gray, *Productive Men*, 1–24.

44. Jesus Cruz, *The Rise of Middle-Class Culture in Nineteenth-Century Spain* (Baton Rouge: Louisiana State University Press, 2011), 53–59.

45. Margaret P. Schaller, *An Alternative Enlightenment: The Moral Philosophy of Jeanne Marie Leprince de Beaumont (1711–1780)* (PhD diss., Florida Atlantic University, 2008), 3.

46. Alessa Johns, "Reproducing Utopia: Jeanne-Marie Leprince de Beaumont's The New Clarissa," *Historical Reflections* 25 (1999): 312; Patricia A. Clancy, "Mme Leprince de Beaumont: Founder of Children's Literature in France," *Australian Journal of French Studies* 1 (1979): 281–86.

47. Victoria Pine, *Jeanne Marie Leprince de Beaumont: Women's Epistolary and Pedagogical Fiction in the Eighteenth Century* (PhD diss., University of Missouri-Columbia, 2010), 16; 17.

48. Jeanne Marie Leprince de Beaumont, *Letters of Madame du Montier*, vol. 1 (London: 1798), 12–13.

49. Jean Louis Flandrin, *Families in Former Times: Kinship, Household, and Sexuality*. Translated by Richard Southern (Cambridge: Cambridge University Press, 1976), 122–28.

50. Tina Yiuwen Chen, *Reason and Femininity in the Age of Enlightenment* (PhD diss., University of California, Berkeley, 2007), 170; Patricia Clancy, "A French Writer and Educator in England: Mme le Prince de Beaumont," *Studies on Voltaire and the Eighteenth Century* 201 (1982): 195–208.

51. Schaller, *An Alternative Enlightenment*, 194.

52. Schaller, *An Alternative Enlightenment*, 199.

53. Hersche, *Musse*, vol. 1, 219–20.

54. Tuttle, *Conceiving the Old Regime*, 156; 163;

55. Tuttle, *Conceiving the Old Regime*, 126.

56. *Catechism of the Council of Trent for Parish Priests*. Translated by John A. McHugh and Charles J. Callan (Rockford: Tan Publishing, 1982), 343–44.

57. *Catechism of the Council of Trent*, 346.

58. Flandrin, *Sex in the Western World*, 95; Fernanda Alfieri, "Urge without Desire? Confession Manuals, Moral Casuistry, and the Features of Concupiscentia between the Fifteenth and Eighteenth Centuries," in *Bodies, Sex and Desire from the Renaissance to the Present*, edited by Kate Fisher and Sarah Toulalan (New York: Palgrave Macmillan, 2011), 151–67.

59. Lesley H. Walker, *A Mother's Love: Crafting Feminine Virtue in Enlightenment France* (Lewisburg, PA: Bucknell University Press, 2008), 24; 27.

60. Tuttle, *Conceiving the Old Regime*, 137. For the development of Catholic teaching see Agnès Walch, *La spiritualité conjugale dans le catholicisme français (XVIe–XXe siècle)* (Paris: Cerf, 2002); Mary Wiesner-Hanks, *Christianity and Sexuality in the Early Modern World. Regulating Desire, Reforming Practice*, 2nd ed. (Aldershot: Ashgate, 2010), 129–80.

61. Agnès Walch, "Marital Spirituality from the Seventeenth to the Twentieth Centuries," in *Companion to Marital Spirituality*, edited by Thomas Knieps-Port le Roi and Monica Sandor (Leuven, Belgium: Peeters, 2008), 155–66; Walch, *La spiritualité conjugale*.

62. Flandrin, *Sex in the Western World*, 78.

63. Flandrin, *Families*, 171.

64. Joan E. DeJean, *Tender Geographies: Women and the Origins of the Novel in France* (New York: Columbia University Press, 1991).

65. Hunt, *Women*, 217.

66. Veronica Čapská, "Between Revival and Uncertainty—Female Religious Life in Central Europe in the Long Eighteenth Century," in *Between Revival and Uncertainty: Monastic and Secular Female Communities in Central Europe in the Long Eighteenth Century*, edited by Veronika Čapská, Ellinor Forster, Janine Christina Maegraith, and Christine Schneider (Opava: Silesian University in Opava, 2012), 11–34, at 29.

67. Susan E. Dinan, "Confraternities as a Venue for Female Activism during the Catholic Reformation," in *Confraternities and Catholic Reform in Italy, France and Spain*, edited by John Donnelly and Michael Maher (Kirsville, MO: Thomas Jefferson University Press, 1999), 189–213.

68. Mary Peckham Margray, *The Transforming Power of the Nuns: Women, Religious, and Cultural Change in Ireland, 1750–1900* (New York: Oxford University Press, 1998), 1–12.

69. Silivia Evangelisti, *Nuns: A History of Convent Life, 1450–1700* (Oxford: Oxford University Press, 2007), 6; Barbara B. Diefendorf, *From Penitence to Charity: Pious Women and the Catholic Reformation in Paris* (Oxford: Oxford University Press, 2004); Jan Zdichynec, "Quia *sic* fert consuetudo? Die Klausur in den Zisterzienserklöstern der Frühen Neuzeit," in *Between Revival and Uncertainty: Monastic and Secular Female Communities in Central Europe in the Long Eighteenth Century*, edited by Veronika Čapská, Ellinor Forster, Janine Christina Maegraith, and Christine Schneider (Opava: Silesian University in Opava, 2012), 37–68; Choudhury, *Convents*, 18.

70. Čapská, "Between Revival," 26.

71. Margaret Chowning, *Rebellious Nuns: The Troubled History of a Mexican Convent, 1752—1863* (Oxford: Oxford University Press, 2006).

72. Ulrich L. Lehner, *Monastic Prisons and Torture Chambers. Crime and Punishment in Central European Monasteries* (Eugene, OR: Cascade, 2013), 70–72.

73. Chowning, *Rebellious Nuns*.

74. Mita Choudhury, *Convents and Nuns in Eighteenth-Century French Politics and Culture* (Ithaca, NY: Cornell University Press, 2004), 40.

75. Choudhury, *Convents*, 33.

76. Choudhury, *Convents*, 38.

77. Choudhury, *Convents*, 47.

78. Choudhury, *Convents*, 4–5; 33–69.

79. Choudhury, *Convents*, 32–35; Elizabeth Rapley, *A Social History of the Cloister: Daily Life in the Teaching Monasteries of the Old Regime* (Montreal: McGill-Queen's University Press, 2001), 66–77.

80. Linda Lierheimer, *Female Eloquence and Maternal Ministry: The Apostolate of Ursuline Nuns in Seventeenth-Century France* (PhD diss., Princeton University, 1994); Emily Clark, *Masterless Mistresses: The New Orleans Ursulines and the Development of a New World Society, 1727–1834* (Chapel Hill: University of North Carolina Press, 2007), 89; Colin Jones, *The Charitable Imperative. Hospitals and Nursing in Ancien Regime and Revolutionary France* (London: Routledge, 1989); Elizabeth Rapley, *The Dévotes: Women and Church in Seventeenth-Century France* (Montreal: McGill-Queen's University Press, 1990); Olwen H. Hufton, *The Poor of Eighteenth-Century France 1750–1789* (Oxford: Clarendon Press, 1974).

81. Clark, *Masterless Mistresses*, 121.

82. Clark, *Masterless Mistresses*, 5–6.

83. Emily Clark, *Voices from an Early American Convent: Marie Madeleine Hachard and the New Orleans Ursulines, 1727–1760* (Baton Rouge: Louisiana State University Press, 2007).

84. Bianca Premo, *Children of the Father King: Youth, Authority, and Legal Minority in Colonial Lima* (Chapel Hill: University of North Carolina Press, 2005), 82–91.

85. Choudhury, *Convents*, 137.

86. Colleen Gray, *The Congregation de Notre Dame, Superiors, and the Paradox of Power, 1693–1796* (Montreal: McGill-Queen's University Press, 2007), 32; Premo, *Children*, 150; Choudhury, *Convents*, 137.

87. Stefan Benz, "Geschichtsschreibung der Frauenklöster Zentraleuropas im 18. Jahrhundert," in *Between Revival and Uncertainty: Monastic and Secular Female Communities in Central Europe in the Long Eighteenth Century*, edited by Veronika Čapská, Ellinor Forster, Janine Christina Maegraith, and Christine Schneider (Opava: Silesian University in Opava, 2012), 241–66; cf. Asunción Lavrín, *Brides of Christ: Conventual Life in Colonial Mexico* (Stanford, CA: Stanford University Press, 2008), 334. For the spiritual biographies of sisters, see

Kristine Ibsen, *Women's Spiritual Autobiography in Colonial Spanish America* (Gainesville: University Press of Florida, 1999).

CHAPTER 4

1. Karl Schmitt, "The Clergy and the Enlightenment in Latin America: An Analysis," *The Americas* 15 (1959): 381–91; John Tate Lanning, *The Eighteenth-Century Enlightenment in the University of San Carlos De Guatemala* (Ithaca, NY: Cornell University Press, 1956).
2. Susanne M. Zantop, *Kolonialphantasien im vorkolonialen Deutschland, 1770–1870* (Berlin: Erich Schmidt, 1999), 188–89.
3. Margaret R. Ewalt, *Peripheral Wonders: Nature, Knowledge, and Enlightenment in the Eighteenth-Century Orinoco* (Lewisburg, PA: Bucknell University Press, 2008), 113.
4. Ewalt, *Peripheral Wonders*, 95–140.
5. Charles E. Ronan, *Francisco Javier Clavigero, SJ, 17311787. Figure of the Mexican Enlightenment* (Chicago: Loyola University Press, 1977), 83–87; Richard E. Greenleaf, "The Mexican Inquisition and the Enlightenment, 1763–1805," *New Mexico Historical Review* 41 (1966): 181–96.
6. Antonello Gerbi, *The Dispute of the New World: The History of a Polemic, 1750–1900* (Pittsburgh: Pittsburgh University Press: 2010 [1955]).
7. Ronan, *Francisco*, 250.
8. Ronan, *Francisco*, 341.
9. Jorge Cañizares-Esguerra, *How to Write the History of the New World: Histories, Epistemologies, and Identities in the Eighteenth-Century Atlantic World* (Stanford, CA: Stanford University Press, 2001), 281–307; Fiona Clark, "Read All About It: Science, Translation, Adaptation and Confrontation in the *Gazeta de Literatura de Mexico*, 1788–1795," in *Science in the Spanish and Portuguese Empires, 1500–1800*, edited by Daniela Bleichmar et al. (Stanford, CA: Stanford University Press, 2009), 147–77.
10. Felix Becker, *Die Politische Machtstellung der Jesuiten in Südamerika im 18. Jahrhundert. Zur Kontroverse um den Jesuitenkönig Nikolaus I von Portugal* (Vienna: Böhlau, 1980), 11.
11. Becker, *Die politische Machtstellung*, 24.
12. Maura Jane Farrelly, *Patriot Papists: The Making of American Catholic Identity* (New York: Oxford University Press, 2012).
13. Luca Codignola, "Roman Catholic Conservatism in a New North Atlantic World, 1760–1829," in *Religious Conflicts and Accommodation in the Early Modern World*, edited by Marguerite Ragnow and William D. Philips (Minneapolis: University of Minnesota Press, 2011), 153–207, at 159.
14. Joseph Agonito, *The Building of an American Catholic Church: The Episcopacy of John Carroll* (New York: Garland, 1988), 211.

15. Agonito, *The Building,* 30–31.

16. Patrick Carey, *People, Priests and Prelates: Ecclesial Democracy and the Tensions of Trusteeism* (Notre Dame, IN: University of Notre Dame Press, 1987), 108.

17. Codignola, "Roman Catholic," 178; Carey, *People.*

18. Carl F. G. Zollmann, *American Church Law* (St. Paul, MN: West, 1933), 112; 143–45.

19. Agonito, *The Building,* 197.

20. Thomas S. Kidd, *God of Liberty: A Religious History of the American Revolution* (New York: Basic Books, 2010).

21. Agonito, *The Building,* 251.

22. Scott McDermott, *Charles Carroll of Carrollton: Faithful Revolutionary* (New York: Scepter: 2004).

23. Jonathan Wright, *The Jesuits. Missions, Myths and Histories* (New York: Harper, 2004), 183.

24. D. E. Mungello, *The Great Encounter of China and the West, 1500–1800* (Lanham, MD: Rowman & Littlefield: 1999), 21.

25. Ronnie Po-chia Hsia, *A Jesuit in the Forbidden City: Matteo Ricci, 1552–1610* (Oxford: Oxford University Press, 2010).

26. Anthony E. Clark, ed., *A Voluntary Exile Chinese Christianity and Cultural Confluence since 1552* (Bethlehem, PA: Lehigh University Press, 2013).

27. John Dragon Young, "Chinese Views of Rites and the Rites Controversy," in *The Chinese Rites Controversy: Its History and Meaning,* edited by D. E. Mungello (Nettetal: Steyler Verlag: 1994), 83–110, at 94.

28. Eugenio Menegon, *Ancestors, Virgins and Friars: Christianity as a Local Religion in Late Imperial China* (Cambridge, MA: Harvard University Press, 2009), 178–205.

29. David E. Mungello, *Curious Land: Jesuit Accommodation and the Origins of Sinology* (Honolulu: University of Hawaii Press, 1989); Mungello, *The Great Encounter,* 68–74; Johann Riedl, *Das Heil der Heiden nach Röm 2* (Mödling: St. Gabriel Verlag, 1965).

30. Claudia von Collani, "Das Problem des Heils der Heiden," *Neue Zeitschrift für Missionswissenschaft* 45 (1989): 17–35 and 93–109.

31. Michael Buckley, "The Suppression of the Chinese Rites," in *The Chinese Rites Controversy: Its History and Meaning,* edited by D. E. Mungello (Nettetal: Styler Verlag, 1994), 281–85; Henri Bernard-Maitre, "Die Frage der chinesischen und malabrischen Riten," *Concilium* 3 (1967): 551–58.

32. Knud Lundbaek, "Joseph Premare and the Name of God in China," in *The Chinese Rites Controversy: Its History and Meaning,* edited by D. E. Mungello (Nettetal: Styler Verlag, 1994), 129–48, at 145.

33. Josef Metzler, "Ein Mann mit neuen Ideen. Sekretär und Präfekt Stefano Borgia," in *Sacrae Congregationis de Propaganda Fide Memoria Rerum* vol. 2 (Herder: Rom and Freiburg, 1973), 119–53.

34. David E. Mungello, "Confucianism in the Enlightenment," in *China and Europe*, edited by Thomas H. C. Lee (Hong Kong: Chinese University Press, 1991), 99–130. One of the few Enlighteners who relied on Figurism was the maverick of Catholic philosophy, the Scotsman Andrew Michael Ramsey (1686–1743), who used it to project his own, universalist philosophy of religion.

35. André Ly, *Journal D'André Ly: Prêtre Chinois, Missionaire Et Notaire Apostolique, 1746-1763* (Hongkong: Imprimerie de Nazareth, 1924).

36. David N. Lorenzen, "Marco della Tomba and Brahmin from Banaras: Missionaries, Orientalists, and Indian Scholars," *Journal of Asian Studies* 65, no. 1 (February 2006): 115–43, at 119.

37. Wright, *Jesuits*, 111.

38. Ines G. Županov, *Disputed Mission: Jesuit Experiments and Brahmanical Knowledge in Seventeenth-Century India* (New Delhi: Oxford University Press, 1999).

39. C. R. Boxer, "The Problem of Native Clergy in the Portuguese and Spanish Empires from the Sixteenth to the Eighteenth Centuries," in *Christianity and Missions, 1450–1800*, edited by J. S. Cummins (Aldershot: Ashgate, 1997), 161–75; Kenneth Maxwell, *Conflicts and Conspiracies: Brazil and Portugal, 1750–1808* (New York: Routledge, 2001), 77–79.

40. Owen Chadwick, *The Popes and European Revolution* (Oxford: Clarendon Press, 1981), 133.

41. Boxer, "The Problem," 186.

42. Jeffrey D. Burson, "Chinese Novices, Jesuit Missionaries and the Accidental Construction of Sinophobia in Enlightenment France," *French History* 27 (2013): 21–44; Menegon, *Ancestors*, 141–42.

43. Maria de Jesus dos Mártires Lopes, *Tradition and Modernity in Eighteenth-Century Goa, 1750–1800* (New Delhi: Manohar, 2006), 182; 205; *Magnum Bullarium Romanum*, vol. 11 (Luxembourg: 1753), 1–4.

44. Lopes, *Tradition and Modernity*, 40–44; Maria de Jesus dos Mártires Lopes, "The Sisters of Santa Monica in the 18th C.: Details of their Daily Life," in *Goa and Portugal: History and Development*, edited by Charles J. Borges (New Delhi: Concept, 2000), 238–47; Joaquim Heliodoro da Cunha Rivara, *Goa and the Revolt of 1787* (New Delhi: Concept, 1996), 82.

45. Lopes, *Tradition and Modernity*, 118.

46. Lopes, *Tradition and Modernity*, 191.

47. Lopes, *Tradition and Modernity*, 180–93.

48. Lopes, *Tradition and Modernity*, 285–90.

49. Lopes, *Tradition and Modernity*, 356.

50. Lopes, *Tradition and Modernity*, 370.

51. Rivara, *Goa and the Revolt of 1787*.

52. Simon Ditchfield, *Papacy and People: The Making of Roman Catholicism as a World Religion, 1500–1700* (Oxford: Oxford University Press, forthcoming).

CHAPTER 5

1. Immanuel Kant, *Religion within the Boundaries of Mere Reason* [Nachlass], Akademieausgabe (AA), vol. 23, 104.

2. Immanuel Kant, *Critique of Judgment*, AA, vol. 5, 295.

3. Sarah Ferber, *Possession and Exorcism in Early Modern France* (Florence, KY: Routledge, 2004), 15.

4. Giorgio Caravale, *Forbidden Prayer: Church Censorship in Renaissance Italy* (Aldershot: Ashgate, 2012), 191–223, at 194; Euan Cameron, *Enchanted Europe, Superstition, Reason and Religion, 1250–1750* (Oxford: Oxford University Press: 2010), 287–89.

5. Maurice Andrieux, *Daily Life in Papal Rome in the Eighteenth Century* (London: George Allen and Unwin, 1968), 16; 119.

6. Rebekka Habermas, *Wallfahrt und Aufruhr: zur Geschichte des Wunderglaubens in der frühen Neuzeit* (Frankfurt [am Main]: Campus, 1991).

7. Franz Meffert, *Der heilige Alfons von Liguori—Der Kirchenlehrer und Apologet des 18. Jahrhunderts* (Mainz: 1901), 220.

8. Andre Vauchez, *Sainthood in the Later Middle Ages*. Translated by Jean Birrell (Cambridge: Cambridge University Press, 1997 [1981]).

9. Jacyln Duffin, *Medical Miracles: Doctors, Saints, and Healing in the Modern World* (Oxford: Oxford University Press, 2009), 12–36.

10. Fabian Campagne, "Witchcraft and the Sense-of-the-Impossible in Early Modern Spain," *Harvard Theological Review* 96 (2003): 25–62, at 56; Jonathan Israel, *The Radical Enlightenment: Philosophy and the Making of Modernity* (Oxford: Oxford University Press, 2001), 401–3.

11. Duffin, *Medical Miracles*; Catrien Santing, "Tirami Su: Pope Benedict XIV and the Beatification of the Flying Saint Guispee da Copertino," in *Medicine and Religion in Enlightenment Europe*, edited by Ole Peter Grell et al. (Aldershot: Ashgate: 2007), 79–100.

12. John Chinnici, *The English Catholic Enlightenment: John Lingard and the Cisalpine Movement, 1780–1850* (Shepherdstown, WV: Patmos Press, 1980), 137–39.

13. Ludovico Muratori, *Delle riflessioni sopra il buon gusto nelle scienze e nell'arti* (Venice : 1736), ch. 4, par. 7.

14. Ludovico Muratori, *De Ingeniorum moderatione in religionis negotio* (Augsburg: 1778), lib. 2, ch. 14.

15. Jürgen Jensen, *Kirchliche Rituale als Waffen gegen Dämonenwirken und Zauberei. Ein Beitrag zu einem Komplex von Schutz-und Abwehrritualen der Katholischen Kirche des 17. und 18. Jahrhunderts in Italien* (Münster: LIT, 2007); Cameron, *Enchanted Europe*, 287–89; Caravale, *Forbidden Prayer*, 202–3.

16. Ludovico Muratori, *The Science of Rational Devotion* (Dublin: 1789), 13.

17. Muratori, *The Science of Rational Devotion*, 161.

18. Ludovico Muratori, *Della regolata divozion de' cristiani* (Venice: 1742), ch. 24, 353: "inventate . . . per farne qualche traffic temporale"; "di sola apparenza e non di sostanza," ch. 36, 374.

19. Rainer Beck, *Mäuselmacher oder die Imagination des Bösen: ein Hexenprozess 1715–1723* (Munich: Beck, 2012), 440.

20. Ludovico Muratori, *De Superstitione Vitanda* (Venice: 1740).

21. Muratori, *The Science of Rational Devotion* (Dublin: 1789 [1747]), 205–6.

22. Caravale, *Forbidden Prayer*, 207.

23. Benedict Werkmeister,*Vertheidigung des von Herrn Pfarrer Brunner für aufgeklärte Christen* (Frankfurt: 1802), 34.

24. Werkmeister,*Vertheidigung*, 34–35.

25. Vitus Anton Winter, *Versuche zur Verbesserung der katholischen Liturgie* (Munich: 1804), 215.

26. Charles Anselm Bolton, *Church Reform in 18th Century Italy: The Synod of Pistoia, 1786* (The Hague: Nijhoff, 1970).

27. Francis Young, *English Catholics and the Supernatural, 1553–1829* (Aldershot: Ashgate, 2013), 69,

28. Henry Charles Lea, *A History of the Inquisition of Spain* (London: Macmillan, 1907), vol. 4, 203.

29. Lea, *A History*, vol. 4, 203–4; Henry Kamen, *The Spanish Inquisition: A Historical Revision* (New Haven, CT: Yale University Press, 1998).

30. Staatsarchiv Bamberg: Signatur: Hochstift Bamberg, Zent- und Fraischgericht, Nr. 172; Johannes Dillinger, ed., *Zauberer–Selbstmörder–Schatzsucher* (Trier: Kliomedia, 2003).

31. Haus-, Hof-und Staatsarchiv Vienna: HHStA LHA 215–2.

32. Hohenlohe Zentralarchiv Lauenstein: La Bü 1454; Johannes Dillinger, *Magical Treasure Hunting in Europe and North America* (Houndmills: Palgrave Macmillan, 2012).

33. Rainer Decker, *Witchcraft and the Papacy: An Account Drawing on the Formerly Secret Records of the Roman Inquisition* (Charlottesville: University of Virginia, 2008), 40–44; 132; 213; James Maxwell Anderson, *Daily Life during the Spanish Inquisition* (Westport, CT: Greenwood Press, 2002), 82; Lea, *A History*, vol. 4, 235.

34. Lea, *A History*, vol. 4, 202.

35. Timothy Dale Walker, *Doctors, Folk Medicine and the Inquisition: The Repression of Magical Healing in Portugal during the Enlightenment* (Leiden: Brill, 2005).

36. Maria Tausiet, "From Illusion to Disenchantment: Feijoo versus the 'Falsely Possessed' in Eighteenth-Century Spain," in *Beyond the Witch Trials: Witchcraft and Magic in Enlightenment Europe*, edited by Owen Davies and Willem de Blecourt (Manchester: Manchester University Press, 2004), 45–60, at 46.

37. Tausiet, "From Illusion," 53.

38. Josef Müller, *Der Freiburger Pastoraltheologe Carl Schwarzel, 1743–1809* (PhD diss., Freiburg i.B., 1959, digitized 2007), 51.

39. Israel, *The Radical Enlightenment*, 377–404.

40. Erik Midelfort, *Exorcism and Enlightenment: Johann Joseph Gassner and the Demons of Eighteenth-Century Germany* (New Haven, CT: Yale University Press, 2005).

41. Felix Anton Blau, *Ueber die Wirksamkeit der gottesdienstlichen Gebräuche in der katholischen Kirche* (Frankfurt: 1792), 49–51; 194.

42. Manfred Probst, *Der Ritus der Kindertaufe. Reformversuche der katholischen Aufklärung des deutschen Sprachbereichs* (Trier: Paulinus, 1981), 171.

43. Michael Ostling, *Between the Devil and the Host: Imagining Witchcraft in Early Modern Poland* (Oxford: Oxford University Press, 2011).

44. Israel, *The Radical Enlightenment*, 377–404.

45. Decker, *Witchcraft*, 110–12.

46. Lodovico Antonio Muratori, *Della Forza della fantasia umana, trattato di Lodovico Antonio Muratori* (Venice: 1745).

47. Lea, *A History*, vol. 4, 246.

48. Edward E. Evans-Pritchard, *Witchcraft, Oracles and Magic among the Azande* (Oxford: Clarendon, 1937); Cameron, *Enchanted Europe*.

49. Muratori, *Della Forza*, ch. 10, 109–10.

50. Ostling, *Between the Devil*, 60.

51. Beck, *Mäuselmacher*, 451; Young, *English Catholics*, 96.

52. Moshe Sluhovsky, *Believe not Every Spirit: Possession, Mysticism, and Discernment in Early Modern Catholicism* (Chicago: University of Chicago Press, 2007), 235; Nicky Hallett, *Witchcraft, Exorcism and the Politics of Possession in a Seventeenth-Century Convent: "How Sister Ursula Was Once Bewitched and Sister Margaret Twice"* (Aldershot: Ashgate, 2007).

53. Anton Memminger, *Das verhexte Kloster* (Würzburg: Memminger, 1908); for forcing men and women to take monastic vows, see the excellent book by Anne Jacobson Schutte, *By Force and Fear. Taking and Breaking of Monastic Vows in Early Modern Europe* (Ithaca, NY: Cornell University Press, 2011).

54. Claudia Sussmann-Hanff, "Maria Renata Singer von Mossau–die letzte Hexe von Würzburg," *Frankenland. Zeitschrift für fränkische Landeskunde und Kulturpflege* 47 (1995): 25–36.

55. Ulrich L. Lehner, *Theologie ohne Hexen und Zauberer* (Nordhausen: Bautz, 2007), xxi.

56. Rainer Decker, *Witchcraft and the Papacy*, 40–49; Cameron, *Enchanted Europe*, 193–95.

57. Cf. Gábor Klaniczay, *The Uses of Supernatural Power: The Transformation of Popular Religion in Medieval and Early-Modern Europe*, translated by Karen Margolis (Princeton, NJ: Princeton University Press, 1990), 130–31.

58. Klaniczay, *The Uses*, 187.

59. Benito Feijoo, *Cartas eruditas y curiosas* (Madrid: 1774), iv: carta xx, § 29, 278; Fernando Vial, "Ghosts of the European Enlightenment," in *Rethinking Ghosts*

in World Religions, edited by Muzhou Pu (Leiden: Brill, 2009), 163–82, at 169; Fabián Alejandro Campagne, *Homo catholicus, homo superstitiosus: el discurso antisupersticioso en la España de los siglos XV a XVIII* (Madrid, España: Miño y Dávila Editores, 2002).

60. Klaniczay, *The Uses*, 181.
61. Louis Antoine de Caraccioli, *La vie du Pape Benoit XIV* (Paris: 1783), 192–93.
62. Vial, "Ghosts."
63. Vial, "Ghosts," 178.
64. Klaniczay, *The Uses*, 171.
65. Klaniczay, *The Uses*, 172.
66. Edmund Kern, "An End to Witch Trials in Austria: Reconsidering the Enlightened State," *Austrian History Yearbook* 30 (1999), 159–85.

CHAPTER 6

1. Massimo Leone, *Saints and Signs: A Semiotic Reading of Conversion in Early Modern Catholicism* (Berlin: De Gruyter, 2010).
2. Ronnie Po-Chia Hsia, *The World of Catholic Renewal, 1540–1770* (Cambridge: Cambridge University Press, 1998), 137.
3. Nigel Aston, *Art and Religion in Eighteenth-Century Europe* (London: Reaktion Books, 2009), 288–89.
4. Aston, *Art*, 47.
5. Thomas DaCosta Kaufmann, *Painterly Enlightenment: The Art of Franz Anton Maulbertsch, 1724–1796* (Chapel Hill: University of North Carolina Press, 2005), 84. Yet another example is the Bolognese artist Guiseppe Maria Crespi (1665–1747) and his series of seven pictures depicting the sacraments of the Catholic Church. Instead of visualizing the sacraments with the help of biblical allusions and the portrayal of the obviously supernatural, such as Jesus healing the sick, he conceives the sacraments as normal activities in the everyday life of the church. Instead of seeing an apostle performing baptism, one sees a domestic room and family where the sacrament is celebrated. Likewise Pierre Subleyras (1699–1749) refused to paint St. Camillus's saving of the sick in a hospital with any reference to the supernatural. Instead, one perceives the "quiet determination" of Camillo and his helpers when removing the patients and saving them from the tides of the Tiber. There was no need to depict the supernatural, since the mind and soul of the saint were considered the center of all supernatural transformation. See Christopher M. S. Johns, "Gender and Genre in the Religious Art of the Catholic Enlightenment," in *Italy's Eighteenth Century: Gender and Culture in the Age of the Grand Tour*, edited by Paula Findlen, Wendy Wassyng Roworth, and Catherine Sama (Stanford, CA: Stanford University Press 2008), 331–45; see especially Christopher M. S. Johns, *The Visual Culture of Catholic Enlightenment* (University Park, PA: Pennsylvania State Press, 2015).

6. Peter Hersche, *Musse und Verschwendung: europäische Gesellschaft und Kultur im Barockzeitalter* (Freiburg: Herder), vol. 1, 601–633; Ulrich L. Lehner, "The Many Faces of the Catholic Enlightenment," in *Brill's Companion to the Catholic Enlightenment in Europe*, edited by Ulrich L. Lehner and Michael Printy (Leiden: Brill, 2010), 1–61.

7. Chadwick, *The Popes and European Revolution*· (Oxford: Clarendon Press, 1981), 32.

8. Benedikt Maria Leonhard von Werkmeister, *An die unbescheidenen Verehrer der Heiligen, besonders Mariä: Eine Belehrung nach der ächtkatholischen Glaubenslehre* (Hadamar: 1801), 18.

9. Werkmeister, *An die unbescheidenen Verehrer*, 64.

10. Werkmeister, *An die unbescheidenen Verehrer*, 164.

11. Ulrich L. Lehner, *Monastic Prisons and Torture* (Eugene, OR: Cascade, 2013); Chadwick, The Popes, 294.

12. Joseph Weisskopf, *St. Johannes von Nepomuk* (Vienna: Reinhold Verlag, 1931).

13. Ludovico Muratori, *Lusitanae ecclesiae religio in administrando poenitentiae sacramento . . .* (Modena: 1747).

14. Aloys Bach, *Urkundliche Kirchen-Geschichte der Grafschaft Glaz. Von der Urzeit bis auf unsere Tage* (Breslau: 1841); "Miszelle," in *Stimmen der Zeit* 39 (1890): 221–24; August Josef Nürnberger, *Neue Dokumente zur Geschichte des P. Andreas Faulhaber* (Mainz: 1900).

15. Manfred Weitlauff, "Die selige Crescentia Höss von Kaufbeuren," in *Bavaria Sancta*, vol. 2, edited by Georg Schwaiger (Regensburg: Pustet, 1971), 242–82.

16. Andreas Weileder, "Die heilige Crescentia von Kaufbeuren im Spiegel der ersten Befragung durch Eusebius Amort and Giovanni Bassi im Jahre 1744," in *Die heilige Crescentia von Kaufbeuren*, edited by Andreas Weileder (Thalhofen: Bauer-Verlag, 2001), 6–123.

17. Weileder, "Die heilige Crescentia," 52.

18. Weileder, "Die heilige Crescentia," 59.

19. Otto Weiss, *Weisungen aus dem Jenseits? Der Einfluss mystizistischer Phänomene auf Ordens- und Kirchenleitungen im 19. Jahrhundert* (Regensburg: Pustet, 2011).

20. Weileder, "Die heilige Crescentia," 118–22.

21. François Boespflug, *Dieu dans l'art: Sollicitudini Nostrae de Benoît XIV (1745) et l'affaire Cresence de Kaufbeuren* (Paris: Editions du Cerf, 1984).

22. Agnes de la Gorce, *Saint Benedict Labre*, translated by Rosemary Sheed (New York: Sheed and Ward, 1952), 28.

23. Thomas Worcester, "The Classical Sermon," in *Preaching, Sermons and Cultural Change in the Long Eighteenth Century*, edited by Joris van Eijnatten (Boston: Brill, 2009), 133–73, at 142–43.

24. Hersche, vol. 2, 748–93.

25. Gorce, *Saint Benedict Labre*, 66–67.

26. Rebekka Habermas, *Wallfahrt und Aufruhr: zur Geschichte des Wunderglaubens in der frühen Neuzeit* (Frankfurt: Campus, 1991); Hersche, vol. 2, 794–844.

27. Gorce, *Saint Benedict Labre*, 98.

28. Gorce, *Saint Benedict Labre*, 194.

29. *Der Deutsche Zuschauer* 3, no. 8 (1785): 173–80.

30. *Deutsche Zeitung*, issue 36 of September 10, 1785.

31. Christian Gotthilf Salzmann, *Ueber das menschliche Elend*, part 5, edited by Carl von Carlsbad (Carlsruhe: 1787), 61.

32. Théodule Rey-Mermet, *Alphonsus Liguori: Tireless Worker for the Most Abandoned* (Brooklyn, NY: New City Press, 1989); Théodule Rey-Mermet, *Moral Choices: The Moral Theology of Saint Alphonsus Liguori* (Liguori, MO: Liguori, 1998); *Alphonsus of Liguori, Selected Writings*, edited by Frederick Jones (New York: Paulist Press, 1999)

33. Rey-Mermet, *Moral Choices*, 2.

34. Frederick Jones, "Alphonus de Liguori," in *Alphonsus of Liguori. Selected Writings*, 9–56, at 49.

35. Charles E. Curran, *Catholic Moral Theology in the United States: A History* (Washington, DC: Georgetown University Press, 2008), 6–7.

36. "Ueber die Verfassung der Geistlichkeit in Frankreich," *Schlözer's Stats-Anzeigen* 8, issue 30 (1785): 129–52, at 150.

37. Richard A. Sokolovski, *Matrix omnium conclusionum. Den Augustinus des Jansenius lesen* (PhD diss., University of Fribourg/Switzerland, 2007).

38. Brian E. Strayer, *Suffering Saints: Jansenists and Convulsionnaires in France, 1640–1799* (Brighton: Sussex Academic Press, 2008), 236–65.

39. B. Robert Kreiser, *Miracles, Convulsions, and Ecclesiastical Politics in Early Eighteenth-Century Paris* (Princeton, NJ: Princeton University Press, 1978).

40. Strayer, *Suffering Saints*, 245.

41. Strayer, *Suffering Saints*, 263; Dale Van Kley, *The Religious Origins of the French Revolution: From Calvin to the Civil Constitution, 1560–1791* (New Haven, CT: Yale University Press, 1996).

42. Jennifer Herdt, *Putting on Virtue: The Legacy of the Splendid Vices* (Chicago: University of Chicago Press, 2008), 221–82.

43. Timothy Tackett, *Religion, Revolution and Regional Culture in Eighteenth-Century France: The Ecclesiastical Oath of 1791* (Princeton, NJ: Princeton University Press, 1986), 34–58; Jonathan Israel, *Revolutionary Ideas: An Intellectual History of the French Revolution* (Princeton, NJ: Princeton University Press, 2014), 180–203.

44. William Bush, *To Quell the Terror: The Mystery of the Vocation of the Sixteen Carmelites of Compiègne Guillotined July 17, 1794* (Washington, DC: ICS Publications, 1999), 41–42.

45. Dan Edelstein, *The Terror of Natural Right: Republicanism, the Cult of Nature, and the French Revolution* (Chicago: University of Chicago Press, 2009), 35.

46. Bush, *To Quell*, 109.

47. Bush, *To Quell*, 208.

48. Timothy Tackett, *The Coming of the Terror in the French Revolution* (Cambridge, MA: Belknap Press, 2015).

49. A step in the right direction is the insightful book by Jennifer A. Herdt, *Putting on Virtue: The Legacy of the Splendid Vices* (Chicago: University of Chicago Press, 2008); cf. Richard Bruch, *Ethik und Naturrecht im deutschen Katholizismus des 18. Jahrhunderts: von der Tugendethik zur Pflichtethik* (Tübingen: Francke, 1997).

50. Cf. Michel R. Barnes, *A Man of the Church: Honoring the Life, Work and Theology of Ralph Del Colle* (Eugene, OR: Wipf and Stock, 2012).

51. Gustavo Gutierrez and Gerhard L. Müller, *On the Side of the Poor: The Theology of Liberation* (Maryknoll, NY: Orbis: 2015).

52. See the important work of Joseph F. Byrnes, *The Priests of the French Revolution: Saints and Renegades in a New Political Era* (University Park: Pennsylvania State Press, 2014). Widely ignored because of its strong anti-Enlightenment narrative but nevertheless invaluable because of the amount of archival resources researched is Georg May, *Das Versöhnungswerk des päpstlichen Legaten Giovanni B. Caprara. Die Rekonziliation der Geistlichen und Ordensangehörigen 1801–1808* (Berlin: Duncker & Humblot, 2012).

53. Hopefully, the *Oxford Handbook of Early Modern Theology, 1600–1800*, edited by Ulrich L. Lehner, Gregg Roeber, and Richard Muller (Oxford: Oxford University Press, 2015) will contribute to a change.

CHAPTER 7

1. Andrew S. Curran, *The Anatomy of Blackness: Science & Slavery in an Age of Enlightenment* (Baltimore, MD: Johns Hopkins University Press, 2011), 14–15.

2. David Eltis, "The Volume and Structure of the Transatlantic Slave Trade: A Reassessment," *William and Mary Quarterly* 58 (2011): 17–46.

3. In Christopher L. Miller, *Blank Darkness: Africanist Discourse in French* (Chicago: University of Chicago Press, 1985), 43.

4. Nicole Priesching, *Von Menschenfängern und Menschenfischern. Sklaverei und Loskauf im Kirchenstaat des 16.–18. Jahrhunderts* (Hildesheim: Olms, 2012), 17.

5. Nicola Spedalieri, *De' Diritti dell' uomo libri VI* (Assisi: 1791), book 5, ch. 16, par. 20.

6. Don Jordan and Michael Walsh, *White Cargo: The Forgotten History of Britain's White Slaves in America* (New York: New York University Press, 2007), 145.

7. Jordan, *White Cargo*, 231.

8. Curran, *The Anatomy of Blackness*, 76–95.

9. Curran, *The Anatomy of Blackness*, 198.

10. Ann Thomson, "Diderot, Roubaud et l'esclavage," *Recherches sur Diderot et sur l'Encyclopédie* 35 (2003): 69–93.

11. Thomas Nutz, *Varietäten des Menschengeschlechts: die Wissenschaften vom Menschen in der Zeit der Aufklärung* (Cologne: Böhlau, 2009), 141–42; Christine Küchler Williams, *Erotische Paradiese. Zur europäischen Südseerezeption im 18. Jahrhundert* (Göttingen: Wallstein, 2004), 62–63.

12. Jean Tarrade, "Is Slavery Reformable? Proposals of Colonial Administrators at the End of the Ancien Regime," in *The Abolitions of Slavery: From Léger Félicité Sonthonax to Victor Schoelcher, 1793, 1794, 1848*, edited by Marcel Dorigny (Paris: UNESCO and Berghahn, 2003), 101–10, at 106; Curran, *The Anatomy of Blackness*, 119.

13. Ann Thompson, *Bodies of Thought: Science, Religion, and the Soul in the Early Enlightenment* (Oxford: Oxford University Press, 2008), 242–43.

14. Henri Grégoire, *An Enquiry Concerning the Intellectual and Moral Faculties, and Literature of Negroes*. Translated by D. B. Warden (Brooklyn: 1810), 252–53.

15. The most easily accessible Latin-English version is in Hugh Charles Clifford, *Christianity versus Slavery* (Dublin: 1841), 54–65; cf. Samuel Miller, *Portugal and Rome: An Aspect of the Catholic Enlightenment* (Rome: Università Gregoriana, 1978), 52–58.

16. Priesching, *Von Menschenfängern*, 86–155.

17. Priesching, *Von Menschenfängern*, 159–232; Robert C. Davis, *Christian Slaves, Muslim Masters: White Slavery in the Mediterranean, the Barbary Coast, and Italy, 1500–1800* (Houndmills: Palgrave Macmillan, 2003). Molly Greene, *Catholic Pirates and Greek Merchants: A Maritime History of the Mediterranean* (Princeton, NJ: Princeton University Press, 2010).

18. Priesching, *Von Menschenfängern*, 159–232. On the relief and exchange of prisoners in the Mediterranean, see Heike Grieser and Nicole Priesching, *Gefangenenloskauf im Mittelmeerraum* (Hildesheim: Olms, 2015). On Livorno's fascinating religious landscape, see Francesca Bregoli, *Mediterranean Enlightenment: Livornese Jews, Tuscan Culture, and Eighteenth-Century Reform* (Stanford, CA: Stanford University Press, 2014); Stephanie Nadalo, "Negotiating Slavery in a Tolerant Frontier: Livorno's Turkish Bagni, 1547–1747," *Mediaevalia* 32 (2011): 275–324.

19. Priesching, *Von Menschenfängern*, 223.

20. Priesching, *Von Menschenfängern*, 235–430.

21. Conquered towns were given as *encomiendas* to conquistadors and early settlers—the *encomenderos*—as recompense for their service to the crown. The *encomenderos* had the right to collect tributes and personal service from the natives, whom they practically treated as slaves.

22. Felix Becker, *Die Politische Machtstellung der Jesuiten in Südamerika im 18. Jahrhundert. Zur Kontroverse um den Jesuitenkönig Nikolaus I von Portugal* (Vienna: Böhlau, 1980), 11; Peter Claus Hartmann, *Der Jesuitenstaat in Südamerika, 1609–1768: eine christliche Alternative zu Kolonialismus und Marxismus* (Weissenhorn: Anton H. Konrad, 1994); Julia J. Sarreal, *The Guaraní*

and Their Missions: A Socioeconomic History (Stanford, CA: Stanford University Press, 2014); Miguel de Asúa, *Science in the Vanished Arcadia: Knowledge of Nature in the Jesuit Missions of Paraguay and Rio De La Plata* (Leiden: Brill, 2014).

23. Joseph Calder Miller, *Way of Death: Merchant Capitalism and the Angolan Slave Trade, 1730–1830* (Madison: University of Wisconsin Press, 1988), 271.

24. Arnold Bauer, "Christian Servitude: Slave Management in Colonial Spanish America," in *Agrarian Society in History: Essays in Honor of Magnus Mörner,* edited by Mats Lundahl and Thommy Svensson (London: Routledge, 1990), 89–107.

25. Thomas Murphy, *Jesuit Slaveholding in Maryland, 1717–1838* (New York: Routledge, 2001), 16–21.

26. Murphy, *Jesuit Slaveholding,* 24.

27. Murphy, *Jesuit Slaveholding,* 34.

28. Murphy, *Jesuit Slaveholding,* 36.

29. Murphy, *Jesuit Slaveholding,* 156.

30. Geoffrey Wettinger, *Slavery in the Islands of Malta and Gozo, ca. 1000–1812* (Malta: PEG, 2002), 78.

31. Julia Gasper, *Theodore Von Neuhoff, King of Corsica: The Man behind the Legend* (Newark: University of Delaware Press, 2013), 154; 163; 177; 143–44.

32. James H. Sweet, *Domingos Álvares, African Healing, and the Intellectual History of the Atlantic World* (Chapel Hill: University of North Carolina Press, 2011), 28.

33. Sweet, *Domingos,* 37.

34. Sweet, *Domingos,* 48.

35. Robert Edgar Conrad, *Children of God's Fire: A Documentary History of Black Slavery in Brazil* (University Park: Pennsylvania State University Press, 1984), 161–62.

36. Conrad, *Children of God's Fire,* 152.

37. Conrad, *Children of God's Fire,* 181; Josè Joaquim de Cunha de Azeredo Coutinho, *Analyse sobre a justiçia do commercio do resgate dos escravos da Costa da Africa* (Lisbon: 1798; 2nd ed. 1808); Leslie Bethell, *The Abolition of the Brazilian Slave Trade* (Cambridge: Cambridge University Press, 1970), 6.

38. Hugo Fragoso, "A Pioneer of Abolitionism in 18th Century Bahia?" *História [São Paulo]* 31 (2012): 68–105.

39. Fragoso, "A Pioneer of Abolitionism in 18th Century Bahia?" Bethell, *The Abolition,* 5; João Pedro Marques, *The Sounds of Silence: Nineteenth-Century Portugal and the Abolition of the Slave Trade* (New York: Berghahn Books, 2006).

40. David Brion Davis, *The Problem of Slavery in the Age of Revolution, 1770–1823,* 2nd ed. (Oxford: Oxford University Press: 1999), 542–43.

41. Raymond Harris [Hormaza], *Scriptural Researches on the Licitness of the Slave-Trade, Shewing Its Conformity with the Principles of Natural & Revealed Religion, Delineated in the Sacred Writings of the Word of God* (London: 1788), 20.

42. Harris, *Scriptural Researches,* 70–74.

43. Kenneth Maxwell, *Conflicts and Conspiracies: Brazil and Portugal, 1750–1808* (New York: Routledge, 2001), 77–79.

44. See, for example, Dagmar Bechtloff, "Wirtschaftliche Aktivitäten kirchlicher Laienvereinigungen im Neuspanien des 18. Jahrhunderts," in *Überseegeschichte. Beiträge der jüngeren Forschung*, edited by Thomas Beck (Stuttgart: Steiner, 1999), 152–63.

45. Kathleen J. Higgins, *"Licentious Liberty" in a Brazilian Gold-Mining Region: Slavery, Gender, and Social Control in Eighteenth-Century Sabará, Minas Gerais* (University Park: Pennsylvania State University Press, 1999), 102.

46. Sweet, *Domingos*, 89.

47. Mariza de Carvalho Soares, *People of Faith: Slavery and African Catholics in Eighteenth-Century Rio de Janeiro*, translated by Jerry D. Metz (Durham, NC: Duke University Press, 2011), 138.

48. Júnia Ferreira Furtado, *Chica Da Silva: A Brazilian Slave of the Eighteenth Century* (Cambridge: Cambridge University Press, 2009), 183.

49. Soares, *People of Faith*; Sweet, *Domingos*, 87; Furtado, *Chica Da Silva*, 178–83.

50. Soares, *People of Faith*, 155.

51. Linda M. Heywood, "Slavery and Its Transformation in the Kingdom of Kongo, 1491–1800," *Journal of African History* 50 (2009): 1–22.

52. John Thornton, "On the Trail of Voodoo: African Christianity in Africa and the Americas," *Americas* 44 (1988): 275; John Thornton, "The Development of an African Catholic Church in the Kingdom of Kongo, 1491–1750," *Journal of African History* 25 (1984): 147–67.

53. Sue Peabody, "A Dangerous Zeal: Catholic Missions to Slaves in the French Antilles, 1635–1800," *French Historical Studies* 25 (2002): 53–90.

54. Peabody, "Missions to Slaves," 82.

55. Peabody, "Missions to Slaves," 90.

56. Peabody, "Missions to Slaves," 66–67.

57. Sweet, *Domingos*, 33.

58. Arthur L. Stinchcombe, *Sugar Island Slavery in the Age of Enlightenment: The Political Economy of the Caribbean World* (Princeton, NJ: Princeton University Press, 1995), 143–44.

59. Emily Clark, *Masterless Mistresses: The New Orleans Ursulines and the Development of a New World Society, 1727–1834* (Williamsburg, VA: Omohundro Institute of Early American History and Culture, 2007), 161–87.

60. Prospere Eve, "Forms of Resistance in Bourbon," in *The Abolitions of Slavery: From Léger Félicité Sonthonax to Victor Schoelcher, 1793, 1794, 1848*, edited by Marcel Dorigny (Paris: UNESCO and Berghahn, 2003), 17–39, at 30.

61. Caryn Cosse Bell, *Revolution, Romanticism, and the Afro-Creole Protest Tradition in Louisiana, 1718–1868* (Baton Rouge: Louisiana State University Press, 1997), 14; 66.

62. Clark, *Masterless Mistresses*, 54–57; 74.

63. Brett Rushforth, *Bonds of Alliance: Indigenous and Atlantic Slaveries in New France* (Chapel Hill: University of North Carolina Press, 2012), 15–72.

64. Rushforth, *Bonds of Alliance*, 271–72.

65. Conrad, *Children of God's Fire*, 162.

66. Rushforth, *Bonds of Alliance*, 271–72.

67. Clark, *Masterless Mistresses*, 164.

68. Susan Sleeper-Smith, "Women, Kin, and Catholicism: New Perspectives on the Fur Trade," *Ethnohistory* 47 (2000): 423–52. One effect of the women's missionary zeal was that hardly an Indian man was willing to undergo instruction to become a catechist.

CONCLUSION

1. John McManners, *The French Revolution and the Church* (New York: Harper, 1969), 17; Nigel Aston, *Religion and Revolution in France, 1780–1804* (Washington, DC: Catholic University of America Press, 2000); Nigel Aston, *Christianity and Revolutionary Europe, 1750–1830* (Cambridge: Cambridge University Press, 2002).

2. See Timothy Tackett, *The Coming of the Terror in the French Revolution* (Cambridge, MA: Belknap Press, 2015); Aston, *Religion and Revolution*.

3. Dan Edelstein, *The Terror of Natural Right. Republicanism, the Cult of Nature and the French Revolution* (Chicago: University of Chicago Press, 2009).

4. Reynald Secher, *The Vendée. A French Genocide*, translated by George Holoch (Notre Dame, IN: University of Notre Dame Press, 2003), 250.

5. Secher, *The Vendée*, 250.

6. Mark Levene, *The Rise of the West and the Coming of Genocide* (London: I. B. Tauris, 2005), 103–61.

7. David Sorkin, *The Religious Enlightenment: Protestants, Jews, and Catholics from London to Vienna* (Princeton, NJ: Princeton University Press, 2008), 261–310.

8. Dale van Kley, "The Abbé Grégoire and the Quest for a Catholic Republic," in *The Abbé Grégoire and His World*, edited by Jeremy Popkin et al. (Dordrecht: Kluwer, 2000), 71–107; for Grégoire, see also the important book Joseph F. Byrnes, *Priests of the French Revolution: Saints and Renegades in a New Political Era* (University Park: Pennsylvania State University Press, 2014).

9. Byrnes, *Priests of the French Revolution*, 59.

10. Pasi Ihalainen, "The Enlightenment Sermon: Towards Practical Religion and a Sacred National Community," in *Preaching, Sermon and Cultural Change in the Long Eighteenth Century*, edited by Joris van Eijnatten (Leiden: Brill, 2009), 219–62; Jonathan Israel, *Revolutionary Ideas: An Intellectual History of the French Revolution from the Rights of Man to Robespierre* (Princeton, NJ: Princeton University Press, 2014), passim; Byrnes, *Priests of the French Revolution*, passim.

11. Franz Berg and Gregor Zirkel, *Predigten über die Pflichten der höheren und aufgeklärten Stände bey den bürgerlichen Unruhen unserer Zeit* (Würzburg: 1793), 12–14.

12. Berg, *Predigten*, 15.

13. Berg, *Predigten*, 17.

14. Berg, *Predigten*, 17.

15. Berg, Predigten, 26; cf. Darrin M. McMahon, *Enemies of the Enlightenment: The French Counter-Enlightenment and the Making of Modernity* (New York: Oxford University Press, 2002).

16. Berg, *Predigten*, 28.

17. Emile Perreau-Saussine, *Catholicism and Democracy. An Essay in the History of Political Thought*, translated by Richard Rex (Princeton, NJ: Princeton University Press, 2012), 45.

18. Klaus Unterburger, *Vom Lehramt der Theologen zum Lehramt der Päpste? Pius XI, die Apostolische Konstitution "Deus scientiarum Dominus" und die Reform der Universitätstheologie* (Freiburg: Herder, 2010).

19. Perreau-Saussine, *Catholicism and Democracy*, 67–68.

Index